Undead

A MEMOIR OF MY SUICIDE

MADELINE VOSCH

BEACON PRESS, BOSTON

BEACON PRESS
24 Farnsworth Street
Boston, Massachusetts
www.beacon.org

Beacon Press books
are published under the auspices of
the Unitarian Universalist Association of Congregations.

Many names and identifying characteristics of people mentioned in this work have been changed to protect their identities.

Printed in the United States of America

29 28 27 26 8 7 6 5 4 3 2 1

This book is printed on acid-free paper that meets the uncoated paper ANSI/NISO specifications for permanence as revised in 1992.

Text design and composition by Kim Arney

Library of Congress Cataloging-in-Publication Data is available for this title.
ISBN: 978-0-8070-1655-8; e-book: 978-0-8070-1656-5;
audiobook: 978-0-8070-2328-0

as from a sapling log that catches fire
along one of its ends, while at the other
it drips and hisses with escaping vapor,
so from that broken stump issued
together both words and blood

—Dante's *Inferno*, Canto XIII

CONTENTS

PREFACE

The summer after I tried to kill myself, I spoke to almost no one of what happened, of what I did. It seemed such an impossibly large, crushing thing to say. A boulder thrown into a conversation, impassible and unwieldy. I could not find the words, could not find a way to fit my mouth around this, could not find the appropriate time or place to confess to friends what, really, had happened, and where, really, I had been.

Maybe that isn't that strange. But in those months, I lived as in a chrysalis: separated from the world through a film, peering through a thin layer, distant from everything and everyone, unsure if anyone could see a difference in me.

My life was cleaved in two by that moment of rupture. There were the months, the years that led to my suicide. Then, I tried. Then, I failed. It was as if finally, truly trying to die was what opened the door for the chance that something else might happen. For years, it felt inevitable that I would kill myself. The only question had been when. When I lived, this central fact of myself was thrown into doubt.

The summer after I tried to kill myself, I couldn't find the language I needed. I wrote long poems about people in a place with no exit. I wrote about places that do not exist where those people will be safe. After I left the hospital, I kept trying to fit it all in poetry. I blanketed it all in metaphors, images of wolves tearing at plants, *time without boxes*, phrases that gesture without saying something outright. In writing poetry, I thought, there was less risk. There was the speaker of the poem, who was different than me, the writer, the person.

A friend had a house that was unimaginably large for Cambridge. She had turned the third floor of the house into a makeshift music venue. The ceilings were tall, the wooden floors just a little uneven. There was a support beam almost exactly in the middle of the room. A few weeks before I moved out of Boston, she agreed to host a reading there. A friend would read part of her own chapbook. A musician would perform their music as a kind of intermission. I would read last. I'd made a chapbook of the poems that I wrote that spring, that summer. I got thick paper, bought an awl, and sewed the books together by hand.

I stood at the microphone in a room full of bodies. Strangers and friends seated, others standing in the back. Somewhere in the crowd, my ex, my former beloved. I read these words about a girl whose mouth was full of cloth, who couldn't speak and had no one to speak to. "There is a place," I read, "that does not exist where she will be safe."

With bright lights in my eyes, I couldn't make out who was there in the crowd. Speaking in poetry, reading to a faceless crowd, was the only way I knew to let this story out. There was no chance for conversation, no chance for questions.

"Where is god in this place with no days?"

After, there were hugs from friends and strangers. I sold every copy of the chapbook. I promised to make more. There was something there. In that room in Cambridge, I began to think that it mattered, maybe, to learn how to say it. That maybe as much as I needed to say it, there was someone who needed to hear it.

I went to graduate school for an MFA, thinking that I would find a way to make this sayable. I started the program sure of what I would do. I had a plan. I would write a long poem, a book-length poem, something capacious and encompassing, something about the not-dying, about the hospital, about the fog that follows. There was a phrase that bumped around in my head, a critique someone had leveled against a book of nonfiction: "The author cannot see outside of her own subjectivity." I was not going to fall into that trap. I would make something intricate, a text so thick with meaning that it wouldn't matter, really, that anything gestured to in the pages had any relation to my actual life.

I made poems from the language of Massachusetts Section 12, the law on involuntary hospitalization. I wrote poems dense with images and metaphors. I wrote a twenty-page poem about trying to die and never used the word suicide. After months of writing these poems, I wanted to tear the pages and slam my laptop into the wall. I hated them. I hated myself for writing them.

I'd built metaphors to hide inside and began to see them for what they were: pretty trinkets made to distract from the things I wanted to say. Intricate language to mask the deep insecurity that perhaps, if this story was not wrapped in poetry, it would just be a paltry little nothing, too personal, too subjective, just another woman writing confessional literature. I thought that the poetry was what made it interesting, what made it worthwhile. But I hated the words, how afraid they were, how they danced in circles around this story that waited at the center.

I was a coward. My writing was made of that cowardice. So, I started to write this book instead.

I needed to ignore all the critics in my head, all the familiar denouncements of women writing about their lives, all the worn-out phrases about navel-gazing. I needed to claim myself as subject, to claim my own perspective, my own life, as messy as it may be. I needed to stop appeasing my imagined hostile readership. I needed to stop being a coward, to tell the truth as clearly as I could. The book you hold in your hands is my attempt to do that. Not just to make it sayable, but to be as honest as I can be about the haze that followed my suicide attempt and all the days leading up to it.

I'm sure that there are ways that this book fails. Maybe aesthetically, maybe in its argument. But I have learned over the years that sometimes telling this story out loud is worth all the risk that comes with it. I have learned that sometimes failing is the best thing that you can do.

PART I

An Archeology of That Silence

The thing they don't tell you about coming back from the dead is that it happens slowly. It is not a single moment, eyes snapping open, full of energy to greet a bright new morning.

You wake with eyelids heavy, rub something other than sleep from your face. Your body is not yours. The morning is a stranger. The hours are bright and unfamiliar. You wake up alone and there is no one to remind you that you are real.

There are a million ways to die, outlined in history books, medical texts, easy to find on the internet. There are countless websites that detail the steps, how it feels to die of one of many afflictions, how to take it into your own hands.

There were none to show me the way back.

The thing they don't tell you about coming back from the dead is that it's easier to die. To end the story there. How is a person supposed to live after dying? What is it supposed to feel like, the coming back? Who can you tell? Where do you go?

I have read more books than I can name that take the reader down, step-by-step, into that dark place, to show the moment a person chooses to make their own ending. These books end in mourning, in dirges. I have never found a book that holds at its core not just the dying, but the coming back.

I am trying to answer the silence.

When I say that there were no stories to show me the way back, there is the inevitable refrain: *But what about the ancient Greek heroes, like Orpheus, who traveled to the underworld and returned? What about the article in the* New York Times, *about the people who jumped off bridges and lived, who testified to their regret? What about the canon of Buddhist literature and thought, in which resurrection, reincarnation, is a fact of life?*

Those months after I lived, I read everything, and saw myself nowhere.

There was nothing, no book, no pamphlet, no novel, no blog post, about how a person is supposed to live in the first months after they tried very hard to die.

I searched on the internet. Suicide survivor support groups. These searches followed the same pattern. I would find an in-person group, an online forum, get excited. I would go to the website and read the same description over and over: *This is a group for those who have lost a loved one to suicide*. These are the suicide survivors, the ones who are left behind, the ones who mourn.

And what of those of us who live?

And what about Sylvia Plath? someone asks. *Have you read her work?*

The Bell Jar ends just as the narrator leaves the hospital. Plath does not offer a path after, only a path toward.

In those months after, when my body was a live wire, when every breath was miracle and surprise, I looked everywhere, and the world was quiet. I read every book I could find on depression, on suicide, on hospitalization. There was nothing to answer the question: How is a person supposed to feel, how is a person supposed to live, when they sincerely meant to die, and didn't, and woke up to a world that has not changed?

Sometimes, a hero is so good, so important, that a story cannot continue after their death. The story relies on their resurrection. *Superman was killed by Doomsday and was brought back through some miraculous Kryptonite.* This is not what I'm talking about. *The Christian god is murdered and comes back through some divine mystery.* This is not what I am talking about.

I am talking about a creature, a needling thing, who screams into thick air, who has never been a hero, who never will be a hero, who looks in the mirror and knows this, who wants more than anything for the narrative to find a resolution, for their story to be over.

You know what I'm talking about.

When Christ died and came back, he was brought to God through the ascension. This death meant something. Friends, family, strangers marked this death, this rebirth. The wounds were visible on the body. The holes in his hands, his side. This body, bearing the marks of death, walking again through the world.

When you leave the hospital, you go to the same apartment in which you died, peel the sheets back, and lay in the bed. The room has not changed.

You walk past people who do not notice, you talk to friends like it has been a week like any other. You are the same, but you are not, no, no, no, you are not the same.

You breathe. This, this is the first and most important thing. You breathe.

You look up facts and statistics and carry them in your chest. The reports and articles stating what is trembling in your heart, that *people are one hundred times more likely to kill themselves after being released from the hospital for trying to kill themselves.*[1] You look people in the eye and hold this close. The days are vibrating around your body and all the things you can't fit into words.

The thing they don't tell you about coming back from the dead is that you get to choose what happens next. The world breaks open like never before. In one direction that same path, once traveled, beckoning again. And there, unspiraling, a million directions you have never imagined.

My logic is thin. The knees of my logic are shaking. Don't push too hard.

The thought: I tried. They told me what should have happened. It didn't happen. Now it is time for something else.

There is a small brown box in my bedroom. In this box, there is a dried leaf. There is the bud of a bougainvillea, plucked from a pot that hung on a friend's porch. There is a letter. There, taped to the underside of the lid, is a Band-Aid with numbers written in permanent marker. There is a triangle of paper, folded over and over itself, covered in tape. There are two bracelets, one from the emergency room, the other from the locked ward. Mostly, though, mostly there are empty orange bottles. I will not tell you how many.

Once, I tried to do the math. I took out the empty pill bottles and read the numbers printed on the outside. Estimating. How many of what had I swallowed that night. I multiplied. I added. I checked websites. *What is a lethal dose?* I started to choke. My hands were shaking. I put the bottles back and closed the box. I promised not to tell.

The thing they don't tell you about coming back from the dead is that you now have two birthdays. The day you were born, and the day you didn't die.

Those first weeks after I did not die, I marked each month as a ritual. Every thirty days I went to the same flower store, spent money I didn't have to adorn my house with color. I walked through the streets haunted by ghosts I couldn't name and bought flowers to honor them. I walked through Harvard Square in a gauze of petals and phantoms. The midday sun, the light that used to press down into my lungs so that I couldn't breathe, the midday sun became a song. I walked with my head up. *Look at me, in it.*

Where are the stories of those of us who lived, we who were not heroes, we whose faces were ugly, crumpled and crying, we who breathed deeply in lungs miraculous, who stared into eyes of friends and could not say, not really, where we had been, we who woke up again and again and again to mornings terrifying and bright, mornings that opened in every direction?

I walked through the world haunted by unsayable things. I ran into strangers, acquaintances. We are all so stressed about finals, we said to each other. The night they took me away, I was supposed to be throwing a party. I apologized to friends for disappearing, for the last-minute texts saying the party was canceled, laughed it off. They asked what happened and I couldn't tell them. Is it worse to tell the truth or to keep laughing? Outside, walking through campus, clocking in at work, every moment was a lie. How could I tell coworkers, colleagues, bosses, professors, friends that for the last week I had been sitting in locked rooms, brushing knees with strangers, sharing the worst, ugliest parts of myself with women who might never see me again?

Let me try that again.

I walked through the world haunted by unsayable things.

Those first days out, when I could come and go as I pleased, I realized that no one was checking to see if I was going to outpatient or returning, whether I'd eaten or decided to skip a meal, whether the pills were in my blood or beneath my tongue. The world was trilling. The bus stopped one block over from my house, took me down to a big street in the heart of Boston that seemed to split the world in two. I stared out the window as we crossed the bridge, looking at the waters I used to dream of drowning in.

Before I left the locked ward of the hospital, I told a girl where they were sending me for outpatient. She snorted. She had been sent there before. All they did was sit and talk. I readied myself. I would hate it. It would be a waste of time, and then it would be over.

The first morning I arrived, a woman came to lead me to her basement office for intake. The room was tiny and windowless. She sat on a medicine ball with her back to me and went through the questions.

"Do you have a history of depression or suicidal ideation?"

"Yes."

"Any attempts?"

"Yes."

"When?"

"April 20."

"So," she looked at a calendar. A week and a half ago. Her movements did not stiffen. "Recent."

"Yes."

She turned to look at my face.

"Did you intend to die?"

"Yes."

She exhaled. Met my eyes for a moment before turning back to the screen.

"Woof."

We laughed, soft and embarrassed, sharing something sweet and raw between us.

She did not tell me that I would be okay. She did not tell me anything. She led me upstairs, to the suite of rooms where the world would crack open, and I began to think that this place would not be like any I had been before.

The thing they don't tell you about coming back from the dead is that more people would care if you died. You imagine the Facebook posts, the digital acts of mourning, the people coming together for your funeral. But there you are, breathing, and in front of friends choking on words that aren't there. Because you lived, because your pulse beats a rhythm in your still-being body, you are unremarkable. You blend in.

A few weeks after I didn't die, I traveled to a wedding. I gathered with friends I had known since I was a child, went to a place tucked in the Catskill Mountains. In snatches, in side conversations, I asked in a voice that did not know how to speak, "Something big happened; can we talk?"

Heads shook. "Is it something heavy? We probably don't have time."

I swallowed myself. I gulped down wine and buried the secret of my breath in my heart.

———

One by one, the doctors tell me.

Lethal doses, they say.

My therapist tells me that he does not understand how I am alive. The things I took, the number of them. I had been drinking. I had barely eaten. He tells me it works like this: This combination of things slows your systems, slows your breathing, until eventually your breath comes in such long intervals, the breaths get so spaced out, it happens that you exhale and before you can inhale again, you die from lack of oxygen. The time between breaths so long that they stop coming. If you don't die, there is brain damage.

I do not know what to say to this. I am sitting in front of him and I am breathing.

If you had been down on the floor, he tells me, you would have crushed your nerves. Laying in one place for twenty hours, the body immobilized. If any part of you had been pressed against any hard surface, the nerves would have crumpled against it, the nerves would have never healed. Parts of you would have been paralyzed.

At the end of our session, I get up and walk home.

Outside a bar, a stranger makes a joke about suicidal ideation. I watch their mouth and try to copy the way they laugh.

There is no agreement on exactly what happened to Jesus those three days after the crucifixion. I imagine him waking in the tomb, alone. His hands, moving slowly to touch his own face. His eyes adjusting to the sliver of light that sneaks under the stone that has been rolled to cover the entrance. His fingers feeling, exploring. This rock. This body. These ribs. The motion of a belly moving inward and outward with breath. How many days there, alone in the silence of the tomb, relearning, reexperiencing, what it was to be alive when everything in the world says you are supposed to be dead.

I am not comparing myself to a god. I promise.

When it happened, I was living on the second floor of an apartment in Somerville. The house sat on a hill. From the back porch I could see the Boston skyline, the way the clouds hung over the city. The floors in that apartment were bright chestnut, linoleum in the kitchen. My own room had hardwood floors that I worried about scratching. The landlords lived on the ground floor, had grown up in the building. My housemates speculated that at one point, every room in the house had been a child's bedroom. My room was not a room. My room had wide glass doors that opened to the living room. I covered them with a black sheet, pushed a bookcase in front of them in a gesture toward privacy.

The house was lovely, lucky, affordable. The house was supposed to be safe.

There was something wrong in the house.

———

I became obsessed, for a while, with the story of the Christian god. How, in the beginning, this omniscient being decided to create thingness, timeness, the boundedness of bodies, knowing that this would require the god to be killed. If this god knew everything, this god would know his own story, how it was going to end. How maybe, in the forever of the outside, this god started to long for an ending, for a way out. How maybe, this god created the whole of everything so he could have an exit, however brief. How all of creation was made to facilitate a god's death. How in the beginning, this god made his own ending.

Call me a heretic, it's okay. I've been called worse.

———

In the throes of my obsession, I was haunted by the Christian afterlife. How inescapable, how trapped that vision of the world seemed. How, in the Christian imaginary, once you come into being there is no way out. When you die there is heaven or hell, an eternal existence. I thought it unimaginably cruel. Even in death, there was no ending. This seemed a hell worse than any I could dream up.

Was there no way out of this?

I thought of the cosmists, Russian theologians who believed that when the resurrection came, there would be no spirit separate from the body. The body would rise from the ground and step toward heaven or hell, forever embodied, forever the same flesh one was born into. I couldn't imagine what could be worse, forever myself, forever my body, trapped and judged as this self that I couldn't stand to be. I prayed to a god I did not believe in: *Please god if there is a resurrection do not let it be bound to this body, if there is a resurrection bound to this body may some mercy exist and leave me out of it. If some mercy exists please god just let me sleep let me be done, let me be safe. If there is some redemption please god let mercy exist and leave me out.*

When I closed my eyes, I dreamed of an emptiness without color, without form.

Let me say it plainly. I closed my eyes and dreamed of nothing. I lay in bed and imagined how to get there. I thought of getting a rope, leaving a note on the door for my housemates to call the police so they wouldn't see my body. I thought about hanging myself from the staircase. I thought of hanging myself from the balcony. I thought of sneaking to the river at night, leaving my shoes on the shore, filling my pockets with stones. I thought of the pills the university pharmacy gave me, one bottle after another. Some days, this dream was the only comfort I had.

People talk about it all the time.

Or, maybe I just notice it more now.

No, people talk about it all the time.

It comes up at dinner parties, casual brunches, offhand at gatherings, walking next to a friend. The word is said as if it knows you are there. The word is said as if to find you out.

What can you do, when you have done the thing that cannot be taken back, when you have held your own hand down that road, when you thought you would be gone, and then you woke up, and then you woke up and someone else looked down at you where you lay, took you to overheated rooms, and slowly, slowly, days blended into days, and you fought to find some soft thing to hold onto, some small growing reason to keep opening eyes in the morning, to rise from your bed even while the body begs for an ending?

What can you say, when friends, strangers, acquaintances, bosses, begin to talk about a person they have lost, when the spine freezes, and the thought turns and turns in one's head, the wonder, the question, repeating, *Is this how people would have talked about me?*

When I first met my beloved, they were gentle and besotted. I came back from a friend's wedding; my beloved had fixed my bike while I was gone, my beloved had replaced the tubing so we could ride together to campus. There was a night I came home from a conference and there was my beloved, waiting for me, so excited to see me that they would rather sit outside in the autumn wind than at their own house. Sitting next to my beloved, walking with my beloved through Cambridge, this became the most important thing in the world.

Walking toward me on the balls of their feet, a saunter in their step, used to living on the upper floors of buildings, careful so that the footfalls would not disturb downstairs neighbors. In summer, soft palms cupped to hold frozen peas, held up in offering to me. A favorite snack, kept in the freezer, eaten like candy, the snap of them melting on our tongues.

In winter, in a room of sawdust. Dismantling the bed built with those same soft hands, hammering and sawing to make the frame bigger, so that it could fit a mattress that would hold two bodies. So that it would better hold my body next to theirs. I sat among the tools and dust, watching my beloved as they measured and sanded, and could hardly believe this was all for me.

Later, as winter dragged on, my beloved began to keep me at a distance. My beloved flew home to Ohio in the middle of a semester to get away from the force of my need. My beloved's callousness could be so mundane, so pedestrian. My beloved didn't want to see me on our one-year anniversary and I knew this was my fault. I knew I needed to be something better than I was to deserve them.

After my beloved left me, they told me they would be with me again if I could get better, if I wasn't so depressed, if I wasn't so suicidal. My beloved began to date someone else, and still my beloved walked home with me, still repeating that they were waiting for me to get well. How badly I wanted that, to no longer be *crazy*, *unstable*, to be the person my beloved wanted me to be, to be a person worthy of their love.

My beloved found my body, found the room with pill bottles scattered on the floor. I didn't mean for that to happen. I didn't think I would wake up. I didn't want anyone to find me. It was them, this beloved who had broken my heart, who came running across town to my house when I didn't answer the phone, who found me drugged and slurring, who called 911. It was my beloved, standing between the police and firefighters, watching as they strapped my body to a gurney and carried me away.

It happens more often than you would think. A conversation on a long car ride turns to dying. *If I die in my apartment, no one would find me for three days. I've thought about it.*

After enough time, my stomach stops dropping. My hands don't tighten around the wheel. My heart does not beat any faster than normal. I stay silent. What is there to say?

When they found me, it was too late. Twenty hours had passed since I had closed my eyes. Twenty hours in the same place in bed, unmoving, unseeing.

When they found me, the drugs were still in my blood. It comes back in snatches, in bursts. My room full of people in dark uniforms. My beloved, there, among them. There were voices. Police officers. Firemen. I worried they would steal the money I had left out on my shelf. My room was too small for so many people. "Why did you do it?" a cop asked.

"Why the fuck do you think," I spat back. That's what they told me I said, anyway.

Strange hands moved my body. The world blurred and twirled. They took me outside. The streets were dark. Later, my beloved told me that they felt like a hero in that moment, for knowing what to do when they found me, when they watched me stumble from the door to my bed, for not making things worse, when the worst had already happened.

My house looked strange, the sky distant, as I rode backward, strapped onto the gurney and into the ambulance. Drugged, dazed, I texted friends, *have to go to the hospital, be back in an hour, sorry for delay.* I was supposed to throw a party that night. I told them all that I would be back soon.

The hospital was bright. I said I could pee on my own. I got lost walking to the bathroom. I couldn't stand up. I fell. A nurse followed me. She said she was going to help me. I said louder that I could pee on my own. The light was harsh and no one was kind. In the bathroom, I peed and fell against the wall and stumbled out. I couldn't find my way back. Someone stared at me, someone led me to bed. My beloved was there. They stayed, late, sat upright on the edge of the bed and let me wrap myself around them. My beloved's grandfather had just died. Or was about to die. I curled my body in a C shape around them, my head on their lap, stomach pressed to their back. I couldn't follow what they said but asked them to keep talking. The words floated above my head, meaningless, unconnected. I fell asleep there, curved around them, listening to the gentle hum of their voice.

———

When they came for me, it was too late. There was nothing in my stomach to pump. Nothing for charcoal to absorb. They pricked my arm with an IV, for fluids. They watched. It was too late. I was alive.

———

Sometimes, when I talk about it, when I say these words aloud, there's an almost unavoidable assumption: I must not have meant it. I must have been relieved. It must not have been that serious. If I had really meant it, when I found myself alive, wouldn't I have tried again?

Once, when I said the words *there were no stories to show me the way back*, someone reminded me of a story published in the *New York Times*, a story of people who jumped off bridges, who survived, who said they regretted it on the way down.

I cocked my head to one side, tried to understand the connection between those stories and my own.

I did not jump off anything and I did not regret it.

When the pill bottles were scattered and empty around my room, I lay down, pulled the sheet over my body and thought about what I would do if I woke up. I went to the kitchen and got the biggest knife I could find, just in case.

I put it on my bedside table and scribbled a note in red ink on a scrap of paper.

give all my money to my mother

I lay back down. I closed my eyes. I smiled. Relief spread over my body, warm and clean, and I thought that finally, finally, things were going to be okay.

How many books have been written about Lazarus, this sainted, beloved by this god? This chosen man, whom Christ awakens from death? How many articles, how much exegesis, to make meaning out of this holy man's life, his rebirth? Remembered, sainted, beloved.

There is a girl in the Christian gospels who is not given a name. She is known by the name of her father, Jairus. She is known by the blessing the god gives her.

There is a moment in the synoptic Gospels where a man comes running to the Christ figure, desperate. His daughter is dying. He begs the god to come and make her well. In that moment a woman, sick for the last twelve years, reaches out to touch the cloak of the god, knowing that just by brushing her fingers against the hem of his garment, she will be healed.

The god pauses, turns, asks the crowd who touched his clothing. The woman comes forward, trembling in fear. She has taken what was not even hers to ask for. The god tells her that her faith has made her well, she need not hide what she did. In the time it took to identify the healed woman, the child, Jairus's daughter, dies.

Strangers come to deliver the news, to tell the god not to bother going to Jairus's house, there is no longer a person there to heal. The god shakes his head and goes to the house anyway, passes a crowd of mourners, women wailing, and goes to the place where the girl lays.

Talitha koum, the god says. Little girl, get up.

She opens her eyes. She gets up. She walks.

The girl is not named. The girl, resurrected, does not speak. After she is brought back, the god leaves her to the living, surrounded by mourners-turned-celebrants. Her voice unheard, this little girl who felt death move through her body, left to live.

Talitha koum, the god says.

And then what? The text is silent, the question echoes. And then what?

I looked for essays, I looked for books, for theology, for scraps. I found one essay on the imbrication of the story of Jairus's daughter and the sick woman who reaches out to touch the god's cloak, how these stories were doubles. I found a copy of a sermon from 1845. I searched academic databases. How do you find a girl with no name? I have seen whole essays written on the use of a single word in scripture. I have seen pages dedicated to unpacking a single phrase. The silence around this undead girl thrums like a hollow cave. What happened to her? Where did she go? What did she do?

If this god was omnipotent, if this god knew he would face his own death, I began to suspect that he let this little girl die, knowing that he would raise her up again. Her death, her resurrection, used to demonstrate the powers of this god. To show that for this god, death was nothing but a kind of slumber, a sleep from which he could awaken anyone at will.

But what, I wondered again and again, what about this little one, this unnamed child, used by a god to showcase his might? What about the rest of us, those who were not raised up to reveal anyone's glory, those of us whose lives kept going unblessed, tainted by what we were, by what we had done?

The little girl's silence screamed to me, and I wanted to scream back. The words on the page surrounded her, suffocated her. Did she know she had been chosen? Did she know her life became miraculous? Did anyone ask her how she felt at all?

Strapped to the gurney, my backpack full of schoolbooks. My friends Ted and Rachel had brought me things from home, were there watching as they took me from the emergency room, transferring me to a different hospital. Ted had brought me a peanut butter cookie and a large, hot coffee, that I did not know would be my last for days. The stuffed animal I've had since I was a baby, given to me when I was barely older than a year. As big as my body, given to me when I was brought in for an eye surgery. Over twenty years later, the pig retained its shape, its form. Wilbur, a red ribbon tied around its throat. Some pig. I felt ridiculous, bordering on grotesque. Not allowed to walk, I was made passive, wearing the same clothes as the day before. I was carted away, through the big doors into the unyielding April morning.

In the back of the ambulance, a man who looked barely older than me sat, his hand on the gurney, steadying it.

"Can I ask," I said, "do you know, will this ambulance ride be covered by insurance? I'm on MassHealth."

He was sitting, looking up, out the window, glancing back down. "Normally, in cases like these, when doctors ordered it, normally it's covered. Don't worry about it," he said. He coughed. I asked where they were taking me. "Probably McLean," he said.

"How long have you been an EMT?" I asked.

"Couple of years," he said. "My girlfriend and I moved to Boston a few years ago. I'm training to be a medical assistant."

"The hours must be exhausting."

"Yeah, I work overnight a lot. We're not supposed to work shifts longer than eight hours, but everyone does. For the overtime. When we don't have anything to do, I can sleep in an ambulance. It's not so bad."

He had a face that made me want to protect him. "Do you have a union?" I asked. He laughed.

Outside, one of the first warm spring days was blossoming through Cambridge. Through the back window, I could see trees with white buds, the branches reaching up and away to the sky.

"I guess we're taking you to Walden," he said.

They were gentle with me. Rolled me down the hall, into the elevator. The sun was bright, streaming in through the windows. I thought they were just moving me for another checkup. I thought I would be home soon.

They rode with me in an elevator, pushed me out into the hall. "Do you know which wing?" one of them asked.

"Probably to the left," the other said. They pushed me to the side, pressed a large button. "Hello?" We waited. A woman appeared on a video monitor. "We've got someone for you."

She shook her head. "We're not expecting anyone. Try across the hall."

They pulled me to the other end of the hall, another set of double doors, another bell. A woman came out to take me. The men helped me out of the gurney, sat me in a chair. The one who had ridden in the back looked at me like he knew something I didn't. "Good luck," he said. He glanced over his shoulder as he left. I smiled, waved. He didn't smile back.

It was a Sunday night. It was a Sunday night before my last week of classes at graduate school, when I should have been studying or at work, but instead, there were doors closing behind me.

A woman with dark hair led me past the double doors, doors that I realized too late I could not return from. Doors that locked and stayed locked. She led me through a large, open room, back to another hallway, a small room where she turned her back and told me to change. She took my blood pressure, my temperature, my vitals. She handed me a hospital gown that she called a johnny, pointed to a spot on my body. An electrode was stuck to my leg. As she peeled it away, she saw another. "They should have taken these off at the ER," she mumbled. The white, plastic square left behind a patch of gray, a remnant of adhesive, when she pulled it from me.

They took my shoes. I couldn't have laces. They took my belt. They cut the ribbon from Wilbur's neck. There could be nothing sharp, nothing that tied. We were ingenious, they thought, in the ways we found to hurt ourselves.

The days jumble.

When I arrived, I signed a release. To submit to treatment for 72 hours, after which I would be let go. The thing they didn't tell me, the thing I heard from stories, from the teenagers who sat coloring at the circular table in the main room, is that every three days, they could force me to revoke it. To sign a new one, consent to a new cycle. There is no limit for how long they can do this.

If a person declines, if a person insists on leaving, they can take you to court, which guarantees at least four more days locked there as you wait for your appointed time in front of a judge, where the doctors who have seen you for half an hour can argue *too depressed to know what's good for them, just wants to get out to try again*, and you will stand alone in front of them, every word you say tainted by who you are, by what you have become.

The ward was like this: One long hallway with two sets of double doors that were the entrance and exit. The cafeteria attached to one side of this hallway. The sensory room that could only be reached through the cafeteria. Across the hall from the cafeteria was the medicine window, the wooden Dutch door, where the nurses would lean out the top, would hand pills across the threshold as we stood on the outside, waiting.

The hallway led to the main room. The nurses' station looked out over this room, a U-shaped desk, behind which we could see binders with our names on the outside. The room had one large, circular table, and a scattering of chairs. There were two small purple couches. From a certain angle, it looked like there was a column almost in the middle of the room. From another angle, it was clear that they were phone booths. There were two dial-up telephones attached to the walls. These were the only phones we were supposed to use while we were there. The walls were covered in carpet, maybe so the sound couldn't escape, so no one could eavesdrop, maybe so that no one could smash the handset into anything solid, maybe so that no one could punch any walls.

There was another hallway, on the other side of the nurses' station, that led to the group rooms. Everyone's room was connected to the main room. Everyone had a roommate, many of us more than one.

There was nowhere to go, there was nowhere to be.

I was in the bed closest to the door, pushed up against the wall. There were two other women who shared my room. There was a sink in the room, a mirror. A bathroom with a door that couldn't lock.

There was a girl who was placed in my room a few days after I got there. She was close to my age. She was going to college in Boston. Diane, who came carrying *Little Fires Everywhere* and told me about her girlfriend. Who told me so many things I wanted to ask her to shut up. Diane had been here before, across the hall in the eating disorder unit, the place the EMTs had tried to take me first.

She told me stories about how bad it got there. In the eating disorder unit, they measured how much each person ate, they weighed everyone daily. They would release patients when they got to a certain weight. The people locked up there would gain as much weight as they could as quickly as they could, planning how they would lose the weight as soon as they got out. One girl hated it there so much, she shat behind a couch in the main room of the ward, and no one noticed it for days.

Diane was indignant. She wasn't supposed to be here. "I didn't even try to kill myself," she said, gesturing at me. Every conversation I had with Diane was the same one. This place was bad, we did not belong here, how long until we could get out?

We studied Section 12 of Chapter 123 of Massachusetts state law as if we could logic our way out of where they locked us, as if we could find a loophole, as if we could understand what they wanted from us. *Section 12(a) allows for an individual to be brought against his or her will to such a hospital for evaluation.*[2]

You sign a paper letting them hold you for three days. They can make you sign a new one when your three days end. Except, weekends don't count. Holidays don't count. You can tally the hours of your life, stare out of windows and count the seconds until you can get out, but they can decide that those seconds don't count. Your Saturdays are no longer days. Your Saturdays, your limbo in which time doesn't pass and you are not sure when it will begin to move again. They control your time, they name your days for you. They have their own tools for measuring your life. It doesn't matter if their rules don't make sense to you. Your time, your days, are not yours. You wait in this limbo until they decide you don't have to. Your judgment is worthless. It's not clear if you exist at all.

In the mornings they brought us to the group room, herded in like cattle. They marked off who was there, who wasn't. They watched us. I stared at the people in the room, in pajamas, in johnnies, the people older than me, the teenagers, all of us huddled in our chairs.

"What are your goals for the day?" they asked. We would go in a circle, say how we were feeling, state what we hoped to accomplish that day. They wrote it down so that in the evenings, we could gather again and share if we had met our goals.

I'm going to finish a puzzle. I'm going to go to one of the groups. I'm going to go outside.

In the mornings, I sat there and made up goals I didn't care about. I spoke like a machine, automatic and cold. Beneath it was the goal that beat like a pulse behind my eyelids, that screamed through my blood.

My goal is to get out.

I looked into the eyes of a girl who had been kept there for six months, who was forced to sign a new three-day every three days. Time contracted. They took away my body. They kept track, they kept watch. They kept count of how many groups a person goes to, how they participate.

The first time I was called in to see the doctor, in her small office on the ward, she prescribed me a range of medications that I did not want. I was to wait at the med window, hold out my hand and swallow. I told her that I had a psychiatrist, that I didn't want new medicine. She told me it didn't matter. I told her that I couldn't sleep here. She said I could get Benadryl at night.

They had taken my weight, taken my history, thought there was a risk. Maybe anorexia, maybe something wrong with food. They put me on a regimen. Three bottles of Ensure every day. Every morning at five a man came, shook me awake long before vitals were called, before the sun rose, when the room was dark and I could hear the snores from the other beds. I opened my eyes to a cup of brown liquid inches from my face. I shook my head. "Let me sleep," I said.

"So, you're refusing treatment?" he said.

"I just want to sleep." I closed my eyes and they took their notes.

They had me on fifteens. One person, constantly circulating, checking where everyone was at all times. The door swung open at night as they came to check on us. In the moments just before sleep, someone came and shined a light on me, marked off my name on the list. Checked the other two I shared a room with. The door swishing behind them.

In the bathroom, I reached up and held onto the place where the doorknob should be, held the door closed. The staff would come knocking.

"Checks," they said.

"Here," I said.

I stayed in bed more than I should have. I knew they were watching, that the more groups I went to the sooner I might get out, but I did not have the energy, did not have the spine, to sit in the group room and listen as they repeated empty platitudes meant to make us into other people, meant to make us normal.

———

If a person comes here on purpose, if you submit to this place out of your own free will, you can leave when you want. Except, even then, the hospital can say that you can only leave during work hours, no weekends, no holidays, no evenings. If they bring you here against your will, there is a form you can complete, a petition to change your status from involuntary to voluntary. No one will tell you about this form. No one will sit you down, explain to you a quicker way out. A hospital can change your status from voluntary to involuntary. A hospital can petition for commitment. No one will explain to you how the hospital decides this.

The law says they have to tell you how to contact a public attorney, someone who will represent you, someone to stand next to you if you need to go before a judge. No one at the hospital will tell you this. No one will mention a lawyer. They put a paper in front of you, they tell you to sign it. The countdown clock begins again.

———

When we sat in the cafeteria at night, when we sat in the large open room during the day, we said everything we could remember about the laws, about how to get out. When my beloved came to visiting hours with copies of Section 12 in their hands, I read the ways they defined me, the names they gave me. I was *a likelihood of serious harm.* I was *a substantial risk of harm* to myself.[3] My judgment was impaired. I could not protect myself from the risk of my own self. Then, the language shifts. The confined person, the law says. The individual, the risk, the involuntary patient. The confined person.

———

In the evenings, some of us gathered in the cafeteria. After the sun fell, after everything was over, we could have desserts. We were allowed two items but had to get them one at a time. Every night I went hoping for small Styrofoam cups of chocolate ice cream, with a flat, thin piece of wood to scoop it out. They didn't always have them. Those nights with no ice cream, I settled for small packages of Oreos or off-brand peanut butter cookies.

It felt different at night when those few of us gathered quiet and soft in the room. I ate as slow as I could and listened. We went through the same routines.

"How was your day?" someone would ask.

"It was okay; I'm trying new meds," someone would say. "Makes me want to sleep all day."

"I really think I'm improving," someone else would say.

"Tomorrow I'm off one-to-ones," someone would say. "I'm nervous." If a person is on one-to-ones, a med tech follows them in every moment of every day. Every second they are watched.

"One-to-ones sound hard," I would say, thinking of the doors left open when I used the bathroom, when I used the shower, never an instance alone, watched and observed every waking and sleeping moment.

"You get used to it," someone would say.

I ate my ice cream, the others ate their graham crackers. It could have been summer camp, young campers getting their last treats from the canteen and staying up late to share secrets. It was sterile like a night in a hotel where you stay up late, the smell of cleaning solution on everything, but there you can wake up and drive into the sunrise the next day.

In another age, they would have locked me in a place that no one could see. All alone, in a cage next to others. Locked away, to be punished for the crime I had committed, trying to take my own life, trying to destroy something that belonged to God. Hidden, quarantined to keep the rest of the population safe from me. In another age, I would be held captive according to the law, for my own benefit. A thing not human, a thing best kept out of sight. An unwilling patient.

A person who can't see how sick she is. A person needing fixing, a person needing to be confined.

In the mornings, we were allotted two hot beverages in eight-ounce Styrofoam cups. Some mornings I got two cups of watered-down gritty coffee, some mornings I got one cup of coffee and one of tea that I could make as strong as I needed. Once, I mentioned caffeine headaches and asked for more.

"Sorry," said the worker passing out food, "everyone just gets two." I did not understand why it was important that we only got two hot drinks in the morning. I did not understand what risk it was to us. I did not realize that it might have been a risk to them. What could we do with two cups of hot liquid. What could we do to them, each other, ourselves. What could we do if we had too much caffeine, if we had uncontainable energy in this place with nowhere to go. We were risks that needed to be caged, to keep everyone safe. All of us knew that this place was not made to help us. This place did not exist to make any of us better, to help any of us start to find a path to a better life. This place was only to keep us behind its doors, to find us new medications. This place existed to keep everyone else safe from us.

I kept my head down and drank my two cups of hot liquid in the morning and thought that at least without the caffeine I could go back to sleep after breakfast.

Sometimes, one of the nurses went on coffee runs and brought back cardboard carriers full of lattes, Frappuccinos, cold brews.

"Why do you get to have that when we can't," Kara said. Kara was in high school. Kara was young and refused to eat anything. She spent the days sipping Gatorade from plastic cups. "Why do you get to have that when we can't?" Kara repeated, standing by the nurses' station, watching them drink from impossibly large Starbucks cups.

The nurse shrugged. "I don't make the rules."

I thought about begging, just a sip, please just a sip. I thought about waiting until someone had their back turned, snatching a cup, hiding it beneath the counter, sneaking to the bathroom, how good it would taste, so hot, so bitter, how the caffeine would flood my body after so many days of dregs. I watched the nurses drink. If I asked, they could make a note for my doctor to see, a mark against me. Every request was a vulnerability, something they could weigh against you, everything seen through the knowledge that you are uncontrollable, that you need to be controlled. I sat quiet, staring at the nurses as they drank.

They brought my phone from the place they had locked it with all other contraband. They would let me use it there, at the nurses' station, where they could see me.

There were a few texts asking where I was. Rachel, checking if I needed anything. A voicemail from Miriam, my boss at the café. I missed a shift Sunday morning. "Madeline, where are you? I can't believe you would do this." Somewhere, days ago, she was angry. "You were supposed to be here half an hour ago." I listened again to the message, the message she left while they were putting me in the back of an ambulance, transferred from the ER to this place. I had never missed a shift in my life.

I was going to lose my favorite job. Down a side street from campus, tucked away, this small café managed by five siblings, staffed by their friends. In the fog of jobs, of classes and stress and not enough money, this place had been a blessing. On the days I worked, I walked from campus quicker. Excited to go to this place where no one cared about how much I was working because everyone was working. Where they accepted me like rain, laughing and joking, treating me like one of their own. Where they made me sandwiches and coffee, gave them to me for free even when I wasn't on the clock.

I looked at the nurses. I did not cry. I would not cry in front of these people, these people who decided if and when I could contact anyone, if and when I could use my phone, if and when I could touch the guitar kept on the ward, if and when I could finally leave. If they saw me cry, they might say I could not use my phone anymore, could not access my laptop. Too upsetting, they might say. Detrimental to improvement.

I wrote emails to my bosses. *Medical emergency, in the hospital, I won't make my shifts for a while.* I turned off my phone, handed it back to the nurses. Walked back to the room I shared with two strangers, looked out over the city. It was gray. I closed my eyes, curled tight in a ball, and waited for something like sleep.

I thought of nothing beyond getting out. I had made it through almost two years of a master's program; there was no way I was not going to graduate on time. I convinced the nurses to let me have access to my laptop. They said it was okay as long as I stayed at the nurses' station, as long as they could see my screen, as long as it was only used for school. They looked over my shoulders as I wrote my final papers. I read essays on contemporary Russian poetry. I was writing about a Russian poet whose book cover featured a sculpture of a naked dead man. I taped a piece of paper over the image so the nurses wouldn't take the book from me. I read a book on religion in South Carolina. I wrote papers where there was no "I," where I could disappear behind the analysis, where I could pretend that I was okay. I wouldn't tell my professors, wouldn't tell anyone, wouldn't share the shame of where I was with them. Nothing would be late. They would never know that these papers were written in stolen moments, sitting in a locked ward, unwashed, in clothes I had slept in, glancing up at the nurses watching me, checked on every fifteen minutes.

I was sitting at the nurses' station, writing a paper on the principles of trauma-informed care. A man who worked there, a tech who worked the swing shift, who was gruff, angry with all of us, was pacing behind the counter. That day, a woman in hijab had been admitted to the ward, had gone straight to her room, and had not come out.

"They're trying to impose their Sharia law," he was saying, loudly. He was scowling. He was shouting into every room.

My throat closed. I stared at the words on the screen, unmoving. Later, when I was released, when I was no longer a ward of the state, when I was no longer just another *crazy*, when I had some semblance of credibility, I reported him to his supervisor, yelled that he should not be working here, and began to cry.

Sitting there, staring at my half-finished essay, I said nothing. Terrified of what he could to do me, what he could write in my files, I did nothing. All of us, silent, as he said again that those people were coming into our country. Those people had no right to be here. These people were a threat.

There is a story in the Christian Bible of a man possessed by hundreds of demons. The townspeople tried to restrain him with shackles and chains, to lock him up where he could no longer shatter their nights and days with his howling. He wanders in the distance. His clothes are ragged. He beats himself with rocks. This man is supposed to stay locked up. This man keeps breaking every chain they put on him. When Christ encounters this man, he asks for his name.

"My name is Legion," the many-voiced man says, "for we are many."

The hundreds of demons speak through this man in one voice. They ask Christ to not send them back to the abyss. The god splinters the demons, divides them, takes their spirits from the man, puts them in the bodies of pigs. The pigs, their bodies no longer theirs, run into the ocean to die.

We are meant to cheer for the godhead as he banishes the demons, as they rush into the water to drown. We are meant to be in awe of this power, that with just a phrase from the god, the horde of demons is vanquished. We are not meant to think of the man, wandering alone, the townspeople afraid of his screams. We are not meant to ask why the only answer to his howls was locking him up. We are not meant to ask why many demons cry in one voice. We are not meant to think of this man who beat himself with stones. This man, unclean, this man whose voice carries from the tombs, this man who only beats at himself, who does no harm to others. We are not meant to ask how a multitude of demons made a home in one man. We are not meant to ask what happens to the pigs after they run into the ocean, if the saltwater fills their mouths, if they scream as they drown. We are not supposed to ask why the only solution was a slaughter. We are not supposed to hear ourselves in the many-voiced howls.

Sam didn't say how long they'd been there. Sam spoke in a voice like bells. Sam's short hair had been dyed, once, before, and had faded to dusty shades of turquoise and lilac. Sam dragging a feeding tube after them. They were always hooked up, the tube sneaking up through their nose. Sometimes, when they were upset, when they didn't want it, they would take out the tube, and the nurses would have to force it back in. I didn't like to think about the way it would feel, the way they would fight, how even when they didn't want to eat, they couldn't stop the drip of the things being put in them.

The first time my three-day was revoked, when time unhooked itself around me, when it was not clear how long I would be there because they could keep me as long as they wanted, my beloved came to visiting hours and sat with me in a corner. I wept. I begged. I was so scared I was trembling.

"You have to help me get out of here," my face crumpled. "Please." My legs tucked beneath me, in the same johnny I had worn the day before. We were in the dining room. Other people were there with their visitors. "Please." My legs ached from not moving, from so many hours curled tight in a ball.

My beloved took my hand in theirs. They promised. It would be okay. It was just a matter of time, of days.

Shame pulsed through my body like a second heartbeat. "Promise you won't tell anyone where I am. Why I'm here." My beloved already thought I was crazy. Their family thought I was crazy. My beloved promised, again, not to tell anyone why I was there, trapped.

My beloved sat with me, holding my hand and promising, until visiting hours were over, until they had to leave, to take the bus back to Cambridge. I watched them pass through the double doors with their head down.

I went to the med window and asked for two Benadryl. The nurse handed them to me in a paper cup, wrote a note in her logbook. I took the pills with no water and stared into the nurse's eyes as I swallowed.

—

The pounding silenced the ward. When it started, we all got quiet, we all knew what it was. The steady thump as Sam slammed their head against the wall in their room. Sometimes they aimed for the corners, where the walls met. Sometimes they did not aim at all.

We looked at each other, we looked toward their room, and waited.

The man who had shouted about Sharia law walked to their door.

"Talk to me," he said in a gruff voice.

"No." Sam was crying, mucus and tears audible and thick.

The man was getting angry. The man was a hard edge.

"If you won't talk to me, I don't know what you want me to do," he said. Everyone in the ward was silent, listening to him yell.

"Leave me alone," Sam said. The pounding was a steady rhythm. The man wanted Sam to talk. Sam wanted him to leave.

"Fine. You don't want my help?" His footsteps were heavy as he stalked to the nurses' station. He shouted to the other nurses. He couldn't believe how Sam was talking to him. He used the wrong pronoun. We listened to him shout, we listened as no one corrected him.

This man who yelled, this man who hated us, could make notes in our binders, *acting up*, *bad behavior*, *uncooperative*, could tell our doctors that we were behaving terribly, that we were unwell, that there was something wrong with us, and he would be believed with no question.

We kept our heads down, we stayed quiet. This place was supposed to help us. They knew what we needed, and if we didn't listen, if it didn't work, that was our fault.

We are judged by the people who hate us. Judged by people afraid of us. People who want to lock us up so they do not hear us scream. People who think the only way to heal us is to kill whatever demon is inside of us. We, legion, there among the tombs, shouting. They do not ask us why we are shouting. They have their chains for us. They have their places for keeping us far away from them. They want to banish every bad thing that lives inside of us. It doesn't matter how those things got there. We are not people with stories. We are not individuals with lives. We are not Sam, or Kara, or Rick, or Cody, or Jasmine, or Madeline. It does not matter what brought us there. It only matters that we behave, that we take the medicines they give us and do what they tell us, until they say we can leave.

Rick had been released. I didn't know how long he had been there, but I knew it had been weeks. He had gotten what all of us wanted, had gotten out. He promised to come back to see us, promised to walk his dog on the parking deck where we could see.

"It's him! Look at his dog!" someone said.

It was sunny. I had to shade my eyes to see him there, on the top level of the concrete garage, across the gap that separated the building from where we were. It was hard to recognize him at that distance in the glare of the sun, but no one else in the world would have been there, walking their dog so we could see its head and tail, those two small puffs of fur. He waved to us, his dog at his side. They walked back and forth. Rick held his hand in the air. The dog wagged its tail.

The days they brought us the therapy dogs were the best days. Even for someone like me, who didn't like dogs, the days they came to see us were the happiest days.

Every morning one of us would ask the others, "Are the animals coming today?" We would scan the schedule, written in red on the whiteboard. The days they were coming, Sam, usually so quiet, so afraid, would perk up. They would tell the story we'd all heard before, about the last time they brought dogs, and what they looked like, and what their names were. Before he left, Rick would tell stories about his dog, the dog he promised to bring to us when he got out, even though it wasn't allowed in the ward and none of us were allowed out.

When they brought in the dogs, it was all Sam could talk about. Normally, in goals group, when they said out loud what their goal for the day was, their voice shook out the day's intention, "My goal for today is, as always, to stay safe." That day, they had two goals. "My goal is to stay safe, and to pet the dogs," they said, perched with their feet on the chair, their arms dangling in front of them, their feeding tube and drip behind them, like ghosts.

When the volunteer came later that afternoon with a golden retriever at her side, Sam wasn't there.

We sat in a circle, the dog bounding around us, as the volunteer told us why she chose to come see us. How her daughter had been here, not in our ward, but the one across the hall, the one they almost took me to, the one Diane told me about, where a girl shat on the floor.

"It helped my daughter so much, being here," she said. "It's important to me to give back." I thought about a woman who hated this place so much she left a pile of shit steaming in the common space, about the ways the techs spoke to us, like we were children to be tamed. I thought about how we couldn't leave.

At dinner, as we tried to eat stuffed shells with plastic knives and forks, no one said a word about how ridiculous it was, even as the flimsy plastic broke while we sawed at the pasta and we could not get the shells into our mouths without using our hands. Sam asked how the dog was. Sam had been put on a new combination of drugs and slept through the dog visit. "It licked my face," Jasmine said, and Sam giggled as if they had been there.

Sometimes, Sam would remind us all about how Rick had walked his dog for us, how cute his dog was, how fluffy the tail. I thought about the way he walked back and forth, waving. If anyone else had seen him, they would have thought he was crazy. A man with a dog, pacing back and forth, waving to an open sky. But he was out there, on the other side of the glass, where no one was watching, tracking, keeping notes. And we were here.

In some places, in some times, to be insane was to be closer to God. Not encumbered by the laws of reason. Speaking in prophecies, something akin to speaking in tongues. A holy fool. A person could walk through town, saying words in rhythms that no one could understand. A person could tear their clothing. Blessed, the others would say. They would feed her. She could go crying, weeping, lurching through the streets; a sign from God, maybe mourning for the sin of the world, maybe grief for all of our failures.

Then, things changed. Reason became God. Those without reason, those outside rationality, were damaged, frightening. An affront to God's order, an affront to an Enlightened society. The babbling, the mad, those of us who did not behave, were taken, chained up. Chains around necks, around wrists, attached to cell walls. There were so many things they could use. Straps to tie us to chairs. Jackets to tie back our arms. Shackles around our ankles. Solitary confinement. Lunatics, all. Those of us who tried and failed were subject to "wicker cages with a hole for the head, with the hands bound, or the 'wardrobe' which enclosed the subject up to his neck, with only the head protruding."[4]

Locked in basements, dungeons, where no one could see us, where we could disturb no one. Dangerous to others, dangerous to society, we were confined. The hospitals not hospitals. The hospitals places to lock us up. The doctors our guards, our wardens, there to correct our behavior. The early asylum was a prison with no exit.

Time was passing and I was frantic. My beloved was supposed to come. They were late. In the phone booth, I called, and no one answered. Did they forget about me? I imagined them at dinner, at a restaurant, telling someone a sad story about an ex of theirs who was in the hospital. I thought about the first night we kissed, when they told me a sad story about their best friend back in Ohio, who was in the hospital, who was starting electroshock therapy. I had become another sad story, another tragic woman they had learned so much from, another troubled girl who taught them empathy, another anecdote to share over dinner as they refilled their date's water.

Then they were there, appearing in the room. I ran to them. "I thought you weren't coming," I said. My arms were clamps at their neck.

In the cafeteria we sat looking at the sunset. The evenings blended together. There were times they didn't talk much, times when I would glance around the room to see if Jasmine, or Sam, or Cody, or Kara were looking at us, if anyone saw how little my beloved spoke to me. What would everyone say about the way we sat in silence? What did it say about me, that my most frequent visitor had nothing to say to me? There were times when they brought printouts of Massachusetts laws on involuntary hospitalization. Some days, in the quiet, I asked what my beloved was thinking about. There were times when they looked at me with heavy eyes and told me about issues with housemates, about the things that were troubling them. I wanted to be useful. I wanted to be good. I listened and comforted them and did not remind them where we were, why we were there.

The doctors weren't there on the weekends. We squirmed, we counted the minutes that didn't count toward our release. No medication changes, no doctors' notes, no oversight. We waited, we colored, we started new puzzles.

There were rules they didn't tell you, things you could only learn by being there. Once a day, if you had a note from your doctor, you could join a nurse who led a group on fifteen-minute walks. I learned this after I saw my doctor, when it was too late to get a doctor's note, when it would be three more days before I saw her again. For all the days I was there, I could only go outside once, to sit in a small garden for ten minutes.

There was a guitar kept in the group room that I was only allowed to play in the morning. The staff on the afternoon and evening shifts shook their heads when I asked for it. I didn't have a note in my file from a doctor, they said. A thing like that, with taut, sharp strings, was too dangerous for me to hold. I didn't mention that the nurses brought it to me in the mornings.

"I guess music therapy isn't a thing here," I said. They shrugged.

In the mornings, when the staff didn't check my file, I took the guitar to a room designed to hold sound, the designated room for people to go when they were screaming, yelling, so they did not disturb the other patients.

In the guitar case, there was a capo but no pick. It was too dangerous, a piece of plastic small enough to be swallowed. One of the morning nurses ripped out a sheet of paper from a notebook, folded it over and over into a compact triangle, covered it in tape. In that little room with the door closed in the locked ward with a pick made from paper, I played the only song I knew by heart. I plucked at the strings, rhythmless. Head pounding from lack of caffeine, I stared out of the window and played the same song, slow and out of tune, over and over and over.

In my room there is a small brown box. In this box there is a piece of paper, folded and folded and folded over itself. For years, I didn't have a guitar of my own. It didn't matter.

This little scrap of paper and tape, this gesture of kindness, given to me in a place with no way out.

There was going to be a conference call, to determine if I could leave. If the call went well, I could be released that day or the day after. I had six people ready, friends from my graduate program, waiting by their phones to join the call, to say that they would be part of my support network. My beloved texted me. They were ready for me to call, whenever I needed. They would do anything to help me get out.

I sat in a small room, in the chair farthest from the door. The room was crowded with bodies. There was the social worker who had met me once. There was the doctor with thick, Botox lips, who had seen me once, who had told me to try new meds. There was a new doctor, with short black hair, who had taken over from another doctor, who told me I needed mood stabilizers. I didn't know any of their names and they didn't know mine.

My hair was thick and matted after days of washing with the thin stream of water and sample-size standard-issue shampoo. I was wearing the clothes I had worn the day before. I was so close. I was so close.

My brother and sister were on speakerphone, the first to join the call. "I'm just worried," my brother said. "Why won't she take the new medication?"

My stomach dropped. They looked at me. Three strangers who would decide how long I was trapped there. Panic shot through my gut.

"We're concerned about that too."

"I don't need mood stabilizers," I said. "I have a psychiatrist outside of here; he doesn't think I need them." My friends texted. Did I need them? They were waiting, ready to call. O*ne minute, I'm not sure.*

"She's not even invested," one of the women waved her hand at me. "She's just on her phone."

"I've got people waiting to call in. I'm texting them." My voice was getting higher. The note of panic, the edge of desperation. There was a group of people waiting, a group of people who had agreed to help, who the doctors said could call. "I'm just telling them it will be a minute." I could hear myself beginning to sound crazy. I texted my beloved. They were waiting, they had made sure to be free. I was inconveniencing them. I did not know how to be what anyone needed me to be.

"Put the phone down. You're not taking this seriously," another woman said.

The woman with dark hair met my eyes. "You're too depressed to know what's good for you," she said. "You're too depressed to think straight." They all looked at me, quiet and blinking. They waited, weighing what I would say, how I would say it, how I would hold my body. They would decide if I was good enough to be let out, if I could meet their expectations, if I could sound the way they wanted me to sound. If I could sit up straight, make my voice steady.

I was cornered. Hair greasy and tangled. In dirty clothes, a wild creature.

"You have to let me out. This place isn't good for me."

"You don't know what's good for you."

"I don't need mood stabilizers. I have antidepressants."

"Those have been working great for you," she spat. "If those had been working you wouldn't be here to begin with."

I was trapped, ragged. I stared at the doctor and had nothing to say. If I were to tell the truth, that this thing had been coming, that it would have happened without these pills, they would know that the problem is me, the problem sat at the core of me, unmoving. They would keep me here longer. There were no words to say. They wanted to remake me to fit their definition of health, their understanding of okay. In their eyes I was unstable. The unreliable narrator of my own life.

My phone vibrated in my hands. My friends, my beloved, asking when they could call. People who would have told the doctors that they were waiting for me, that they would be there when I got out, that I had a support system, that I had hands waiting to catch me. I didn't understand why the doctors wouldn't let them call in.

The conversation kept going, circling. They talked over me, around me. Why wouldn't I take the medicine? Why was I so intent on getting out? The social worker looked at me with sad doe eyes, silent. I texted my friends. *Never mind, I think the call is off. Thanks for offering to help!*

They asked again and again, why was I so insistent on getting out? They were rational, and to them, wanting to die was profoundly irrational, and they could not let someone like me leave this place.

I would stay in this place, observed, a thing, a creature. A thing like me couldn't know what it needed, what would make it normal. The room was crowded and small and watched. I wished I had thought to get the campus therapist to join the call, to hear his calm voice cut through their demands. I balled my hands into fists. I tried to swallow tears. Notes taken of my reactions, every move I made, all of it evidence that I couldn't be let go. *Her anger. Unstable.* Somewhere far away, I heard my brother telling me to call him from the main phone after this was done.

There was nowhere to go. There was nowhere to cry. They were coming on rounds, on checks. What would they write if they saw me, curled in my bed, holding a stuffed animal and weeping?

I stood in the hallway near the medicine window, trying to disappear. Jasmine paused as she walked past. We kept track of each other's days, which day out of our three, knew each other's counts, we knew how close, how far, the steps each one of us would have to take to leave. She knew about the call, she knew I'd had a chance.

"How did it go?"

I looked at my feet and started to cry. She didn't move. She didn't reach out to touch me. "It's okay," she said, in a voice calm like snow. "I know. It's okay." She waited, standing at a distance. "It gets to be so much." She stood watch, this woman I barely knew, this woman who had been trapped there so much longer than I, who understood the grief, the powerlessness, the anger.

"I just want to go home." I cried like a child.

"I know," she said, "I know."

Later, I will learn that the people from graduate school who knew where I was thought I was there for an eating disorder. Google search the hospital, the information for the eating disorder ward across the hall comes up. There is nothing about the place where we were. Later, I will not tell them the truth. I will think it's better for them to assume that I couldn't eat instead of thinking of all the pills I could swallow.

When I remembered how to steady my breath and harden my jaw, I went to the phones, dialed my brother's number, curled my legs beneath me. I drew shapes in the carpeted walls as it rang. None of us knew what to do.

I didn't say that I had tried to tell him, tried to warn him that if he brought up any reason to keep me here, they would hang on to it, cling to it. I didn't remind him that I had asked for him to follow my lead, that this was not the time to ask questions. To be in a place like this was to be uncredible from all sides. What kind of person, involuntarily hospitalized, would know what was good for them? To be there, locked, a ward of the state, was to be made a thing unreliable, a thing who surely could not think straight.

"So, what, you want me to come out there?" he said.

"I don't know," I said. "Yes?"

Three days later he was sitting across from me in the cafeteria, staring at his hands. I couldn't remember the last time I saw him in person. He looked so large, so solid in the hospital chair.

"My three-day's up tomorrow," I told him.

"Are they going to let you out?" he asked.

"I don't know," I said. "I think it'll help that you're here."

He was staying at my house in Somerville—a half hour Lyft ride away, an hour and a half on public transit. It didn't seem worth it, for him to come all the way out and spend the day waiting downstairs in the lobby, just in case they let me out, just to ride in back in another cab with me. If I was released, he would be waiting at my house. If I didn't get out, he would come to visiting hours in the evening, we would make a plan, figure out what to do next.

When Christ came back from the dead, he hadn't even been dead for three days. He died on a Friday afternoon. Stayed dead on a Saturday. Came back on a Sunday. No one knows what happened to Christ while he was dead. He doesn't tell anyone. No one in the gospels asks where he has been, they only care that he came back.

When you leave the hospital, when your three upon three upon three days are up, there will be no crowds to greet you. When you leave the hospital, you won't know how long you were there. When you leave the hospital, you are supposed to go back into the way time moves, hour to hour, day to day.

In his *Inferno*, Dante, guided by Virgil, comes to the seventh circle of hell and finds the Woods of Suicides. A place where the soul of the person who sinned against God, who took their own life, is trapped inside a knotted sapling, whose bark is pecked and eaten by harpies. The cursed trees feel every bite, awake to the talons and claws and beaks. Their bodies transformed into lacerated stumps, bleeding, broken. Somewhere between life and death, the trees, ungrowing, rooted in suffering. This is their punishment for violence against the self. For killing one of God's creations.

Trapped forever in these woods, their bark torn by sharp beaks, only able to speak if the tree-self is damaged, if a twig is snapped off, if through this painful act, an opening is made. These trees in their limbo, unable to speak to the others just like them, their limbs unable to touch, unable to commiserate. Frozen, alone, so close to others who could share their pain. On the Last Day, when everyone else will rise from the dead for judgment, these cursed souls will remain as twisted stumps, neither living nor dead, ensnared eternally.

When I read this, I thought it was the worst and truest story.

It was the morning that my latest three-day was expiring. They woke me like normal, plastic cup of thick protein shake shoved in my face, and brought me to stand in line for vitals. My legs were sore from doing nothing but sitting, from keeping my legs tucked beneath me, making myself smaller. I wanted to tell them that I might be getting out, that they didn't need to take my vitals, that it was okay if I went back to bed or had an extra cup of coffee. Instead, I stood in line for the nurse to take my blood pressure. Until I was cleared, until I passed through those double doors, there was no guarantee that I was going anywhere.

I asked the nurses if the doctors were on the ward. Only the doctors could let me out. The nurse shrugged. "They'll probably have a meeting after lunch."

I sat in the cafeteria, drinking watered down coffee, staring at yogurt. Diane sat across from me, and we talked about what we always talked about. "Your three-day is up today? Do you think they'll let you out? Mine is up tomorrow, I'm really hoping they let me out, my parents have been coming every day, it's clear that I have a support system. If they try to keep me here longer, I'm going to fight it."

That morning, everyone talked. My three-day was up. They hoped it would be today. Did anyone know when they decided? I had someone come to visiting hours regularly, they would consider that. Someone wanted to know what would be the first thing I did when I got out. I didn't know. It didn't matter. Nothing mattered after getting out.

The social worker assigned to my case called me into her office. She flipped through my binder, pulled out a paper. "We've set you up with an outpatient program in Brookline. They'll be expecting you there tomorrow."

"Okay," I said. I tried not to hold on to this word, tomorrow. I tried not to hope.

She passed a paper along the table to me, a form with the seal of the hospital at the top. Safety Plan. "Take a minute to fill this out, I have to go meet with someone else and I'll be back."

There was a place to list my name and address. There was half a line to answer what I would do in a moment of crisis. Spaces to list numbers, names, people I would call if I decided to try again. Phone numbers for hotlines printed across the top of the page. A space to make a list of things to do instead of dying. I wrote too many phone numbers to fit on the page, kept writing them on the back of the paper, to prove that I had support, that this will not happen again, to guard against them finding another reason to keep me.

She came back, looked at the sheet, tore off the top page so I was left with the yellow carbon copy of this liability waiver. The hospital was free of any responsibility; this was my safety plan, the steps that I agreed to follow. If I were to try again, if I were to succeed, the hospital would not be at fault. It would be me, alone, my fault, my responsibility.

They took me to the room where they kept everyone's things locked up, stored in small cubbies. They handed me my backpack, the clothes they had taken. After so many days barefoot, in slippers and socks, my shoes, fitting snugly wrapped around my feet, felt strange and tight. They opened the doors and I tried to walk slowly, their eyes on my back. It was not until I was in the elevator, alone, that I could exhale.

They don't tell you when you are going to leave. They don't give you notice, don't give you time to call family, friends, to arrange a ride. They don't give you money for the train or a taxi. Once the doors close behind you, you are on your own, unless you misstep, unless you are dragged back there again.

Outside was gray, foggy and damp. I rushed through the hospital foyer, waited in the open air for my Lyft driver. I had forgotten to say goodbye to Sam. I paid thirty dollars for a Lyft from the hospital to my front door. Desperate for a door I could lock, a hot shower, a rough loofa, real soap, the weight of a metal utensil. Guilty in the face of the money I could have saved by taking the bus, then the train, then another bus. I couldn't justify the cost, but I didn't care.

I was starving for real food and ate every piece of candy the driver had placed within reach. Wintergreens, lifesavers. I had never tasted anything so sweet.

I came home to the same house in which I had died, and there was my brother, waiting. I took a shower and told myself I would never again take for granted the hot rush of water, the pressure on my head, my body, the luxury of a bathroom door that locks.

I took my brother to The Neighborhood, a diner I had heard so much about, hadn't ever been able to afford. We were the only customers. The coffee was strong and bitter. I don't remember what we talked about, but we walked there, down the street together in the middle of the day, and no one was calling to check where I was, no one was taking note of how much of what I ate, and this felt like a miracle.

He stayed for one day, the first day I took the bus downtown to start outpatient. That night, before he left, we made a plan, a real plan, not the liability waiver the hospital had given me. People to call. Other things to do instead of dying.

"We need to figure this out so if something like this happens again it doesn't fuck up my life," he said. Though it was fair, though it was earnest, though he was laughing when he said it, I put these words into a box and placed it next to my heart, wrapped in guilt.

The thing they don't tell you about coming back from the dead is that the not-dying creates problems for others, things you have to learn to swallow, things you bury in yourself.

We went to the kitchen and looked at the knife block. We wrote the numbers of the suicide hotline on Band-Aids in thick Sharpie, stuck them to the side of the wooden block that rested against the wall, where my housemates would never see them. The Band-Aids fell off. We cut pieces of tape. We covered the Band-Aids in tape.

"I swear to God," he was laughing. "You asshole, if you don't call that number." We stood next to the knives, the early summer night thick around us, laughing. It didn't matter that I had called this number before, that the night I tried to die I could have googled that number if I wanted to. What mattered was us, there, laughing at the scraps of plastic and tape. Hidden where my housemates couldn't see, the signs of where I had been tucked away, out of sight.

Months and years later, I google searched the name of the hospital ward, and learned that it is a for-profit institution, run by a hedge fund, and that it had the power to keep me there indefinitely, until my Medicaid ran out, until the bill crested above me.

When I discovered this, I stared at the screen. It took me a moment to realize I was screaming.

In the weeks after I got out, I read every book, listened to every podcast, desperate for anything to reflect my story back to me. I scoured the library. I read fiction, memoirs, psychology books. Nothing was right. The women in *Girl, Interrupted* did not worry about the things we worried about. Kaysen writes of the "day-to-day business of being nuts" in a tone that grates. The women in her book can leave the ward. With supervision they can walk to an ice cream shop. They have their own rooms.

Sylvia Plath's ghost haunts Cambridge. She was taken to the good hospital, the nice hospital, and she didn't have to worry about losing her home, about losing her job. When Sylvia Plath was taken to McLean Hospital, the novelist Olive Higgins Prouty paid for her treatment and went to check on her. Plath's novel *The Bell Jar* traces the gentle, gradual fall into the fog of depression. The main character, Esther, is not working, has a mother who loves her. The novel ends as Esther leaves the hospital. We don't get to know what happens to her, how she does or does not adjust to life after. We see her fall, we see her steady, and we move on. The novel asks us to consider a girl who wants to die, who has material resources, whose treatment is shaped by the way she is gendered, who is supposed to return to being what a proper girl should be. We are asked to consider her despair, her recovery.

Reader, I am asking you to consider me.

I am asking you to consider the rest of us. People who went to hospitals with no safety nets, people who sat in hospitals and worried about jobs, about rent. People who were fired because we missed a shift, we were a no-call no-show. People who left locked wards and had to keep living, whose stories continued without a road map.

How many ways had I failed? Was I a failed suicide, a failed person, or something else entirely? A ghost, a zombie, a thing that should have died, a haunted body who kept living even after its own death.

Different cultures and times have their own ideas and customs surrounding suicide—about altruistic self-killing, or about how a person who kills themselves is the most damned of all. The Catholic church forbids suicide, and, until the 1980s, if a person took their own life, they were denied funeral rites, barred from burial in consecrated ground. A person's body is God's property; to destroy God's property is theft. A person's body is raw material, owned by a more powerful being.

In colonial Massachusetts, "The civil desecration of the corpses of suicides was common, as were attempts to prevent untoward influence upon the living by physically isolating and constraining the body and its potentially dangerous spirit."[5]

I stared at my feet when I walked to work. Down the streets of Cambridge, to the front desk of the language center and back home, up the hill, through the bustle of Union Square, and did not know if I stepped over my buried kin. I didn't know if I could use that word, but there was a connection, unmistakable, between myself and the forgotten dead. Unmarked, unnamed, our dangerous spirits confined to secret gravestones.

"The bodies of those who killed themselves were, in many countries, buried at night and at crossroads. The greater traffic over such crossroads was thought to 'keep the corpses down,' and the intersection of paths, it was believed, would make it more difficult for the spirit to find its way home."[6]

Union Square in Somerville is a maze of intersecting roads and pedestrian paths. There is a small plaza where, in summer and fall, stands are erected for the weekly farmer's market. Music, children running and laughing. A stall that sells iced coffee. A sprawling plant store, bursting at the seams with leaves and vines. I didn't know what was beneath it all. If underneath the footfalls of children, beneath the pavement and sewer pipes, pushed aside to make room for subway tracks, if somewhere hidden, covered, below these crossroads, lay the bones of those whose death made them unknowable, untouchable eternally.

"In early Massachusetts, cartloads of stones were unloaded at the crossroads where a suicide had been buried."[7] The bodies and spirits of those who killed themselves, confined like contaminants. Dangerous, these restless ghosts with no way home.

I walked home from work, sat alone in my bed in the golden hour of a Somerville evening, the soft light turning the world silken. Whenever my housemate was dog sitting, when she brought a new pup to the house, the creature would balk at the door to my room, whining and crying, refusing to go in. "Dogs can see ghosts that people can't," she told me, laughing. "Your room must be haunted." I stood in the middle of the room and looked at the dog, whimpering on the threshold, staring back at me.

I found a scrap of paper among the things the hospital sent me home with. In red ink, scribbled notes. My age. The date they found me. My weight. A list of the things I took. Above it all, the letters TBF.

I brought the note to the therapist who worked at the school counseling center. It was the last time I would ever see him. As a student, I was only supposed to have six sessions with a university therapist per year. He was only supposed to help me find an outside therapist, someone I could afford, someone who would not have to limit our time because of the university policy. After our first session, he scheduled me to see him again. We could only meet once a month. When we passed six sessions, he didn't say anything. I don't know if it was something he could see in my eyes, something in the way my voice shook, but the weeks passed, and he didn't acknowledge that there was a rule we were breaking. But now I had graduated, and this was not a thing either of us could find a way around. No longer a student, no longer eligible for university services.

I brought the note to him during our last session. "Should I have this?" I asked. "What does that acronym mean?"

He hadn't known that I'd been in the hospital at all, that I had tried to die. He looked at the note and looked back at me. I thought for a moment that he would start to cry. "To be followed," he said.

"Oh," I said. We sat looking at each other in silence. I thought of the nurses and aides who stalked behind me, the notes they kept. They all would have known, would have seen this in my files. I was a risk of harm. I was an emergency. A thing that needed watching, a thing that could not be left alone.

"I'm really glad you're okay," he told me. "I would've been devastated if anything had happened to you."

I realized, with the gentle pressure of a throat suddenly tight with the threat of tears, that he was the only person who had said that to me. I looked at him, his blue eyes watering, and thought how earnest he was, how small, in his brown corduroy jacket that was just a little too big. I thought about what it would be like to hug him. The space between us was impassible.

"We have to talk about saying goodbye," he said. "What will happen if we run into each other somewhere. I can't acknowledge you, but if you say hi to me first, I'll say hi in return, but that's it."

"Can I write you a postcard?" I asked. "To tell you if I'm doing well?"

"Yes," he said. "But I can't write back."

I left his office and didn't know where to go. I wandered campus, toward home, watching other people, their faces up toward the sky.

At home, I put the nurse's paper with the rest of the things I had saved from the hospital. The sun was coming in through the windows. There were a thousand things I did not have names for, the day gentle, the light a soothing touch on my skin. Toothless, this day like a blanket, wrapping me inside itself with a secret that no one would know to ask about. Unfollowed, alone, I did not know where to go.

I saved the notes from those days before I tried to die, those weeks where my heart was a feral creature in my chest. In a packet with the papers and forms from the hospital, I collected the evidence that no one else would see.

Sergei Yesenin was a poet who lived through the Russian Revolution, the founding of the Soviet state. The first thing I learned about Yesenin was not his poetry, his fame or popularity, how beloved he was, or his brief marriage to Isadora Duncan, but how he died. In 1925, he was found dead in the Hotel Angleterre in St. Petersburg in an apparent suicide. According to legend, to myth, the day before he killed himself, he wrote one last poem. There was no ink in the room. To write this goodbye poem, he cut his skin, scrawled the words in his own blood. After he died, a wave of copycat suicides swept through the Soviet Union. Some of his works were banned. Too dangerous, too depressing for people to read.

A few days before I tried to make my own ending, I sat in class, writing and rewriting the same poem in my notebook, misspelling words, forgetting declensions.

До свиданья, друг мой, до свиданья.
Милый мой, ты у меня в груди.
Предназначенное расставанье
Обещает встречу впереди.

До свиданья, друг мой, без руки, без слова,
Не грусти и не печаль бровей,-
В этой жизни умирать не ново,
Но и жить, конечно, не новей.

Scribbled over and over, these words incomprehensible to everyone around me, as if to say to classmates and friends who sat close by, I am too far away for you to see. Written in words they could not read, as if to say, I will not implicate you in what is about to happen. As if to say that no poem in my blood, no breath in my chest, could change the direction of this path. As if to say a goodbye that no one could hear.

Goodbye, my friend, goodbye.
Dear one, you are in my heart.
Our predestined parting
Promises we'll meet again in the future.

Goodbye, my friend, without hands, without words,
Don't be sad and don't furrow your brow—
In this life, to die is nothing new,
But to live, of course, is no newer.[8]

A condition of my release from the locked ward was my attendance at an outpatient program, a partial hospitalization at a facility in Brookline. I looked at the glossy brochures, images of women and flowers, and expected nothing. This would be no different than the things that passed for group therapy at the locked ward, I thought, sitting in rooms and waiting for time to pass.

My first morning in Brookline, I was brought to a small suite of three rooms and offices. The room I sat in was dim and windowless. The chairs were pushed against the walls. Women of all ages and backgrounds sat there, some staring at the floor, some looking at each other. We went in a circle, reading the rules for group discussion. *Only use I-statements. Ground things in your own experience. Something that is good for you might not be good for someone else. Don't give advice. Don't interrupt someone when they are talking. If someone says something that resonates, something you agree with, snap your fingers.*

Iman came with heavy eyes, clutching coffee. Cathy was a teacher who spoke like she was drowning. Rana did not speak much English, and we made room for her silences. Jessie was always there, on her crutches. Jessie did not speak. Day after day, she sat looking, silent. When we went in a circle to introduce ourselves at the beginning of each group, she exhaled her name. We held our breath to hear.

On my second morning, before group sessions started, I turned and there was Diane, grinning at me in the hallway.

"They sent you here too!" she exclaimed. She sat next to me, told me about how bad it had gotten the day I left the locked ward, how they found out someone was giving someone else their Xanax, how someone punched a wall so hard they broke their wrist, how glad she was to be out.

When the group leader came in, when she shut the door behind her, something changed. Serious and calm, the air around us settled. One by one, out of order, we began to say things out loud, things we had not said in other places, things we could not say in other places. This room so different from the locked ward. This room where we were not followed, this room that we could leave if we wanted.

There with each other, in that suite of rooms in a hospital in Brookline, we built the walls to safeguard each other. Our vows sacred and unbreakable. We would not interrupt. We would not share what was said with anyone outside of the group. We would not exchange contact information, not phone numbers not last names not social media, until we graduated.

We sat in small rooms together. Bared our worst parts. We sat in small rooms together, chairs pushed to the edges. We were all shaking, separately. One by one, we had lived.

There is a moment when a snap becomes thunder, when the simple action of a woman pushing her middle finger against her thumb becomes crashing applause, yes, yes, you are here and you are speaking and I hear you.

There is a moment, when you speak, and the noise of middle fingers slapping against the bulbous base of uncountable thumbs becomes the sound you have needed for all your life.

Time meant something different there, the moment I spoke. I had been waiting, practicing in my head, rehearsing so the sentences would come out just right. I stared at the floor, my voice shaking, that first time I spoke, when someone listened. I looked around the room. Heads were nodding. Women were meeting my eyes and mouthing yes. Yes. We have been there too. In small rooms, I led them to the darkest parts of the house, where light had never reached, where something so foul was hidden, it did not have a name.

I waited. They waited.

Yes, they said. I have felt that way too. One by one by one by one by one by one, fingers snapping as if to say, we are glad you are here.

There is a woman with dark hair, who I saw twice in my life, who worked in the locked ward, who rolled her eyes at me when I screamed that I wanted to go home. A woman who told me I was *too depressed to think straight*, who thought I couldn't possibly know my own needs, what crazy person could understand their own state of mind, this woman who looked me in the eye and said it would only be a matter of time before I was back, locked away in that place, watched and monitored. It would only be a matter of time before I slipped up, a thing like me too unstable to live on the outside.

I am not saying that spite is the best reason to stay alive, but it is not the worst.

I took the bus through Boston and stared into the morning light. I walked down Commonwealth Avenue, the city waking around me. The students were gone for the summer. I wasn't going to be late; I was never late. I would arrive at the unit early, would get coffee, get my favorite seat. I would smile as the other women came in. I would smile at the women who lived in that hospital, who couldn't leave. I would drink the watery coffee, grounds floating in the cup. I had my own coffee that morning at home. I could have as much coffee, as much hot water, as I wanted. I would listen in session, I would snap at all the right moments. This place, so similar to the ward where I had been locked up. This place, so different. We left the room when we wanted to. We ate when we wanted to. We were trusted with metal silverware. We could say what we wanted and knew no words we said would be a weapon against us.

Katie asked for clarification all the time, when she didn't understand a phrase, when a therapist said something vague. She asked, "But tell me what that looks like in practice." Diane hated this place, but she could go home when the day was over. These women whose quirks and pain and desperation and hope were the hands that began to put my broken bits back together. These women who I could sit with in those days when the earth and everything in it was startling, like a stranger speaking my name.

When my last days in the program were approaching, I tried to see if I could stay there longer. It was so helpful, so good, I told my clinician. Couldn't I have a few more group sessions?

"Your insurance only covers two weeks," she said, shaking her head.

I was making $18,000 a year in one of the most expensive cities in the United States. Medicaid paid for the ambulances, the emergency room, the locked ward. I was reaching the limit of what they decided a person who tried to kill themselves needed.

All of this, paid for by MassHealth. This is a blessing I can never pay back, a blessing beyond blessings. Because I was poor, the state paid for me. There were women who needed this place. There are women who need this place. There are so many people who need this place. There are some people who are not poor enough to get this covered on state insurance. There are some people whose insurance won't cover it at all. I was so lucky to receive this help. I don't think anyone should have to be.

———

I took the bus home from outpatient and wrote papers all night. My days ruptured in two. There was this place in the heart of Boston where I could say everything out loud, and there was the rest of the world, where I didn't know how to speak.

———

I started sleeping with someone who lived next to the Divinity School. Lewis had nothing to do with Harvard. We would meet at a bar, drink until we were drunk enough, go back to his house, his basement room. In the mornings I climbed up the stairs, opened the door and looked across the street at the gray stones of the Divinity School chapel. I imagined running into peers, classmates, professors, as I walked home from his house, hungover and disheveled, smiled at the pleasure of it. I wanted to be audacious. If anyone saw me, they could think I had spent the night with someone, and they wouldn't think to ask where I had been the last weeks of class.

I threw a graduation party. I wanted to be reckless and young. No one there knew I was supposed to be dead. I talked and laughed with people like there was no secret, like there was nothing at all to know.

After midnight, Lewis appeared next to me, kissed me hungry in front of everyone. His hand around my waist, his body pressing hard and sharp against mine. Lewis, tall and muscular, holding on to me like we were already alone. It was intoxicating, to be wanted like this, publicly, by someone who didn't know me at all, someone who couldn't see the creature that I was.

In another age, someone would have shoved an ice pick up my nose, underneath my eyelid. In another age, someone would have locked me away and never let me out. In another age, I would have been excommunicated, worse than dead, damned forever.

In the weeks and months after I lived, I kept myself quiet. The word too big. Commit. I tried to commit. They tried to commit me.

People say it almost without thinking. They *committed* suicide. To what other acts do we give that verb? To commit an act of genocide, to commit murder, to commit adultery. Horrible, sinful acts.

To someone on the outside, the desire to kill the self can be unfathomable. Strange and big, necessitating a strange and big word to match it. But it is in this word, in this phrase, that the shame sneaks in.

There are people who are careful in how they say it, knowing what the words carry. In certain circles, with people who work in mental health or people who have been through the system, the phrase *commit suicide* has been retired, replaced. When people do say it, the hard edges of *commit* throw me off-balance.

It is not that everyone means to call this thing shameful, to call this thing monstrous, I don't think. It is the phrase that most of us have heard our whole lives. Whether we mean to or not, the shame slips in, settles, there between the lines.

Though we no longer cut the heads off of people who have killed themselves, though we no longer bury them at night, though we no longer try to make sure their corpses and ghosts will never find the way home, still we bury them in language of sin, of shame. In our words we mark them as strange, as other, as doing an incomprehensible action that defies our idea of rightness.

I started going back to work, picking up shifts at the library and the café, sitting at the returns desk at Widener Library. It happens so often, if you're listening for it.

"Well, it's the same with being involuntarily committed," the girl behind me said. She was studying to be a therapist. "It's a lot easier to get out if you voluntarily commit yourself," she said. "From what I've read. It's not good to keep patients there if they don't want to be there."

"Yeah totally," another girl said.

"There's a lot of writing about the differences between patients who commit themselves voluntarily and those who don't; it's interesting how they're treated differently."

The two girls talked for longer than I thought was possible. They asked each other questions about hospital policies, about the literature. I stared at nothing and said nothing. They kept talking, not stopping to think that anyone around them could have ever been in a place like that, that anyone near them could know every word of Section 12. I sat, fresh and vibrating, the scent of the ward on my tongue, staring silent ahead.

The thing that haunts, the needling doubt that pushed at me in the mornings, in the sharp light of day, when I close my eyes at night, is that no one will be honest. People might assume I didn't really mean it, people might assume I am relieved, but no one will assume that there in my mind, tossing, daily, is the question: Is it okay that I lived?

I woke up and my mistakes were still there. I woke up and lived inside the memories of every time I misspoke, every time I got too drunk and began to cry at a party. I woke up to a newfound complication. If I share this fact of myself, *I wanted so badly to die*, will people think I am begging for attention? Will people think I'm broken? One more reason to stand at a distance from this sharp-edged girl.

The day before my health insurance mandated that I leave the outpatient program, there were ten minutes left in the group. I raised my hand, shaking, looking at nothing. "I tried to kill myself, and the doctors don't know how I survived, and I don't know who I can talk to about it outside of here, and everything feels so surreal."

Across the room, Katie leaned forward in her chair. Before the group leader could respond, could direct the conversation, she spoke. "I have been there too," she said. I stared into her eyes. "I know that feeling. I promise, you will start to feel normal again. After a while, it doesn't feel so surreal. And I just want to say, I'm so glad you're still here."

I wished the sound of snapping could turn into something physical, a worry stone, a pebble, so that in those moments, in the weeks after I was no longer in outpatient, when the doubt came sharp and cruel, it would be there to hold on to.

What would it mean, to refocus the gaze, to shift the vocabulary?

No longer *commit*, no longer locked away, no longer a single person acting irrationally, but something else.

We say that someone died from a heart attack. Most of us don't say that someone died from suicide. To align self-killing with "natural" or accidental deaths is to point fingers in all directions. Where were the doctors who could have stepped in to help? Where were the signs, who noticed, who didn't? What were the causes?

To say that someone did not *commit* but rather died by suicide is to say that it might be comprehensible. A venture, a guess at understanding, a step toward acknowledging that the causes can lie outside a person as much as inside. That maybe this thing does not need to be so covered in shadows, maybe it does not need to be so hidden in shame.

Mark E. Button writes that such an understanding of suicide, one that takes at its core that a person is acting in response to the conditions of their life, should evoke *an existential and institutional crisis*, as we turn the gaze back to ourselves, to the world we have built and ask: What is it about this place that makes people want to die?[9]

No longer an individual floating in a void, staring into an existential question, *to be or not to be*, unplaced in time and space. Instead, a person in relation to their environment, a person whose death is an indictment of us all.

In June, weeks after I left outpatient, I went to meet Iman at the vegan diner in Central Square. Perched on too-tall chairs, seated across from each other, the joy of our meeting brighter than anything. How had we been doing? Had anyone heard from Katie? What about Diane? Were we on new medication? What was it like, what were the side effects? Between us, invisible and electric, the shared knowledge of where we had been. I told her I had a crush on someone, that he was texting me.

"Oh my God, invite him, I want to meet him," she laughed. It was the night of the Cambridge city dance party, where hundreds of people would gather outside city hall, where someone would play music and the lawns and streets would turn into a dance floor.

He came, sat close to me at the table meant for two. "How do you two know each other?" he asked. Iman and I stared at each other across the table and began to laugh like this was a joke, a shared secret that we would not let anyone else in on.

"I go to the café she works at all the time," she said. "Right Madeline?"

"Yeah," I said. He didn't believe me, but it didn't matter.

Outside, the music was loud. The music poured out from a speaker in front of city hall. Neon lights flashing on our faces. The street was thick with bodies, heavy with laughter, and there we were, there I was. For a moment, for a night, dancing with Iman, with this boy I couldn't stop smiling at, in the crush of people, my secrets not so bad, not too horrible to know, right there in the middle of it all.

Because I was on MassHealth, because I was living on $18,000 a year in one of the most expensive cities in America, I qualified for a program where I received free therapy through a local hospital, from a doctor who was in their last year of school. I was a test subject, a dry run.

Because I was on MassHealth, because I got therapy for free through the training program, because my therapist knew the constraints with which I lived, he would tell me where I could go to get my medicine for free. Once a month, on the way home from work, I made a detour, went to the same hospital where I had been in the ER. To get to the pharmacy, a person had to follow a winding hallway, turn at all the right places, take the elevator to the second floor, turn left, and follow the signs. The pharmacy was small, with a makeshift waiting area nearby.

I would wait in line, documents ready. At the window, it always followed the same pattern. They would get the medication, the antidepressants, and antianxiety refills. They would tell me how much it cost, a number I couldn't afford. I would tell them that I was on MassHealth, that it should be free. The pharmacist would go to speak with their supervisor. I would wait, checking the time on my phone, scrolling through Twitter. So often, those of us who need help have to know exactly how to demand it, where to go, who to talk to, the exact words to say.

The pharmacist would come back, type things into the computer. "Six dollars," they'd say. I would walk out the door, refills in hand, and try not to think how much of this was chance. I tried to feel lucky, instead of precarious.

It was a beautiful, clear Boston morning. I sat on my back porch, looking over the highway. If I held my head just right, I could see the skyline. In the sun, coffee in hand, I clicked through my mandatory graduate school loan exit counseling. I filled out how much I owed in loans from undergrad, how much I had in the bank. The website calculated, estimated. *You should expect to earn $100,000 per year to keep up with your loans.* I stared at the numbers and laughed harder than I thought was possible. I should plan to earn more money per year than I had ever seen.

There was a power in the knowledge that they would not have gotten a single penny if I had died. I was so close to them getting nothing at all. The knowledge made me giddy. My best joke. I was there in the sun, I was breathing, and for a while, I believed they couldn't touch me.

I carried death in my mouth like a tongued pill. Hidden, pressing on my jaw, waiting for someone to come and ask me to share it. No one did.

The people who knew where I had been were too polite, too decorous to ask what had happened. The people who hadn't noticed my disappearance would have no reason to think that anything was different, that there was something there, in the way I carried my body.

The days pricked my skin, the moments full of the pressure of not knowing. Every day was a year, and no there was no one to share this wonder with.

How strange, to be alive and breathing in the mornings.

I started seeing someone who didn't drink, and I began to prefer sparkling water to beer. I went to bed early. I got my job back at the coffee shop, looked forward to my shifts, where the family who ran it took me into their fold, invited me to their parties, took me swimming on days off.

And still it was there, waiting for someone to ask, for someone to tell, undissolved, the fact of it. I wanted to sit in a room of people who would look at me and know, who would gasp, who would sit with me in this feeling that refused to dull, who would watch as I opened my mouth, and this thing would come out.

In the months after I lived, I waited for something to go wrong. I waited for evidence, for the loss of brain cells to announce itself. I was worse at mental math. The numbers became unfamiliar and unwieldy. I used to have a good memory, but now I was forgetting things, had to triple-check my work schedule, suddenly unable to recall details in the stories friends told me. When I met new people, their names slipped away. I mixed up Isaiah and Isaac, forgot which name was attached to which face the moment I learned it. Was this memory loss because of what happened, or just from getting older? I could still write a paper; I could still write a poem. I waited for a day when the words would stop coming, when I wouldn't be able to spell or make complete sentences. I made strong, bitter coffee in the mornings. I sat on the back porch, I walked to work. I went on dates. I got used to seeing my beloved in the distance, the way my stomach would drop. I went to therapy and didn't ask if I was running out of time to see this community therapist, since I was no longer a student and might not qualify for the free program anymore. I thought I saw one of the doctors from the locked ward at Market Basket and ran home with my groceries.

In the magnificently air-conditioned Cambridge Public Library, I pulled book after book off the shelves. Susanna Kaysen, *Girl, Interrupted.* Yiyun Li, *Dear Friend, From My Life I Write to You, in Your Life.* Leslie Jamison, *The*

Recovering. Terese Mailhot, *Heart Berries*. Julia Kristeva, *Black Sun: Depression and Melancholia*. Ann Cvetkovich, *Depression: A Public Feeling*.

I sat on a bench outside in the sun. I flipped through the pages. *Am I here?* I asked again and again. I wanted a conversation with anyone who could understand, who had been where I had been, who was not afraid of what it might mean, who would not judge, someone who had closed their eyes and did the thing that there was no taking back, who came back anyway. I wanted to find a way to return to those rooms in Brookline, the woman who brushed knees and shared secrets, but all I could afford were the pages beneath my fingers.

Every winter I watch *It's a Wonderful Life*. If not on Christmas itself, near it. George Bailey, driven to suicide after his uncle misplaces money for the family business, when they are coming up short, when the great jaws of capitalism are closing around his throat. The angel Clarence jumps into the water before George can, because he knows that George will save him, that he will be too distracted to try to end his own life. Clarence brings him into an alternate reality in which George never existed. Not what would have happened if he died that night when he stared into the water and jumped, but what it would have been like had he never been at all.

People turn cruel. His younger brother dies in a childhood accident because George isn't there to save him. In this alternate reality, the villain of the film runs the town. Without the Bailey Building and Loan to give mortgages to the poor, the capitalist turns the once picturesque place into a shanty town, with almost everyone living in slums.

It's nice, beautiful, to think about life this way. That one person can have such an effect on the people around them.

George Bailey regrets a life in which he does not exist at all, but the film does not address the jump from the bridge, the plunge into the cold waters, what might have happened had he died that night. George decides that he will take what he has seen and continue living. He returns to the spot on the bridge, clasps his hands, and decides to live.

My story is not so magical. Who, really, would have felt it if I hadn't come back? What might have happened? My mother would've been devastated. I do not want to imagine my sister's response, how she would have cried, how she would have been honest with her children, as young as they are. My father would have found ways to make it about himself, would say it was his fault, would say it was because I did not have Jesus in my life. But what else? The world would have continued, and I would have turned into a story, a life read through its ending.

A girl I was friends with in high school killed herself, how tragic, someone might say.

Do you ever remember Madeline? Do you remember how she was in high school, how pretentious, how quiet?

I grew up across the street from her; she was always morose.

Do you remember those parties in college, when she drank too much and cried, and no one really knew why?

What really would have changed if I had not come back? It is a strange comfort to know that not much would have. If anything, things might have changed for the better. Maybe Harvard would have understood the urgent need for decent mental health care. Maybe other suicidal people on campus would have been reached out to, their friends suddenly aware of the acute nearness of death, this possible action not so far, not so unthinkable.

But I lived, and in the living, there was a silence. There was no heightened awareness, no new suicide prevention programs implemented. A friend of mine knew they could call me if they wanted their world to end, but they had known that before. Nothing outside of my body was different.

When George Bailey runs home through the thick snow of Bedford Falls, he is triumphant. He gets home, dashes upstairs to his children and holds them to his chest. Donna Reed, his wife, opens the front door and looks up to see him. She throws off her scarf in a gesture that I have always thought the most beautiful, the most elegant movement in human history. She ushers in crowds of people, friends, neighbors, bringing money, dollars at a time, pennies, combining their spare cents to make up the deficit that Bailey needs. As auld lang syne rings out, he looks in a copy of *Tom Sawyer*, one last gift from his guardian angel, with the note: *no man is a failure who has friends.*

And a woman? A woman who has no one to call?

What happened after the gospels moved on and left the nameless girl, Jairus's daughter, behind? Did she remember that moment for the rest of her life, like a gentle hand on her shoulder, a comforting finger under her chin, the knowledge that she was special, chosen? Or did it blur into the background of her life, a dream of a stranger standing over her, a man's voice ringing in her ear?

I asked someone, once, what they thought of this unnamed girl's story. I asked what they thought happened next. Why does it matter, they said, where the story ends? Maybe it's the mystery that's important. Maybe we are never supposed to know what happened to her, where she went, what she did. Maybe we are supposed to let her fade into anonymity, maybe we are supposed to allow her the freedom of her life. Maybe if someone had told the rest of her story, she would have been trapped in it, forever, for all of time.

I fought back tears. This seemed a betrayal more than I could stand.

I stared between the lines of text like I could force them into meaning something, into answering the question they were not designed to hear. There must be some meaning, some *thing*, in the living.

I went searching for types and found holes where people had been. I went searching for words and found silence. I went searching for narratives and found plots that broke off, sheer cliffs facing empty skies.

Days turned to weeks and still I hunted, desperate for anything, any sentence, any word that could guide me. Still, there was nothing. I began to think that maybe my story is itself nothing, that there is nowhere for it to go. The silence stood at my back and beckoned me into its fold. What is the purpose of a story like this? What is the purpose of a life like this?

I realized I was looking for Jairus's daughter in the wrong places. I was looking for her, alone. I wanted her to be special. I wanted her to be like how I imagined her: blessed, chosen. But Christ raised so many people from the dead; Christ promises to raise everyone from the dead. What, really, made her any different?

The story of Jairus's daughter appears in the middle of a litany of miracles. Before she enters the narrative, the disciples follow their teacher to a boat at sea. Waves rise, the god lifts a hand and calms them. Christ finds the man possessed by demons. Christ steals the demons from the man and kills them all. And there, her story, in the middle of them. Her story, one of many.

Dear reader, I was naive. I had forgotten, I had overlooked, in my frantic search to find the girl, I had missed the last line of her chapter in the Gospels.

In most versions of the story, Christ turns to those who have gathered in the house and orders them to tell no one what they have seen. He holds his finger over the little girl's lips, shushes the room. Again and again the god says: Silence. The waves will be silent, the demons will be silent. The crowd who sees the little girl get up, ordered to be silent.

I was so focused on her, I forgot to see the house she lived in. The god, commanding everyone to keep this thing, this living, to themselves. The disciples, the girl's family. The story was only obeying the god's command. We were never supposed to know how it ended.

My mother flew out to see me for commencement, though I wasn't going to the ceremony. I couldn't bring myself to tell her what happened, not all of it, anyway. "I was in the hospital," was all I could say. She nodded and didn't ask questions.

Graduation was exactly one month since the morning I woke up in the locked ward, but I didn't tell her that. I told her instead that it wasn't worth the money, the hassle, the stress. To rent one of the robes for the week was almost $90. There was a luncheon on campus, tickets priced at $50 a head. This is what I told her, so that I wouldn't have to tell her that I couldn't be around that crowd, the throng of people who had known me before, who had no idea where

I had been. People who knew me as the girl who interrupted class, the girl who glared, who still cried at parties.

The day of commencement, we took the train south to the arboretum. I checked my phone to keep track of how the ceremony was progressing. The moment when my name should have been called, when I should have walked across the stage waving in a last gesture of pretending that this was a place I belonged, my mother and I were in the lilac grove, the purple flowers in bloom. The scent swept over us like a wave. My mother knew it had been hard, she knew that I had graduated. Next to her there in the sun, barely two years after we had lived together in a small, warm duplex on the south side of Des Moines, I knew I couldn't ever tell her what had happened, where I had been.

One of the skills taught in dialectical behavioral therapy is distress tolerance. To learn how to respond to overwhelming emotions in healthy ways. But what if the anxiety, the depression, the fear, is telling us something, calling to us from somewhere inside ourselves?

What is the healthy response to the way the mind glosses, the way the body wears itself down, when there is too much work and not enough of anything else? What is the healthy response to the way the feet ache, the way the heart pounds, when sleep is impossible, when one is working overtime and there is still not enough? What is the healthy response to too many hours on the clock and still not enough food in your stomach? What is the healthy response when you know you need help, when you know you need help that you cannot afford? What is the healthy response to a world where your anger makes you crazy, where, if you name the things that happened to you, you are selfish, you are navel-gazing, you are told that you cannot see past your own subjectivity?

Sometimes, it begins to feel like learning to tolerate a world that is trying to eat you alive.

I started to collect everything I could find, every narrative, no matter how old, that I could read myself in. I threw away the ones that didn't fit. The film *Wristcutters: A Love Story* was disdainful. Those who killed themselves were sent to live in a limbo where no one could smile, then released, saved, redeemed through true love—trapped in a purgatory like Dante's, with romance the salvation. *Ordinary People, Ted Lasso, 13 Reasons Why.* I rummaged, hoarding every scrap that made sense, that helped me understand my own thorned survival.

In the pilot episode of *ER*, we are introduced to a large cast of characters. Among them, the blunt, surly Carol Hathaway. There are hints that Hathaway had a romantic relationship with the womanizing Doug Ross, played by George Clooney. Carol goes home for the night, surreptitiously taking some medicine from a cabinet, a gesture so subtle it's easy to miss. Halfway through the first episode, Dr. Mark Greene gets a call in the dining room. They rush to intake, where they see Carol carted in, her eyes closed, her skin pale. Delicate piano music ripples in the background. As the camera pans across Carol's face, a synthesizer approximating a siren rings out. The hospital lurches to a halt. The doctors, nurses, aides, don't know how to move. Dr. Greene rushes to the operating room, tells the rest of the staff to get back to work, as a few select doctors and nurses set about attending to Carol's limp body. At the end of the episode, it's not clear if she is going to make it.

In the next episode, eight weeks have passed. Carol is alive, and Doug has not gotten up the courage to see her. We are told he feels guilty, like he may have been the cause. Near the end of the episode, he shows up on her porch with a bouquet of flowers. He rings the doorbell. Her mother answers, tells him to leave. From behind her, we hear Carol's voice. "It's okay, Mama." She walks forward, covered in shadow. It is not until she is in the doorway that we see her face in the light. Doug fumbles, tells her she looks beautiful. Gives her the flowers. Asks how she is. "Okay," she says, guarded. He says okay and leaves.

Carol, outside the frame, barely in the episode at all, is incomprehensible. Shrouded in darkness, in silence. We are supposed to focus on the guilt that Doug is feeling. We are not supposed to ask how Carol has spent those eight weeks, what took her to that point. We are not supposed to ask why she did what she did. We are not supposed to get angry that he only came after eight weeks; we are supposed to sympathize with his perspective. We are supposed to understand how difficult it is for him to see her.

She is there, in shadows, shrugging, telling nothing, and we are not supposed to notice the silence.

The thing they don't tell you about coming back from the dead is that people will leave. Some of them will be justified. Some of them won't be. It will take time to learn the difference. You might never know for sure. You might think their leaving is an indictment. One judgment among many.

You might think their departure means that you were right to try, that there is something wrong with you, that you should try again.

The night it happened, I had gotten in a fight with a friend.

I had walked to the party alone. I drank three beers in an hour. I was hungry. I couldn't remember the last time I had eaten a meal.

There was a woman at the party who I had been friends with at the beginning of graduate school. It had been weeks since we'd last spoken. I missed her. I needed help. When she was leaving, I followed her to the room where everyone had piled their coats on a bed, watched her put hers on. I began to cry before I began to speak.

"I feel like you abandoned me," I said.

"Do you really want to talk about this now? Fine, let's talk about it now." Her voice, sharp and snapping. I was crying, still. She told me I had been a terrible friend. I had no words I could say in response. She told me that I never asked how she was. She told me that I didn't understand how hard it was for her. She told me I failed her, and she was right. Still, desperate, I needed someone. I needed someone to tell me that even though I failed them, they would still be there. I needed someone to tell me that even though I failed them, I was still a person with anything like value.

"I don't have time for this," she said.

Something began to go wrong. It was not crying. I was used to crying. Something else was happening. The room was spinning. There were no words in my head. The air was not coming. My hand to my chest. "I can't breathe," I said. Air not in my lungs. Croaked, like a dying frog. Not enough. "I can't," I said. "I can't." Inhuman, the gasps that came out of me.

"I don't have time for this," she said.

How I must have looked in front of this woman, clutching at my body, mouth gaping wide even as my lungs would not work, the noises coming from my throat shuddering. How ugly I must have been, how abject.

"I don't have time for this," she said, and left.

That night, I sat alone and choking. I sat on a pile of clothes and gasped and gasped. I made noises outside of language. Noises like drowning. All the worst things about me were true. Not worth knowing, not worth loving, not worth saving. I heard my beloved's voice, imagined how they would look at me from across the room. What a monstrous, shameful thing I had become. I made the same mistakes, again and again, with person after person. I couldn't interrupt the cycle; I couldn't make myself into a better person.

I left the party, did not look anyone in the face. There, sitting on that pile of coats, I had decided. I knew what would happen, I knew how it would go. The choice had been made. I walked home and thought the spring air was beautiful. Light and full of promise. I called my beloved. I didn't tell them why. I didn't tell them this was the only goodbye I could say.

"I can't really talk now. Is everything all right?"

"Yes," I said. "Yes. Just wanted to say hi. Have a good night."

"You're sure you're okay?"

"Yes," I said, and smiled.

I walked beneath an underpass near the train tracks. There were cars all around. The subway coming and going. I knew what I was doing. I knew where I was going. I wasn't crying anymore. Finally, finally, I would do what I needed to fix myself.

When I got home, I went to the kitchen and filled a coffee mug with water. In my room, I sat on the floor. I put my back to the closed door. I kept the lights off. I put the bottles to my lips, threw my head back and prayed. In my mind the unleavable house, the insurmountable debts, a red face, close, shouting. I saw the person I had become. The thing of myself needed ending. There was only one way out, and I had finally found it.

I didn't follow my plan to call the police so no one else would find me. I didn't think about it at all.

A pounding on my door. I stumbled down the stairs. Opened the door to my beloved. Couldn't walk straight. Stumbled back up. Words slurred out of my mouth. Fell back in bed. My beloved saw everything. My beloved was witness to everything I was, everything I had done. My beloved saw the pill bottles scattered all over the floor. My beloved called the police. Then, there were so many bodies in my room.

I never meant for my beloved to see me like that, never meant for them to find me. I never meant for my beloved to have to be responsible for what happened next. Never meant for my beloved to have to dial those numbers, speak those words into the phone. I never meant for anyone to find me. I never meant to wake up again at all.

I woke up in the ER. I don't know what day, I don't know what time. Still high from the drugs I took or the things the doctors put in me. There was a text from the girl I spoke to at the party, the girl who heard the worst sounds I had ever made. *Last night was a lot. Let me know if you want to talk.*

There were too many unsayable things. If I were to tell her where I was, what had happened, what I had done to myself, she might think I was blaming her. She might think I was avoiding accountability for the ways I had failed her. She might think I was being manipulative, demanding sympathy. I didn't know how to tell her that this, the final push, had been a conversation in which not a single lie had been told.

In the hospital I stared at her message. Words crowded my throat. There was no way to communicate this, no word I could say that was not heavy with meaning. I couldn't respond. I never saw her again.

There is an episode of *ER* when Carol comes back to work after her suicide attempt. She has been given eight weeks off work, eight weeks to rest and take care of herself. The day she comes back, everyone knows. The delicate piano riffs are back. She walks in, looks at the coworkers she hasn't seen in months. "I'm here to unload the new shipment of barbiturates," she says. They turn and laugh. They make jokes, they laugh about her not-dying.

It is gentle, the way it comes. The warmth. The care. The maybe-it's-not-so-shameful.

"I met you on my first day," says the young intern.

"My last," she says, her smile wry, "or so I thought." She doesn't hide it, doesn't care what any coworker, any patient might think of her.

At the end of the episode, she is called into a darkened locker room, told that someone is hurt. She rushes in, the lights flip on. The hospital staff is waiting. It's a surprise party. They cheer. They clap. They put a makeshift hat on her head, made from a neck brace, the words *Welcome Home* written in thick marker. They chant for her to make a speech. They lift her on top of a box, where everyone can see her.

"To say I feel lucky is kind of an understatement," Carol says. They pop open cans of soda like champagne and raise them in toasts to her. George Clooney stands in the doorway, clapping. She thanks them all for saving her life. Interspersed with the festivity are flashbacks to images of her, lifeless on the gurney.

It's the kind of thing I dream about. They are all there, stopping everything they were doing to help her mark this day, to show her that they care, that the fact of her living is a reason to rejoice. There in the locker room, they use what materials they can find to make her a celebration. It is ridiculous, it is lovely. I want to believe that it's real for someone.

What happens to a story that outlives its ending? A story that keeps going, long after it should have ended, a story that eludes, sidesteps, the path it's supposed to follow? In temporal suspense, I floated. Unbound, there was no narrative, no progress. Time was a thread I couldn't follow, a knot I couldn't untie. I was supposed to die that night. I should have died that night. I didn't. Where does anyone go from there?

The story of Lazarus is only told in the Gospel of John. Where Jairus's daughter gets a paragraph, no name, no ending, Lazarus's narrative goes and keeps going.

The god hears that his friend, beloved Lazarus, is sick. The group sets off to his house. "He is sleeping," the god says, though he means the man has died. To this god, death is a short nap that only he can wake someone from. When the god arrives in the town, Lazarus is already dead. In the tomb for four days, alone. The god demands belief and promises resurrection. Lazarus's sisters promise that they believe.

Here, in the middle of this story, the shortest passage in the Bible. *Jesus wept.* The god puts his hands to his face. Tears, wails from the god. This beloved, gone. These tears always seemed to me a contradiction. Why does the omnipotent god cry, already knowing that this man will be brought back? Is it out of love for this man, knowing that he suffered? If so, why does the god not cry for the little nameless girl? Where are the tears for those of us who are not beloved?

When Lazarus is brought back from the dead, he joins Christ for Passover. Lazarus reclines at the table, eating and drinking. His life is a sign of this god's power. Those who hate the god begin to plot to kill Lazarus, for as long as he lives, people will believe. But in Jerusalem the story of Lazarus continues to spread—this man, this chosen one, who was dead and now walks. His story gets to be told, shared. His story is no secret. His story is a celebration.

I don't know what I want from this story. I don't know what there is for me to learn. Lazarus is special, Jairus's daughter is not. I want to know why but no one will tell me. The dead man emerges from the tomb. Christ weeps over the man he loves. I want to know why his death matters, why hers doesn't. Why hers should be secret.

The thing they don't tell you about coming back from the dead is that dying alone isn't so bad. They don't tell you the worst part: the way your lips will clench shut, the way your story didn't end where it was supposed to, the way you lose the narrative of your life. Your voice is still yours; your voice is not something to be trusted. When you leave the hospital, your story is told by someone else, by physicians' notes and clinician reports.

When you leave the hospital, you will not know if the disease of yourself is the same as it was before they attached electrodes to your body. You, a contaminate, a danger. You, an emergency. You, your life, your self, your own catastrophe.

The thing they don't tell you about coming back from the dead is that your living will curse you. Your living will brand you. What you have done to yourself cannot be shared. You know the ways people will look at you. You keep this quiet, your secret, not shared with friends or lovers. People will ask how you are, how the summer has been. You become a liar. Say it's been good. You will know that it's better to lie than to let them see you for what you are. If you were to open your mouth, if you were to open your mouth and let all of this come out, they would see you for the undead thing that you are.

When no one is watching, you read the laws again. All the reasons they could keep you there. All the words they have for you, for what you have become. There, the names you missed before. There, you: an alleged person. Something different, something no longer human. Not after what you've done. Not after you lived. A monstrous kind of living, a thing that goes on walking long after their story should have ended.

PART II

A Place with No Exit

When I was young, when I closed my eyes and imagined my future, I saw a nothing outside time, outside color. I went to a college I couldn't afford because somewhere in my body I knew I wouldn't survive long enough to face the mountain of debt.

The night I did not die, when I sat with my back against the closed door of my room, when I took the lid off bottle after bottle and threw my head back again and again, it was the conclusion to a story that had already ended. Predetermined. It was enacting the inevitable, this thing that I had known for so long would happen. This, the only way out of myself. The only imaginable way to change my life, to make it any better.

What I mean to say is that night when I tried to die, my death was what my whole life had been waiting for.

"'Narrative foreclosure,' defined as the 'premature conviction that one's life story has effectively ended: there is no more to tell, there is no more that can be told.' It is not simply that the person believes she does not have much time left; the traumatic event somehow disrupts her ongoing life story such that the story ceases to be sustainable."[1]

———

I was the smallest made smaller.

The youngest of three, in the background. I was the voiceless ghost, watching from the top of the stairs, hearing from behind closed doors, an unreliable witness, a limited narrator, on the outside looking in, but always there.

No one told me about the gun with the end sawed off. No one told me outright about what happened behind doors that never opened. I listened. I put down my book, stood in the hallway with my ear against the door. The bubbling of bongs, the noises of more menacing things that I did not know the names of. No one told me why my siblings moved out. I crept onto the landing and heard. The voices that seemed so large I thought they were animals. The anger with no place to go, thrown between bodies. The consequences that came thundering, for talking back, for yelling back. The police came and went. The police came and went again. Their fists on the front door, their sure voices that never trembled.

No one told me who the white men were who came one day in summer, baseball bats slapping their palms as they approached the house. No one told me what would've happened if I didn't listen and get upstairs, if I hadn't been quiet no matter what. No one told me where those men went, or why the police didn't come that time, and I spent the summer days looking out the window, wondering if they were coming back, who they were coming for. No one told me, and there was no one for me to tell.

———

A small town, twenty miles south of Des Moines. The fields went on, low, stretching over the gentle rising hills. A girl could drive half an hour in any direction, pass through a town of fifty people, keep going through the aching green country as if there were no towns, no people at all.

Before I was old enough to work, before I spent every evening standing under fluorescent lights at Jimmy John's, I borrowed my stepmother's bicycle, went riding through town, followed the bike path that had been built over the remains of rusting railroad tracks, the bike path that seemed to cut through the center of the world. I pedaled through trees, through empty space. The sky was gray and heavy, the humidity thick.

I met a girl who grew up in a town smaller than mine. I mentioned that I am from a small, nowhere place, and we compared populations. She scoffed at me, said her town was so much smaller.

I did not know how to explain to her that there is a particular kind of suffocation that comes with being poor in a small town, regardless of size. The way it shrinks the world, the fear that leads to taking any job, that leads to doing any drug, that leads to the deep-down knowing that your life does not matter, and will not matter, and no one is coming to save you.

The bike path led northeast, past the cement factory, past the silos and grain elevators that sat in the middle of town. As soon as the bike's front wheels crossed Hillcrest Street, the looming factories vanished, replaced by thick woods. Milkweed and cottonwood, elm and yarrow. The road curved over a small wooden bridge. The hills were long, the inclines barely perceptible. The green fields flowed in every direction, without end, without respite. Sometimes, rarely, I saw another person running or biking.

Mostly, though, mostly, I was alone, there in the middle of this great wide nothing.

Everywhere I looked was fields, empty roads, towns of cement and police and danger. I pushed against the pedals. There had to be something more, I thought, somewhere, a place where I would not be afraid.

I rode down those empty paths until my legs were sore, until I was covered in sweat. I counted mile markers. No matter how far I went, I never found anything new. I turned and rode back to the house that was waiting like an open mouth.

I never knew who called the police, but there they were. They came at night, they came in the mornings when we were still in pajamas, in the heavy summer sunlight, taking my father aside to speak in hushed tones. I never found out who had made the calls, if it was for domestic disturbances or for suspicion of drugs. I never found out if it was a neighbor who heard the yelling and called, or if it was my mother or father, picking up the phone mid-argument. But there they were in the doorway, bringing their order, their law. They told my father he had to do something about our mother. She was out of control. Had to do something about my brother, my sister, had to tame these wild children. The police came, patted him on the back, and left us there until they were called again.

They came for my mother. They came for my brother. They came for my sister. The police looked at me as a child, skinny and small and clutching Tamora Pierce books, and laughed about how long it would be until it was my turn.

I swore to myself that I would prove them wrong. I would never be what they said I was doomed to be. I hid in my room and read books about mystical lands, books where girls were heroes. Books where girls trained to be knights as strong as any man, where girls could shapeshift into tigers, into fierce wolves, where girls were brave and could stand up to dragons.

In the rest of the house, the sirens, the fists on doors, the voices raised and growing larger.

My father was a minister, pastor of a Quaker church in a town of eighty-three people. When we were children, on Sundays we got dressed in our best clothes and drove through empty fields to the little red chapel. The church was small, barely two rooms. A basement, a sanctuary. Ten people on a Sunday morning. Most of the time, my brother, sister, and I were the only children in that place where there were more daddy longlegs than humans.

One Sunday, someone gave us lollipops before the service began. We sat in the back of the church, eating candy and standing backward on the pews to gaze out the window onto the rolling Iowa fields. We made noises, we squirmed, we played. My brother tried to count how many licks it took to get to the center of a Tootsie Pop, whispering a running tally, making notes on scraps of paper.

I don't remember if it started as soon as we got in the car to go home, or if the wrath was held back, just for a moment, until we were driving, until there was nowhere to go and no witness to see. "Beyond disrespectful," he said. "Outrageous," he said. He yelled. His hands tight around the wheel. His hands punctuating the air. We shrank in the back seat. He was the pastor. How did it look, his own children not paying attention? How could she let us behave like this? How could she embarrass him during church?

"I'm sorry," my mother said over and over. "I'm sorry."

In the back we were quiet and didn't know where to look. Guilty, down to our bones. I didn't want my mother to sound so sad, but there was nothing we could do to take it back. It was our fault that she was being yelled at, our fault that her voice shook.

Years later, I told people that I went to Harvard for graduate school because I wanted to study religion in post-Soviet spaces, to read about Platonov and Fyodorov and the cosmists, to study how the Soviet empire affected religions in the Caucasus, to get a PhD. The other reason was too cliché, too banal to say out loud.

I wanted to understand how a person could stand in front of a crowd, could choke as he said that we are called by God to forgiveness, to love each other even when it hurts, and then go home to spend hours yelling at his wife.

How did it start? There is no one to ask and no one to remember. What did the room look like the first time he raised his voice to my mother? Did her eyes focus on a single object? Or did she look all around the room, frantic? Did she yell back, her voice rising to meet his? Did her body shake, or did she, on some level, expect this? Was it one thing that started it? Was it all at once, the sudden hours spent yelling, screaming face red and too close to hers?

Or did it happen gradually? A sharp word over dinner. A rude comment in front of her parents. An angry voice when they were alone. One night just ten minutes spent yelling, accusing. More the next night. More the next night.

There were six of us, really. Father, mother, brother, sister, me, and the fear. The living breathing constant growing hiding-under-shelves fear. The what-will-be-next feeling.

When I was born, before we moved to Iowa, we lived in a small town in northern Wisconsin. A village, a place with dirt footpaths through meadows, where a bear sometimes came to eat from the apple tree behind the parsonage where we lived. On the shores of Lake Michigan, this little place of idylls. A family of five living on a pastor's salary, $20,000 a year. My mother worked in a diner, wearing a pink dress with a white apron even as her belly swelled when she was pregnant with me. Every six months, my mother would pack us in the car and make the drive to Green Bay so we could get our iron levels tested, so we could still qualify for WIC. Outside those trips, it was hard to find the time, the money, to get down to the city to restock on supplies at one of the supermarkets. My mother had a friend who went there more often and would pick up her favorite stain remover. One day, my mother called. She was out of that magic solution, and could her friend pick up some more the next time she was in the city?

Was there a pause? Was there hesitation? Did the line go quiet for a moment as this woman considered her words? Or had she practiced her response, ready for the inevitable call?

"I can't," the woman said. "I have seen the way your husband treats you, and I can't go back to your house."

"Oh," my mother said. "All right, then."

You need to leave a small town to get to the government offices that administer WIC. You need to leave a small town to find a homeless shelter. You need to leave a small town to find a soup kitchen. You will need to leave a small town, drive for miles through corn, to find anything like a therapist.

You will need to check your bank account again and decide if there is enough for gas money. Sometimes, there won't be. Sometimes, you will stare at the sunset, how it turns the cornstalks golden and have nowhere to go. There is no difference between twenty and two hundred miles when there is no gas, when there is no bus, when the bike path that leads away from the town only goes to a smaller town. You will look at the corn like a wall you can't dig through.

Who in that place—first in Wisconsin, then Iowa—who else would believe this woman, this woman who was often late to church, this woman who sometimes drove through town with her coffee cup forgotten on the roof of the car? Who would believe her, that the sentimental pastor, who spoke with a voice cracking from the weight of God's love, could turn to her at night in such wrath? Surely, she was exaggerating. Surely, it was warranted.

First the focus was my mother, then my brother, the oldest of us. She tried, sometimes. Stepped between them, screamed. "Don't yell at him." His voice like thunder, his voice like bellows, his voice like acid thrown in her eyes. "You stay out of this." My sister and I, quiet and there.

Thanksgiving dinner. My brother did not bend his head to pray. "How dare you. How dare you disrespect my God. In my house." For hours, they screamed. My mother cried. "Please, stop," she said. "You stay out of this." My sister and I, crying, holding hands, silent, looking at the food on our plates. I don't remember how it ended. Only my sister's hand in mine, the way she looked at me, as if she wanted to tell me that it was all right but knew that if she spoke this aloud, if she became the focus, it would all be directed at her, at us. My sister squeezing my hand, as if to say that we could hold on through this, even if nothing could stop it.

When we were older, he tracked my brother and sister across town. Stormed into their friends' houses, grabbed their arms, dragged them away. He would make sure they did not drink, they did not smoke, they did not kiss any lips, they did not fall in with the wrong crowd. They would not sin, not when they lived under his roof.

They snuck out while he was sleeping. Once, my sister miscalculated. Came home in the morning when he was already watching television in the living room. Her makeup smudged, wearing the same clothes as the day before. I woke to the shouting.

He was determined. He got a sleeping bag, slept at the foot of the stairs so no one could get out of the house at night.

After the fights, my siblings would be grounded. They would lose access to the car. He hid the keys, he stood in front of the door, he kept us there in the house. The punishments were simple, ordinary. The thing that gets hard to tell, the thing that I frantically searched for words to explain, was that the consequences and punishments didn't really matter. It was the anger, how quick it came alive and crackling and constant, the fury that turned my father's face into a stranger. The inescapable fear that electrified our days.

The fights would break out in the morning, in the afternoon, at night. My body would shake with tension. The fights would last for minutes, for hours. One wrong move, one wrong word, the spark of a storm.

When I was fourteen, when my father filed for bankruptcy, before the banks came for whatever they could get, he took my sister and me to the mall in Des Moines. I don't know where my brother was. My father bought us new coats, brand name from our favorite store. My coat was the most delicate snow blue, and I loved it until it was worn thin and covered in stains. That was the year my father had to ask his parents for money to help us. We couldn't justify those coats, this expense. He bought them for us anyway.

We would spend what we could before it all got swallowed in the bankruptcy. There was no reason not to have one night where we lived like we were rich before it all disappeared. We went to our favorite Barnes and Noble, could get as many books as we wanted. He took us to a steakhouse. I had never been to a steakhouse. It was the dimmest restaurant I had ever been in, and this felt important. The lights were low, candles on the tables. He explained filet mignon, and we all ordered the same thing. I couldn't believe it when it came. The steak, round and thick, soft and tender, wrapped in pale bacon. We ordered cheesecake drizzled in strawberry sauce. I didn't know what it meant that the banks were coming, but that night, I was the richest I had ever been.

Separately, simultaneously, my mother and father filed for bankruptcy, and though I did not understand everything that this meant, I understood that it was bad. The debt collectors called and shouted at me over the phone when I couldn't tell them where my mother was. I told them that she had left, she didn't live here anymore. They screamed, said I was a liar. I was afraid. I didn't know what they could do to her, what they could do to me.

After my parents divorced, after the bankruptcy filing, after my mother moved out, we ate bowls of refried beans for dinner. There were nights we ate jars of olives, forks poking into the brine. Nights where there were salad kits and nothing else. We sat on a broken blue couch, watching reruns of *M.A.S.H.* Most of the time it was just my father and me, refried beans, and Alan Alda proving to us that there were good, courageous people in the world.

There was no one else to tell, so my father told me how we might lose the house, how there was nothing, how there was nothing. "I'm bleeding money." The words thrummed in my blood: There is not enough, there is not enough, there is not enough.

He got a third job, an hour and a half south, near the border of Missouri, still bought us presents that Christmas.

When he screamed at my brother, when he screamed at my sister, I thought they deserved it. They had been drinking, they had been smoking. They got expelled, they got put on parole. Didn't they understand everything he was doing for us? How could they do this, how could they talk to him like that? I sat on the stairs and listened, adrenaline beating like a second heart. There were drugs coming in and out of the house, people coming in and out of their rooms, all kinds of smoke seeping under the door and making our house smell sweet. I listened to the screams, the refrains, how dare you, while you live in my house you will obey my rules, and did not wonder what came first, the drugs or the fear.

I sat next to him in the aftermath and listened to his worry, his fear. I was proud to be his confidant. I, the special one, the good one, the one who understood that it was their fault. I promised myself again that I would not be arrested, I would not be expelled. I would not let the things that happened to them happen to me.

———

After my mother moved out, my brother went with her, tired of the fights, tired of the watchful eyes. When he left, when my sister was older, when it was her turn, when she was the focus of every fight, she didn't take it. On a bright day when she was sixteen, she decided it was enough. "If you live in my house, you will follow my rules." His voice filled the summer day. Outside, in the driveway where everyone could see, she spun to face him, her two middle fingers in the air like explosions.

"Well, fuck you, Daddy," she said, and was gone. With nothing but a cheap cell phone in her pocket, she walked down the street of that small town, away from that house, toward something unknowable. I stared out the window and was too afraid to move.

———

When I was old enough, when I began to act out, when there was no one left in the house to see, there was nothing to tell. Who would believe that this man who worked so hard, who had two and then three jobs, who served as a pastor of a small church, who knew so much about Luther, about

God, about forgiveness, who would believe that this unruly daughter did not, in some way, deserve it? Hormonal, these teenagers. Melodramatic, angsty. Just like her siblings, they might say. Just like her mother.

I got straight A's. My teachers loved me. I never missed class. No one called the police on me. I never got caught shoplifting, drinking, doing drugs, was never late to a shift at work. It turned out that these things didn't matter. If I didn't use a coaster, this foreign object that I had never heard of before my stepmother moved in, if I left a dish unwashed in the sink, if I talked back, if I snapped, made a rude comment, I became what my siblings had been before me, what my mother had been before them. A conduit, a recipient, an empty vessel to hold his rage.

His face, towering and close. Spit landing on my face. Anger sudden and uncontrollable. I began to yell back. The more I yelled, the worse it got. I learned to yell louder. I sharpened the edge of my voice. I fought like a caged animal. Often, loud, and clawless.

"How dare you," he would repeat. "How dare you. While you're in my house," he would shout, "you will obey my rules."

After each fight, I would sit on the stairs and listen. "She can't talk to you like that," my stepmother would say. "Unbelievable," he would say.

I had thought my siblings deserved it. I thought maybe I deserved it. I thought I didn't deserve it. I didn't understand. I didn't know if something was wrong with me. I didn't know who was wrong and had no one to ask.

They built a new mall in West Des Moines. Large, sprawling, shimmering. A little more than twenty-five miles from our house, twenty-five miles through fields and over highways. We were there on a weekday after school. At fourteen, I was too young to drive on my own, still needed a parent to get anywhere. It started like it always started, and then we were there, yelling at each other in the corridor by the food court.

"You can't talk to me like that." My father's voice loud as a gunshot.

I talked to him like that.

"You can find your own ride home," he said, and like that, he was gone.

I watched him walk away, a shadow against the glare of the doors. He wasn't really leaving, I thought. He wouldn't leave me here without a way home. He would come back.

I went to the food court. I wasn't sure how long to wait. Time passed. Fifteen minutes, thirty. I sat in the food court staring at the doors. I didn't have any money. I didn't have a credit card. I had a Nokia phone. I paged my mother at work, 911, emergency. She called within minutes.

"What's wrong?" she said.

My mother left her shift as a home health-care aide and drove across town to find me. From where I sat in the food court, I watched her walk, still in scrubs, feet barely touching the ground, frantic, scanning tables. I stood and waved to her.

"Are you okay?" she asked. Her voice panicked. She looked me up and down.

"I just want to go home," I said. "Is that okay? Do you need to get back to work? Can you drive me home?"

"It's all right," she said. "I got cover. Making sure you're safe is more important."

She offered to take me to her apartment, the cavernous place on the southernmost side of Des Moines, where I could stay as long as I wanted. Where I could sleep on the couch or in one of the three beds in the windowless room my brother and sister shared. The place where every meal was a question.

"I just want to go home," I said. It was a school night, and I still needed to finish my homework.

When I walked in the door, he was in the living room with the television on and did not look at me, did not ask how I had gotten back. We never brought it up again.

Years later, I indulge myself, imagine a different ending. What might have happened if I had talked to anyone who worked at the mall, what might have happened if someone had called the police, this time for him, this time for me.

A face red and close to mine. I was yelling back. I was small. I was skinny. In front of me, a person angry like a force, like a storm, all-encompassing. The room was dim, but there was the face, loud and close. Spit landing on my cheeks. And then I was on the floor. And then I was looking up. And then I saw how close the sharp corners of things were to my head.

"You pushed me," I said.

"No, I did not." A sneering voice. "I never touched you."

I looked at my hand, the places where fingernails had dug into me, had torn the flesh raw. It wasn't a punch, not really. It wasn't violence, not really. It was so small. It was barely even bleeding.

I didn't understand how this man, this man who spent money that we didn't have to buy me coats, clothes, who got nervous every week before he gave a sermon, full of stage fright, wanting to do right by the Lord, who closed his eyes as he stood at the pulpit, who played guitar for us when we were children, laughing as we danced around him, who stood in the autumn sun and talked with me about *Catcher in the Rye*, leading me through my first literary analysis, this man who said that everything he did was for us, how he could watch me cower before him. I didn't understand how this man who said that we were his purpose in life, that he wanted to protect us, this man who promised me I would go to college no matter how much it cost, who coached my childhood soccer team, who asked my permission before he proposed to my stepmom, who took me to Warped Tour when we couldn't and couldn't and couldn't afford it, who went days without eating to be sure we didn't feel the same hunger, I didn't understand how this person who loved me more than anyone else in the world, how he could watch me fall to the floor.

If this man who was my protector, this man of God who knew me from my first breath, if he could watch me fall to the floor and know it was my fault, that he didn't do anything wrong, it must have meant that the fault was mine. I began to suspect that somewhere, deep in my core, in my belly, was something foul beyond language. Something that justified, deserved this treatment from the person who was supposed to love me more than anyone else. Maybe this person saw me for what I was. A monstrosity outside semantics. I, me, all of me, all of who I was, defiled. Tainted by whatever it was that was the foundation of my being.

I began to think that maybe it was possible for a person to be fundamentally, biologically unlovable, the same way that a person can't sprout wings and fly away.

In a class in graduate school on trauma and adolescent development, I read how the developing brain adapts to conditions of constant stress, when every moment of calm is punctured by the knowledge that there is danger, waiting. When the brain is always on the edge of fight or flight, ready to run.

There is a little part of your brain, a little bean, tucked deep in the folds. This bean, the amygdala, is a piece of the fight or flight response. When a shot goes off, the amygdala sends a message to the hippocampus: *wake up we have to run.* An SOS, a distress signal. When the fear is a static hum that ripples through a child's brain, this fight or flight response is permanently engaged. The body, the brain adapts to conditions of threat. The brain is ready for whatever danger will appear. Stress hormones are constantly elevated. Normal, everyday things—a disagreement with a friend, a tense situation at home, a voice raised in their direction, a door slammed shut—can flood the brain with adrenaline. Fight or flight is always prepped. If, for a child, for a developing brain, the tension, the fear, is inescapable, their brain will learn to look around every corner, will react to everything as danger. Untreated, a person can spend their life on edge, waiting, always waiting, ready for the other shoe to drop.

When it was my turn, there was no one left to see. Mother, brother, sister, one by one had left, moved to the apartment in Des Moines. Their disappearances should have been a sign, a warning. But there was no way another body could have fit in their two-room apartment, with one car split between the three of them, each driving the other to work and school and work and school. My father was beginning to approach something like stability. There were conversations about how to scrape together the money for the bankruptcy lawyer, but still there was dinner every night. After he married my stepmom, when there were two incomes, we had cable. The choices were clear even then in my child-mind: safety and freedom but with hungry stomachs and shabby clothes and dropping out of school, or danger and fear with a stable roof and graduating, a better chance at college.

I thought, since it happened to them, they must know what was happening without me having to say. When he grabbed my shoulders, when he pushed me to the floor, when his spit landed on my face, I thought, this is what happened to them, this was inevitable. I didn't tell anyone because there was nothing to tell. There was nothing new, there was nothing at all.

My mother and her boyfriend picked me up from the house. Drove the mile and a half down the road to the town square. "Now, you know," my mother said as we got out of the car, the sky gray and uncompromising above us, "I might be able to help sometimes, a little, but it wouldn't be much, and not every month." She was embarrassed to tell me what I already knew, what I had already counted on. We met a woman on the street who led us past a door I had never seen before, led us up a flight of stairs wedged between two businesses. She opened another door to a small room with uneven wooden floorboards. It smelled like smoke. The paint was chipping. There was a bedroom. I don't remember if there was a kitchen. For $300 a month, it could be mine.

I tried to do the calculations. With minimum wage at $6.25, how many hours a week would I have to work at Jimmy John's? Would I still have time for school? What was it worth, this tiny, smoky haven? Where would I get furniture? I would need a car. Where would I get a car? I didn't know what safety was worth or if there was another way to get it.

I thought of late nights at work, stained with bleach and mayonnaise, coming home to a place like this. A safe place for my friends to gather, to drink and smoke without having to drive out onto unnamed gravel roads. A place for me to leave the television on, to stay up all night reading, a quiet place I could make mine with mess, with dishes in the sink and clothes on the floor.

Mostly, though, mostly, I thought about coming home from work late in the night, smelling like yeast and smoke, closing the door behind me on a dark, quiet room, and breathing in, deeply.

"It's good that we looked," my mother told me as we left, as she drove me home. "It's good to know it's there."

I researched emancipation. I would have had to stand in front of a judge and try to prove the thump jam unsafe heartbeat, the feeling in my chest. There were no marks. There were no bruises. There were no witnesses. There was no evidence. There would be consequences, punishments, for trying, for talking to a judge, for saying these things out loud, and wasn't I just exaggerating, being overly sensitive? What had happened, really, that was so bad?

My father had an office in town with a computer and steady internet, a place where I used to go, a small room surrounded by books, surrounded by quiet. He would give me the key, and I would walk through town in the summer, lock the door behind me, and do small, innocent things. Spent hours on internet forums, writing fan fiction, watching clips of my favorite cartoons there in the silence.

There was a day when I was in the bathroom at home, sitting on the closed toilet lid, the golden key to the office held tight in my hands. I was crying. I don't remember what I did that time. There were fists on the door. Yelling. Then, the door open, the lock on the bathroom door useless. In front of me, over me. Large hands pried mine open. Took the key, held it in front of my eyes. A voice close, too close, too loud. There was nowhere to shrink, there was nowhere to hide. I would never go there again. I was grounded. I couldn't go to my friend's house. Footsteps pounding away, the bathroom door left open. Nowhere in the house to be safe, no lock that could hold.

That night I closed the door to my room, dragged the dresser in front of it. Opened my bedroom window, took out the screen, hid it under the bed. My feet on the slanted roof. The ground sprinkled with snow, the shingles dry. I took a deep breath, inhaled the bitter winter. I jumped. The ground rushed to meet me. I landed beneath the living room window, where the lights were on, where someone sat, talking.

Low to the ground I ran. I ran down deserted sidewalks. I ran past houses warm with light. I ran through the fresh snow. In a stranger's driveway, behind the spine of an evergreen tree, I hid from the road and called Megan to come get me. It was New Year's Eve and she was throwing a party. I would begin this new year leaping away from the house, landing in the snow, running close to the ground. I would begin this new year impossible and free, if only for a moment.

Before your eighteenth birthday, did a parent or adult often or very often swear at you, insult you, put you down, or humiliate you, or act in a way that made you afraid that you might be physically hurt? Before your eighteenth birthday, did you often or very often feel that you didn't have enough to eat, had to wear dirty clothes, and had no one to protect you?

In graduate school, we studied the Adverse Childhood Experience test. The ACE test is a series of ten questions designed to see how many stressors a person experienced before their eighteenth birthday. This is meant as a rudimentary quantification of trauma, a way to measure and research toxic stress. The ACE scores correlate to various health conditions throughout the rest of a person's life. The higher the ACE score, the higher the risk for heart disease, for suicide. If a person scores four or more on the test, their risk of suicide is twelve times higher than that of the general population.[2]

In graduate school, we were given copies of the test. It was meant to be a demonstration. We were all going into ministry, public education, nonprofits. It was meant to show us the extreme conditions that some people lived in, to help us understand, to help us empathize. When we took the test, I covered my paper with my hands. *Yes, yes, yes.*

My score was so high I could not find statistics on what percentage of people received it, and I didn't know if I should cry because of what it meant or from the relief of knowing that I was not exaggerating, that here was something I could point to, that it was real, what had happened, what was happening.

There are criticisms of the ACE test. It is simplistic, reductive, doesn't account for racism, homophobia, how those constant stressors chip away at a person. Flawed as it was, it was something I could hold onto, so that if someone said that what happened to me wasn't really that bad, I could meet their gaze and say, yes, it was.

I appeared on Megan's porch on a January evening, after another fight, after another night like every other night, clutching a trash bag stuffed with clothes and no apology. My mother had come from Des Moines, had driven down to give me a ride across town to a house that might have room for another body.

Where can a person go, where can a person hide, in a town like that? In a town so small the police knew my name, where the grass grew wild in the cracked sidewalk.

Megan opened the door with unspoken questions, but still she and her mother let me in.

In the guest room, I did not unpack my things. I pulled them from the trash bag and thought how fitting, a person like me, a person who was, deep down, a throwaway, living out of a trash bag. I rode to school with Megan, took the bus home when she stayed late for band practice. I set the places for dinner at night. I would earn my keep. Every day I was there Megan's voice grew sharper. Another friend at school told me she had said something, annoyed. How long was I going to be there? I was invading her space, interrupting her routine. The roots of something curled around my stomach. The burden of my self, taking too much from her.

I thought about other friends I could stay with, other people whose parents wouldn't mind another body, an extra mouth to feed. I thought of a friend who lived out in the country and did not have an extra room. Another who lived down a long gravel road, who would have said yes, who would have understood, who had plenty of space. Her mother, who worked nights at a casino in Des Moines, who came home late and made us nachos while she drank margaritas, who would've asked questions with no accusations. I thought of the strain it might put on our friendship, if I were to take the same things I took from Megan, if I were to disrupt her life. I was terrified that they would all see me for what I really was, to see that something about me was wrong.

I took my trash bag and went back, again, to that house that I could not think my way out of, and no one there said anything about why I left. None of us ever mentioned it again, as if it had never happened.

I went home to the place where no door was strong enough, where nothing could not be taken. I went home, laid in bed, closed my eyes, and made a promise. I would hold on, I would go to college, a good college, I would get out of there and after that, nothing mattered. I would wait and hope for an end to it.

One punishment for the arguments, the back talk, the ways I screamed, was being barred from the desktop computer that sat in the corner of the living room. The logic was: Here was something they knew I cared about. Here was something it would hurt to lose.

Alone in that house, no brother no sister no mother, no words, no framework to make sense, I kept the television on.

Those months when the computer was banned, I scribbled on scraps of paper, I lay on the couch and dreamed. Waited until they were at work, or at meetings, or out at dinner. I never went with them to dinner; I was never hungry then. Or, I was always hungry, and if the hunger was loud enough it meant I didn't have to hear anything else.

My father and stepmother had changed the computer password, but this was easy enough to get around. From the start screen there was a way to make my account the administrator, to change the password back. The computer was next to the window, where the road bent, and I kept one eye looking out, ready for when their car turned around the corner. I listened for the grind of the garage door opening, when I would save the file, unplug the computer, and run. Either down to the basement to hide, or to the living room, where I left the television on, muted, so I could unmute and pretend that I had been there the whole time. The stories that came out of me in those moments were bursts, harsh and rough edged.

It wasn't long before they caught on, before they came home one day or woke up in the middle of the night, saw the computer restarting, and knew. Their tactics changed, but I was ready. At night, in the morning, whenever they left, they unplugged the mouse, slipped it into their pocket. I learned how to work a computer using only a keyboard, navigating with the arrow keys. When they started to unplug the keyboard and carry it with them wherever they went, they forgot that when we had come to this house, they had kept a dismembered computer from 1999 in the basement. I waited until they slept, crept to the basement, carried up the secret parts, and connected the pieces of contraband. Tense like live wires, heart racing, I crouched over the keys, fear prickling at my neck, waiting for the noise of a door opening, and wrote stories that only a handful of strangers on the internet would ever read.

I heard a creak, unplugged it all and went running.

The world was closed and getting smaller.

Once upon a time, I stood in front of a crowd and tried to tell.

Of all my drunken confessions, of the lies I told to friends, of bitter and caustic subtweets, of the nights I blacked out, vomited on people I had crushes on, wept in front of people I had crushes on, no utterance, no single act haunts me like the words that came spilling out as I stood beneath the harsh lights of a chapel outside of Story City, Iowa, when I was fourteen.

The Bible camp let me attend for free. Some Christians still believe in helping the poor. I was there for a week. I met peers with frayed bangs and dyed hair who spoke about love and pain in a way that left me speechless. Leah, a tiny, red-haired lesbian, spoke so openly of the drugs and urgency of rural Iowa that I wanted to press her to me, to take care of her, to take her story into mine.

In those spaces, there was a vocabulary that we knew well. Confession, testimony, witness, judgment. We confessed to each other again and again. Confession became the point. In our creed, we confessed, aloud and to each other, the things we believed.

There was a ritual on the Wednesday night of Bible camp, when each camper would sit alone with their counselor and together would talk and pray about the most intimate things in the camper's life. While everyone else was in the dim light of the chapel singing, the counselor would take each of their campers, one by one, lead them to a secluded place where they could still hear the music, and ask the youth what weighed on their hearts. As children, as teens, ushered into those rows, watching our peers return from their prayers tear-stained, faces ruddy, we held hands and knew something special was happening. We sat in long rows with our cabinmates, going one by one to pray with our counselor, our comforter, our intercessor.

Someone had set up a microphone at the front of the chapel and invited anyone to come onstage, to share with everyone in the camp how that week had changed them. People went to the microphone and testified to the ways that God, ever-present in this place, had touched their lives. They cried. Shared things about their lives. I listened to their words, heart in my throat, and thought that yes, I could speak too.

I walked to the microphone in the center of the stage. The lights were trained on me, and I could not see past them. Faces disappeared in the shine of the hard-yellow spotlights.

"I am so thankful for this week."

The words I did not have, the things that filled me with shame. That I had daydreams about him hitting me. That I closed my eyes and imagined him pushing me down the stairs, because at least then there would be a mark. A bruise. Something to point to and say, 'Look, please, he is hurting me.' If it could only be visible, if it could be like what other people talked about, if I could have a language for it. Instead, I had cowering. I had spit on my face. I had the way my shoulders hunched when he began to yell, when he got so close to me I thought I would be swallowed whole. Below it all, the thought that maybe that was what I deserved.

"I am so thankful for this week." I thought of appearing at my friend's doorstep with a trash bag full of clothes, asking if I could stay.

"I am so thankful for this week, helping me find peace." There at the light my voice was shaking.

"My dad hurts me, and this week helped me find peace." Those words together had never left my mouth. Not to my friends, not to my siblings, not to my mother. To say them was dangerous. To say them out loud was wrong. I was bringing the inside things outside. I walked from the stage, my body a wire on fire. I fell into Leah's arms, crying and shaking.

A man stepped onto the stage and announced there would be no more sharing, that was it for the night.

What did I mean when I said I was at peace with the things I lived with? I did not know then and I do not know now. I might have meant: I am fourteen and home is not a safe place. I might have meant: I do not have words for what is happening to me. I might have meant: Help me.

The next day, my counselor pulled me aside. We sat in the grass, near enough to the chapel that we could hear the faint hum of music within. It was the gray-blue of a humid Iowa summer evening that promised rain.

"With something like this, we have to go to the police," she said. She looked at me and I wanted to crawl into myself and never come out. The words I had let slip in the safety of sanctuary were outside, and I could not put them back. What was worse, saying those words out loud, or him finding out that I'd said them? What was worse, saying those words out loud, or being told I was wrong, that I wasn't remembering right? That what was happening to me wasn't really that bad? Or everyone realizing that it was my fault that this was happening to me, that deep down, there was something wrong with me?

Police at the door meant neighbors knowing, meant risking people losing jobs, classmates whispering. Police looking at me like they looked at my siblings, their predictions for me coming true. Other people looking at me. People knowing that I didn't have bruises to show, that I was exaggerating. I would have to move in with my mother. I would have to drop out of school. There was no shelter in town, no place to go if there was no house to live in.

"Please, no police. Please don't tell him. I didn't mean it, I didn't mean it." I begged. I prayed. Already there were conversations about losing the house, about where to find money for gas, for clothes. I couldn't risk anyone losing work, I couldn't risk any of it getting worse. "I didn't say it right," I said. "I didn't mean it like that."

My counselor, this person who had led me in prayers and Bible study, sighed. "We know him," she said, her words coming slow and careful. "Since he's part of the community, if you say so, we won't get police involved."

"Thank you," I said. "Thank you." There in the grass, in the Iowa dusk, I was small but never small enough.

At the end of the week my father came to pick me up from camp, and no one said a word when I got in the car with him to ride the hours south to our town. On the drive, the cornfields spreading out around us, we listened to the radio. Somewhere, halfway home, he said another pastor had told him what I had said. People were talking. I couldn't say things like that. My actions had consequences.

"I'm sorry," I said. "I'm sorry," I kept saying. I had drawn attention to something that was not to be talked about, something that was not to be known, something that wasn't anything at all. I was twisting things. That wasn't really how things were. "I'm sorry, I'm so sorry."

I got home and stopped speaking. I stopped yelling back. I hid in my room, sneaking out when I knew no one was home. I didn't try to run anymore. There was nowhere left to go. There were no words, so I stopped looking for them.

In graduate school, I learned that there is a type of phrase called a performative utterance. The speech act does the thing it describes. Two people approach an altar. The priest stands in front of them and says, "I now pronounce you man and wife." Just like that, because the priest says so, they are man and wife. By speaking these words out loud, the priest changes who they are.

If you tell a child that something in them is wrong, that they are broken, that they have something bad at their core, if you tell them this enough, they will begin to believe you. If you tell a child that they are broken enough times, it is the saying that does the breaking.

Dr. Thomas Joiner, professor of psychology and a theorist of suicide, writes that an important component of suicide is the acquired ability to enact lethal self-injury.[3] Through non-suicidal self-injury, a person can become inured not just to the pain, but to the fear of dying. The repetition of thoughts, the way it might start small, a flash in the brain, that the apartment does have a balcony, that it's not that hard to tie a knot, the thoughts that at first may inspire fear, terror, over time turn into something more familiar, something almost soothing. In Joiner's understanding, suicide is not always a frantic impulse. It can be something worked up to, a thought that sprouts roots, that can vine if left unchecked.

The first time I put blade to flesh, I was in the bathroom in the summer. The door was not closed. Or it was, but it didn't matter. It had already been broken down.

There was nothing else to do so I did it, a few times, just to try it. The slits of the razor shallow. It was only when I pressed at a certain angle that they would bleed. At school, I'd heard people talk about posers, people who came to school with cuts on their arms who didn't mean it, who only did it for attention. I didn't want to be one of them, so I made sure to do it in ways that no one would see.

I closed the door to the bathroom and never locked it. I took a cheap, disposable razor to my inner thighs, to my arms. I begged: *Please let there be a way for these things inside of me to get out.* I needed the tension of my body to break. They weren't cuts, not really. Scratches. Shallow, small. Just enough to draw blood. Just enough to sting.

This would be my secret, this became my comfort. I could walk through school and feel the raw skin in every moment. The soft rub of fabric against the scratches on my wrists. A gentle movement of air that pricked the little marks, that sent waves of discomfort up my arms. The cuts grounded me, held me to my body. They made it bearable. All of the things I had no words for, no way to communicate, made real, tangible. It was as if these secret wounds were portals from which every bad thing could seep out, from which my story poured without me needing to open my mouth. I didn't want anyone else to see the pinpricks of blood. The catharsis of knowing they were there was enough. When anxiety and panic flooded my body, I could breathe deeply, close my eyes, think of those tiny lines, the blood rising to the surface. Overwhelming, the comfort of knowing that I could control how deep the cuts, how many, that I could control how much pain I felt and when.

There was a day when all my long-sleeved shirts were dirty, when the cuffs of my shirt only came to the middle of my forearm. In anatomy class, a friend looked at my arms. "What happened?" she said.

"I tripped on the concrete stairs leading up to my mom's apartment," I said, the lie rehearsed and ready. She raised her eyebrow and did not ask more. I looked up and met the eyes of my teacher, watching us, listening. He stared, silent.

There was a day in the summer when my brother was visiting. We were watching television. He grabbed my arm. "What is this? Don't be a freak. What is this?"

"Don't," I said. "Stop," I said. I tried to cover my arms, tried to get away from him. "I tripped," I said. Or, "My friend has a new kitten." I don't remember which lie I told, but it was enough.

"Don't be weird and try to hide it then," he said. He let go, went back to watching television.

Small as they were, the shallow scratches were too much, too noticeable. I needed it to be unseen. I needed it to be something that no one would say a word about. I needed the pain in my body to be mine. I put the razor down and taught myself hunger. I stopped eating, replaced the scratches on my arms with elbows sharp as knives. I wanted to hurt. I wanted people to hurt when they looked at me. I wanted them to know what I knew, what I taught myself daily as strength and comfort: that no one and nothing could hurt me as bad as I could hurt me.

When a person goes without something they need, when they are deprived for an uncountable time, when that thing is in front of them, sometimes they lose control. When a starving person finds food, they can eat so much, so fast, that they die.

When I met my beloved, all those years later, in the tunnels below Boston, I was so hungry. I was so hungry.

I made a promise to myself. I was going to get out.

I saved as much as I could from work, worked as much as I could. Stayed up late, finished my homework after my shifts. Obsessed over colleges, I started application essays in the summer. In the fall of my senior year of high school, I bought a ticket to Portland to visit a college. The campus was full of large trees and brick buildings. The people there were strange, passionate. I met a girl who recognized me from the prospective student Facebook group. This girl, Alanna, ran up to me and pronounced my name like a friend. No one seemed to think it was odd that I was seventeen and immersed in Dostoevsky. That night, I slept in a dorm room, listened to distant music coming from a group of people spinning fire and thought that this could be a home like I had never known it.

Back in Iowa, in my basement room, I stared at the walls. I would survive this. I would work as much as it took to get into that school thousands of miles away where people spun fire, where people had class outside and talked about writing like it was the most important thing in the world, where no one seemed afraid or ashamed. I could hold on, I could keep going, because this beautiful future was waiting for me.

My father valued education. My father was proud of me. My father said we would find a way to afford it, that we could pay back the loans. He didn't ever explain how. It didn't matter. I got accepted to the college in Portland. I was leaving.

When I arrived at college, I was in awe of everyone I met. They were strange, they were smart; they didn't seem real. They shouted about Clytemnestra at parties when they drank boxed wine. They showed me places on campus where people had hidden tiny figurines for strangers to find. They taught me how to make a honey blunt. I sat in the common rooms of the dorms and listened to the smartest people I had ever met dissect *Heart of Darkness*, and in the same breath, with the same intensity, argue which Kanye album was best. I sat at dinner and stared at all of them, everyone from places that had names—Baltimore, Seattle, Santa Cruz—everyone with stories and lives that seemed so big, so important. These new friends asked me things about my family, where I came from, and I answered in vague, cryptic, sweeping statements. I wasn't there anymore, did anything else matter?

Every day my freshman year, I woke up with a feeling that sent me to the other end of campus in the mornings, through a mist of rain to get good coffee from the smaller, nicer dining hall. There was a giddiness that made me unbearable to be around in the early hours of the day. I met my friends at the main cafeteria. Every morning, we walked together to the 9:00 a.m. lecture for our freshman humanities class. In the drizzle of a gray Portland morning, surrounded by thick trees and brick buildings, I grinned, I practically danced to the lecture.

I met a boy that year. Alex was from Seattle and seemed odd in the way that everyone at that college seemed odd at first, from a world of plaid and grunge and references to an alien culture that I knew nothing about. He would come to our morning class still in pajamas, hair tousled. I have a photo of him from that year, before we kissed, before we dated, when he was just another strange and dazzling beacon of this new life. In the saturated photo he is covered in green paint, his tongue sticking out, pinching his own nipple as he lays on the grass. Alex once told me that when he first met me, he thought I was annoying, naive. In the middle of disaffected New Yorkers and West Coast punks, there I was, inexplicably joyful, delighted by every small thing, earnest and deeply uncool.

I got a job in the campus bookstore. At night, we moved the shelves, blocked off the rows of books so that only the snacks were accessible. We became a tiny convenience store. I worked the evening shifts, I worked the midnight shifts. I met the older students who wandered into the store at one in the morning, coming straight from the library, asked them questions about their work, their lives. I wanted to meet everyone. I wanted to talk to every person I could find. In Iowa, I'd stayed in the library during lunch. I'd kept my head down at Jimmy John's and barely spoke to my coworkers. Introverted, I had called myself. Introverted.

Behind the counter at the bookstore, when it was past midnight and the bosses had all gone home, I played music. I danced. I asked everyone to tell me what bands they listened to. I asked everyone what their name was, where they were from, what they did, who they were. I floated through the days, I bubbled.

This thing, this miracle, that I had no way to explain to strangers, to the people I was becoming friends with: that every morning I woke up, opened my eyes, and was not afraid. Every night I went to bed and did not wonder what the next thing would be, if I would be woken in the night by screams, by yells, by police at the door.

I made it, I thought, I made it.

The thing no one told me, the thing I could not face, was that even though I had traveled hundreds of miles, though I had freed myself from that house, the house was part of me. The thing no one told me was that you can leave the house, and the haunting follows.

I sat in lectures about Herodotus, took classes on literature, majored in Russian, and no one asked what I thought I was doing, what job I could get with a degree like that; in that place, it was worth it for the sake of it. On days when the sun came out, I did classwork outside and thought that everything, everything was worth it for this. The sky crystal blue, the warmth on my arms, the book in my lap.

Every summer I got notices that my financial aid was being cut. The first time it happened, I thought it was a fluke, a mistake. The first time it happened, I cried on a bus in downtown Portland on the way home from a job in a restaurant. I called financial aid. They told me that as a sophomore, then a junior, then a senior, I was eligible for more loans, so the school cut back the grants they had given me since these loans could cover more of the cost. I signed the forms for bigger loans. The second time it happened, I didn't cry. The third time it happened, the school said I was no longer eligible for workstudy. Losing my work study status meant losing food stamps. I took out more loans and tried not to think of what would happen when I graduated, when it would come time to pay them.

My boss changed my schedule, found twenty hours of work per week, so I could re-qualify for food stamps. That year, every year, I scrounged, I lived on food stamps. I tried not to talk about it.

My friends went out to dinner. I would tell the waiter I was fine, just water for me. Blair would frown.

"You have to get something," she'd say.

"I'm not hungry," I insisted. I don't know how many times that happened before they stopped inviting me to go with them. It was small, in so many ways small. I couldn't afford to keep up.

In this place that I loved, in this place I felt safe, this was the first time, really, that I understood that I was poor. I learned a new kind of anger, a bitterness that settled in the pit of my stomach when a girl would mention how much her shoes cost, and I calculated in hours what that meant. Sometimes, at work in my undergraduate library, I cried in the stacks. I shifted the collections of art books and thought about all my classmates who were not working. I began to feel the worry, the suspicion that I would never achieve what other people could, that it didn't matter how smart I was or how hard I worked, I would always end up there, in jobs that would never go anywhere, with loans I could never pay back. That maybe, as much as I loved it, maybe I didn't belong in a college like this, among people that talked about the life of the mind as if the mind did not exist in a body that needed food.

In college, I spent the summers working; I spent the summer nights with friends who became family. Alex, Michael, and Kate, a short girl with curled copper hair, moved into a house a few blocks from my own. I began to spend every free hour on the couch on their porch, every evening laughing with them, amazed that this was my life, that I could let the night fall all around me basking in secondhand smoke. Even if I was poor, even if I was angry, even if I still had no idea who Mudhoney or Shabazz Palaces were, even if I had never heard of the Talking Heads before I met them, they wanted me there, at their house, every day. I belonged, I was beloved. I fell in love with Kate's laugh, with the way she pronounced the word *poetry*, like it had a melody all its own. I rode on the back of Michael's motorcycle as if I owned it. At the Alberta Street art market, overwhelmed and anxious in the crowds, I reached out to touch Alex's back as he walked in front of me to feel the comfort of being there with him.

One night that summer, when everyone else had already gone to bed, I kissed Alex and he kissed me back. Alex, who I ran into one morning outside the library, after he had stayed up all night writing an essay on *Moby-Dick*, whose eyes shone when he asked if he could tell me about it. Who drove a motorcycle and loved poetry, and somehow did these things with such tentative enthusiasm that no stereotype about boys from Seattle fit him.

I tried not to think about the thousands of dollars of debt, the growing interest. As long as I was there, I didn't have to think about where I came from or where I was going. I could pretend those things didn't exist at all. There was Alex, there were my friends, there were the nights spent doing nothing that mattered, because all that mattered was that we were with each other, and I could pretend that none of this would ever end.

The next spring, I walked home one night from a party in Sellwood weeping. Drunk, I had said the wrong thing, had misinterpreted a sign, had gotten in a fight with Blair. The fight was small. She thought I ignored her, snubbed her earlier that day. I had tried to catch her eye, missed, and thought she was ignoring me. It shouldn't have been anything bigger than that, but there it was, all the old feeling.

Deep down, something was wrong with me. I was ruining something that I didn't know how to fix. People were beginning to see me for who I was. It was happening and I couldn't stop it.

I stumbled up the stairs to my attic bedroom. Took the belt off my coat. Tied it tight around my throat. Wrapped the cord around the ceiling light. My fingers fumbling. It wouldn't catch. I tumbled into bed, cried myself to sleep. I kept doing things wrong. I was wrong. I needed to stop. The thing of me needed to be stopped. I was graduating soon and then what? This place, this college, the only real home I had known, was ending. And there I was, ruining the friendships that had made it home.

In the morning, I woke and felt the cloth tight at my throat. I loosened the knot. I got dressed. Put on a different coat. This was the February when it snowed in Portland and the sidewalk was covered in melting slush. I bought two large coffees and a bagel from a cafe. I was trembling, but I would be safe soon. It was only a few more blocks. I wouldn't spill the coffee, I wouldn't drop the bagel. I could hear the television as I walked up Alex's driveway. I knocked on the door. Alex answered in an undershirt and boxers, confused and half asleep. "Can I hang out?" I said. "I brought coffee." I held up the cup in offering, as if to beg forgiveness for asking this of him.

Alex let me into the hot and stuffy living room, where his friends were hungover, in their underwear, hiding under blankets, watching *Adventure Time*. "Are you okay?" he asked. He took a bite of the bagel. "You know you didn't have to bring this?"

I told him I wasn't. Or I asked to take a nap in his room. Or I watched television, and then went to his room, to his bed, and I began to cry.

"Hey, hey, what's wrong?" he said. I shook my head. Alex covered me in patience. "You're welcome to stay here as long as you want, but my parents are in town today, remember? I'll have to go hang out with them for a while." He paused. "Have you eaten today?" I shook my head again, unspeaking. "One second." He went out. I heard him shuffling in the kitchen, his roommates talking. When he came back, he set a plate down next to my head. "You have to eat," he said. He sat next to me and waited as I picked up the grilled cheese sandwich and ate in small, hesitant bites.

"Thank you," I said.

Later, before or after he went out with his family, before or after he fed me leftover burritos, he curled his arm around me and waited until the words came. It was late in the day, the sun dipping low, when I told him about the argument, how I didn't know how to make things right, how I had made a mistake that there was no way to fix. I did not tell him, did not tell anyone, that I fell asleep with a belt tied tight around my throat. That below it all was the knowledge that something was wrong, that something buried deep at the core of me was shameful, dirty, a thing not worth knowing, a thing that, when woken, could only be killed.

When it began to happen again, when, in the spring before I was to graduate from my master's program, I had made too many mistakes with too many people to fix, when I was facing a future drained of all hope, when the thing at the core of me had come back to life, I was so far from that house, from those people, from the memory of those kindnesses, I forgot they had ever happened. They happened to someone else, someone far away. There was no longer a safe house to return to.

After I graduated college, I tried and failed and tried and failed. I won a grant after college. I understood academia, could write a shining grant proposal. In class I was confident, electric, could defend my reading of a text with ferocity and precision. I didn't know how to translate any of that into a job. I didn't know how to talk business, I didn't know how to sell myself. I applied to hundreds of jobs and only got hired in the service industry.

My mother had moved to a duplex on a dead-end street on the South Side of Des Moines. For a few months, when I had nowhere else to go, I moved into the spare room of her house. My mother was working at the airport. She would go in for the first shift sometime around four, when night was still thick, come back home in the late morning to sleep and eat, go back for the midday shift, return to nap, then go back again. She didn't have health care or benefits or retirement money, but it was a job, and we could make rent. The months I lived there I almost never saw her. On my days off from the sushi restaurant where I worked, I would cook dinner for her, leave it out on the stove. I roasted potatoes, topped them with a mushroom sauce, tried to time it so it was ready when she came through the door. My mother hated cooking and ate frozen dinners or mashed bananas when I wasn't there.

The nights I worked late she came to pick me up. I waited outside in the snow, feet aching, hoping that none of my coworkers were driving past and watching as I stood on the empty street corner. There was something wrong with the engine, and as the small red car topped the hill, I could hear the whine. The driver's side window was broken. It was open and couldn't close, and my mother did not have the money to fix it. When she drove, the bitter Iowa air slashed against her face, so my mother wore her warmest clothes and kept a sleeping bag in the backseat to drape over her legs.

In my mother's house there were clocks, all clicking at different times. Uncoordinated, unsynchronized, they chirped. In my mother's house, every inch of wall was covered by photos, cards, our drawings from elementary school. A thirteen-inch television from a garage sale with two long bunny ears to catch the local signals, always on, always noise to drown out the silences of this place. There was a desktop computer, supplied by the low-income, rent-controlled apartment complex. The house had no Wi-Fi, but a DSL cord attached to the computer tower. The cord could not reach far, but if I sat cross-legged, my back to the wall, I could twine the yellow cord, tug it to reach my laptop. I finished my applications for graduate school there, hunched over on the floor.

I was accepted to a master's program at Harvard. I got the email as I ran to my car during my lunch break at the sushi restaurant, trying to shield my phone screen from the relentless spring rain. I had two hours before my next shift. I drove to my sister's house.

"I got in," I said. I squinted. The numbers on the financial aid page didn't make sense.

"They're not paying you?" my brother said. "Don't go if they're not paying you."

"But they're covering most of tuition," I said, pointing at the screen. It was Harvard. How does a person say no to Harvard? How could I say no to Harvard? How could I, working double shifts, living on a dead-end street, so far away from the life I wanted, how could I say no?

I went back to work for the evening shift. One of the sushi chefs, the one with sad eyes, the one who was kind to me, was behind the counter. I motioned him over. Leaned over the sushi bar. "I got into Harvard," I told him. "For graduate school."

"Oh," he said. He nodded. "Okay." He went back to chopping cucumbers. I put on my apron and began lighting candles.

———

Before I left for graduate school, Alex came to see me in Iowa. I was working lunch and dinner every day at the sushi restaurant with a few hours off between shifts. The restaurant was short-staffed, only two servers during the week. No backup, no one to call if the tables were full and the line stretched out the door. On the weekends, we had a busser and another waitress. If anyone got sick, just like that, it was down to one person taking care of every table.

On a Saturday when we had been hit hard, when the lunch rush was never-ending, when it was ticking closer to three and I was still racing dishes back and forth, I looked out of the floor-length windows to see Alex waiting, in the rain, a hood over his head, trying to peer inside. I could not pull out my phone, could not break stride as I rushed another armful of empty dishes back to the sink. I ran between empty tables, wiping them down and snatching empty containers of soy sauce. I watched him cover his phone in the rain, checking the time. Our time together was clipped and circumscribed.

After work, we went back to my mother's house. I told him I was sorry and he said it was okay, and I believed him. I had close to an hour before I had to go back for the night shift. He held me as I napped, quick and urgent, in the small bed that my mother had found for $50 at a garage sale. No box spring, no coils wound tight, so that when a person lay in it, the weight of their body created a crater. When I slept there alone, I stayed to the edges, balancing my body on the inches that stayed taught. It was more comfortable with two people. The dip was bigger and the whole bed became the sag. It was illogical. As the rain dripped outside, and the minutes dragged me closer to the second shift, his hands held me close, in a small, impossible pocket.

Before Alex flew home to Seattle, we drove to the town I grew up in, the house that opened its lips and swallowed things whole. In the years since I'd left, the town had expanded, they'd built more nice houses on the outskirts, had built a new elementary school. We parked in front of the house, its two stories, its brown brick, its wide garage.

"See that window there," I pointed to one of the windows on the second floor. "That's the one I jumped out of when I ran away."

"Damn," he said, and waited, listening. We stayed in the car, and I tried to make the pieces make sense. How, when I lived there, my room was in the basement. There was a small bathroom next to my room. When I showered, little brown bugs, barely an inch long, would crawl around the places where the shower met the floor. I was ashamed. I thought it meant I was dirty, I couldn't clean well, or enough. I didn't tell anyone. I used Q-tips to stab them, to crush them, to kill them one by one.

I told him that when they were trying to sell the house, they discovered that there was nothing beneath the floor. The water from the shower emptied directly onto the Iowa dirt. The bugs came in because there was no foundation, no separation, just the warm and welcoming hush of hot water in the early morning, a stream beckoning the small creatures inside.

Alex and I sat in the car, looking. He listened, his patience a cup waiting to hold the words.

I tried to explain how the bank refused to foreclose on the house, though they couldn't pay for it anymore. How they were aiming for a short sale, and how I still did not understand what that meant.

"I wish I'd burned it down," I said.

"Yeah," he said. He held my hand and looked at me like I was the brightest thing in the world.

That spring, I worked mornings and evenings. Every afternoon I calculated the minutes between shifts. Was there enough time to drive home and take a nap before the night shift? On days when lunch had gone late, when there wasn't enough time to drive home to steal an hour of sleep, I went to a nearby coffee shop. Sat there with my computer, crunching the numbers. How could I make it work? How could I afford it? There was no one to ask, no one to turn to for advice. I made guesses about rent, about how much food would cost. I researched Massachusetts eligibility for food stamps. I wouldn't buy any of my books, I would get them from the library, would scan them all into pdfs. I looked for on-campus jobs, estimated what I might be paid per hour. If I were to get minimum wage, working twenty hours a week, I could afford what I had calculated as the average rent. *This is doable*, I thought, *this is doable*.

I signed a lease for a room in Somerville, paid the deposit for my place in the program. I quit the restaurant when I could no longer take the aching feet, the always short-staffed crunch, being scowled at by men who did not respect me. I got a job at Wells Fargo through a temp agency, where I sat in the middle of a field of cubicles, naive and happy, uncaring that the days were long, that I spent eight hours a day doing data entry, thinking I was going somewhere else soon. I was going somewhere better. I would go to graduate school, I would go into a doctoral program, I would be a professor. I would do something important with my life.

The first time I walked from my apartment to Harvard's campus, I was covered in sweat. I hadn't known it got so hot in Boston, hadn't known the way the sun would compress the world. It was early August, and everywhere I looked there were students with their families. Touring the buildings, preparing to move into the dorms. I wandered onto campus, feet already tired from the two-mile walk from where I lived, shirt stained with sweat dripping down my back, searching for water and an air-conditioned room.

The library doors were heavy, opening to a hall of splendor. A large open room, marble columns rising from the floor, soaring up and up to hold the tray ceiling. At one end of the room was a grand staircase with banisters that shone like gold. Above me, a chandelier. Somewhere up the stairs, past heavy carved doors, lay an original copy of the Gutenberg Bible. There was a gate, a turnstile, a red velvet rope, a group of tourists asking if they could see the library. Even the machines they used to scan your ID were marble and gold.

"How do I get in?" I asked a guard. "I'm a new student."

"Do you have your student ID?" I shook my head. "You need your ID to get in." She spoke with a resigned sharpness, as if she had said the same thing to fifty people that morning and knew she would repeat it to fifty more before her shift ended.

"Is there a bathroom I can use?"

"Across the street, at the bookstore."

"I can't use the bathroom here?"

"You can only get in with an ID."

I hadn't known that a university library could close itself off from the public, that they could hoard books, could offer a glimpse of the wide entrance hall, the carved steps, could taunt with a breath of air-conditioning, could hold it all behind an automated turnstile. I left and began to walk the two miles back home, having seen nothing, having felt nothing but sweat and the pricking sensation that I should not be there.

I got out my phone, began to play an episode of a podcast I had listened to more times than I could count, a man reading "Emergency," by Denis Johnson.[4] I knew the story and this reading of it by heart, the intonations, the moments in the plot. "Emergency" is a story about a man named Fuckhead who works at a hospital in Iowa City. He is not good at his job and does not try to be, mostly focused on swallowing any pills he can find lying around. Fuckhead and his coworker leave their shifts for the night, drive through fields, run over a rabbit and try to save its babies. They get lost in the corn, spend the night sleeping in the car.

I walked through the sweltering campus. I wanted to hold the voice in my hands like a talisman to ward off the doubt that crept up my gut. The story was in my ear as if to say: *Remember where you came from. Remember what it means that you are here.* Making a home of the sounds, of the space. In the stifling air the story murmured: *You can belong here.*

In the financial aid office, I sat in front of a woman who didn't look up from the papers on her desk. I was one of many supplicants. I asked her how it might be possible to get more money, asked why, since I had so many loans from undergrad, since I had so little money to begin with, since I had no family with any money, why my financial aid offer didn't cover everything. There were people I knew who got full tuition coverage, people who got a stipend every month.

"Our aid offers are final." She shuffled papers around her desk. "Grad school isn't for everyone," she snapped. She waited for me to leave.

I went to the nearest bathroom, began to cry. Why did I think I could do this? Why did I think I was special? There was the old fear: that no matter how smart I was, no matter how hard I worked, I did not belong in a place like this. Even here, at the richest school in the world, if a person could not pay to be there, they did not deserve to be there. If I did not merit a full scholarship, if I could not pay my own way, what was I doing there, who was I kidding? I was neither smart enough nor rich enough to justify walking those halls, occupying space in those classrooms.

There was a chip on my shoulder, and it was growing. There was a feeling in my heart, in my chest, that there was something to prove. There was an anger, and it was nesting.

I walked or rode a bike to campus every day. I couldn't justify paying for the bus every day. I had two good feet.

In this place where there was no place on campus to turn with a hungry belly, I waited for my food stamp application to be approved. I waited and waited. It had not been this hard in Oregon. The office of public assistance needed me to fax them something. I had never used a fax machine. I asked campus administrators if there was a fax machine. They pointed me to a basement, asked what I needed it for. I didn't want to tell anyone that I was trying to apply for food stamps. I don't remember what I told them.

In a dark basement, I listened to the whine of the fax machine and hoped these papers were going where they needed to. Days, weeks passed. I got letters in the mail. Nothing was decided yet.

Alex's mother had a weeklong free trial of Blue Apron. She shipped it to my house. I cooked it. I called him. "Alex, who am I kidding?" My anxiety was a forest fire that would not calm. "What am I doing here?" Again and again he told me to give it time, maybe just a semester. I could leave if it was really that bad. It was going to be okay, he told me. It was going to be okay.

I ate pasta with red sauce. I ate peanut butter sandwiches. I ate like a squirrel looking for scraps. Eventually, I got the notice, the card in the mail. I would get $194 per month on my EBT card, this white and blue piece of plastic that became the key to everything. $194 of pasta, of bread and onions. Peanut butter, coffee. I could do this, I told myself. I could do this.

I couldn't square the contradictions. I walked home in the golden September and felt like my whole life was beginning. I sat on the porch in the blue nights and felt walls closing in. I couldn't afford to be here. I deserved to be here. I could prove that I deserved to be here. I needed Alex on the other end of the phone to tell me I could do this. I needed to do this on my own. I needed to start a new life. I couldn't be in two places at once, torn between Seattle and Cambridge.

I broke up with Alex over the phone. I was walking home from campus. "I can't do this," I said. "I feel like I'm trying to be in two places at once."

"Are you kidding?" he said. "After I spent so many hours on the phone with you?"

"I can't do this," I said. The only explanation I could give him, the only explanation I could give myself. All around me, everything was beginning and ending.

To be poor at Harvard was to exist outside logic.

Four classes and three jobs combined to leave me everywhere and nowhere, running between class and work, doing classwork between patrons, counting my life in hours.

I was tired in a way that bent time. I was tired in a way that sharpened my edges. In every moment, I ached, I schemed. When could I sleep next?

To be poor at Harvard was to be nowhere at all.

Before I met my beloved, I went on a date with a boy I met at a party. His father worked as a land appraiser, and I did not know what that meant. He explained and asked what my parents did.

"My mom works at the airport," I said. I sipped the coffee he had bought me as we walked through campus.

"Oh, wow, like, as a pilot?" he said.

"No, she works at the ticket counter," I told him. A silence settled between us, and I let it sit, thick and unmoving.

Once, a friend told me that being at Harvard meant that we'd made it. I wanted to point at my time cards, my food stamps, and ask what he meant.

I got in trouble. As a student, I wasn't supposed to work more than twenty hours a week at on-campus jobs. I got calls from administrators. I got reprimands. I learned to be careful. As long as the hours were split between multiple jobs, the people monitoring such things didn't notice if the hours added up to more than was allowed.

The days were unforgiving. For months, I did not have a day off. I looked at the calendar and tried to breathe beneath the weight of it. The luxury of a slow morning, of a full day off the clock, distant, unreachable. In the evenings, I collapsed.

I was always told that a person is supposed to leave their problems at the door when they enter a classroom. But what if the problem is in the body, stomach clamoring for lack of food, head throbbing for lack of sleep?

I heard other people talk about going to events in the evenings, about study sessions with friends, about late nights smoking together on covered porches.

I was thankful for my jobs, for the large yellow house on Kirkland Avenue where I could brew fresh coffee in the kitchen, where the language professor would wander past, teaching me stray words of Ukrainian as he went, where I could print things for free, where, tucked away, I had a place on campus. I was thankful for my job at the library, where I could listen to music as I reshelved books, where I could sing to myself and dance, just a little, in the stacks. I was thankful for my job at the language center, where I could do homework on the clock, where the boss didn't mind if I left to get a cup of coffee from a nearby café, or to go return a book, or to check the employee lounge for leftovers from events I didn't go to.

I was so lucky, and I was so tired.

When people ask why I did it, why I tried to *find a permanent solution to a temporary problem* I want to tell them about how the fatigue settles in the marrow, how the heart grows bitter and jealous, sitting alone at work, scrolling through images of peers going out to dinner, traveling. How after years of work and hunger, I stared into a future overshadowed by an unpayable debt. I want to tell them that I was just so tired.

I met my beloved in the tunnels below Boston. We were going to a protest against police brutality. We didn't speak until the train ride home, when we discovered that we had both read Maggie Nelson and were too excited to realize this might have been cliché. Breathless, we repeated our favorite parts. We didn't notice another person, forgot that my beloved's roommate was there. Months after we met, we repeated this anecdote to each other as if trying to remind ourselves that we were special, meant to be, as if telling a story that we already knew the ending to.

On our first date at the run-down student bar near the university, neon lights flashed on our faces and I grinned at them over the cheapest beer we could find in Cambridge.

"I'm so relieved," I told them. "I finally got approved for food stamps. The whole process was such a pain in the ass," I said. "Until now I've mostly been eating pasta. I'm so glad it got sorted out." I looked in their eyes, at their hands, and trusted them to hold my story.

They walked me all the way home that night, though I lived two miles from the bar, though it was raining, though their house was another two miles away in a different direction. They held their umbrella over my head, our arms barely touching. We talked like the world was ending or had already ended, and the only things worth knowing, worth noticing, were the things between us. Outside my apartment, in the velvet rain-soaked darkness, they said they didn't want to come in even for a moment to dry off. Instead, they asked if they could give me a hug, there inside the small shelter of their umbrella. I smiled and leaned into them, into their rain-spattered blue jacket, asked again if they were sure they didn't want to come in.

I went to a friend's wedding in New York, and when I got back my beloved was waiting on the porch. My beloved had fixed my bike while I was out of town. This seemed sweet, this seemed like too much. My beloved wanted to talk to me about everything, wanted to see me all the time. There was a day that we did not leave my beloved's bed. Slow, then all at once, our days became each other's.

As winter deepened, my beloved's curiosity, awe, hardened into something I couldn't decipher. By the end of our first semester, we were sitting on the couch across from each other as my beloved plucked a guitar, not speaking to me, and all I could do was think about why my beloved wasn't speaking to me. Something was wrong that I couldn't guess, that my beloved wouldn't say.

The novelty of my stories had worn off. What did it matter, the hours I worked to get here, the hours I worked to stay here. The work and money and food stamps and WIC and Medicaid all blended into a narrative that had already been heard, a narrative that already should have been resolved. I was no longer fun. I no longer had any new insights about books, ideas. No longer interesting, just an anxious girl at the other end of the couch.

Dr. Thomas Joiner, creator of the interpersonal theory of suicide, argues that a key step on the path to suicide and suicidal ideation is thwarted belongingness. The feeling of being among others, alone, alien, unseen, other. He writes that, "The fact that those who die by suicide experience isolation and withdrawal before their deaths is among the clearest in all the literature on suicide."[5]

I walked to work alone. Over winter break, I couldn't work two of my jobs. The language center and the publication where I edited articles were closed for the holidays. I worked more hours at the library. December into January, I walked through the snow, up the grand stone steps into Widener. It was quiet, there in the basement of the library, reshelving the books that so many students had returned when their semesters ended, before they went home for the holidays. I'd told myself I would quit at the library when the spring semester began, when I could work at my other two jobs. But I couldn't count on my other jobs being there in the summer, so I kept working, finding refuge and solitude and loneliness in the basement, one shift among many.

I needed to fax new documents to the office of public assistance so I didn't lose my food stamps. I clutched my coat as I walked through fresh snow to the only place I knew that had a fax machine. My coat was not made for this wind. My shoes were not made for this snow. I got to the building with the fax machine in the basement, pulled at the door handles. It stuck. I shook the handle. Nothing moved. I hadn't thought to check if the building would be unlocked, hadn't thought to call ahead, hadn't ever thought I would walk through the snow and be met with locked doors and dark basements. Later, at home, my socks dripping, my hair wet with melting snow, I saw the documents were damp, drooping, the text illegible, from all of the things that soaked into my backpack. Why did I ever think, I wondered, that I could be at a place like this?

My peers were writing about justice, theology. They attended the summer language institute, spent weeks stumbling over French or Spanish or Arabic while I went to work and went home and looked on from the outside. I imagined what it might be like, to sit in the sun on a porch together, with friends, with peers, to let sweet summer dusk swell around us, to smell the incense on the wind, to breathe deeply with my body next to others, to make flash cards together, laugh at our bad pronunciation, to let time pass and not be afraid. Some nights, some days, I closed my eyes and imagined fantastical things. Cozy in warm rooms with others, them knowing without needing to be told all the things that were wrong with me. Blankets on couches, everyone close, not quite touching. I imagined Ahmed passing me a joint, though it had been weeks since we had talked, though now we only smiled as we passed each other, made small talk in the minutes before class. I imagined Josh, ever the activist, leaning close as I told him how the school perpetuated and was built on divisions of class. I imagined going with Hannah to get coffee, though now I only saw her when we met to plan events. Ashley, sharing bits of her own past over the kitchen table, as if trying to tell me that I was not too far gone. And my beloved, there in the room, seeing that I was loved, that I was a lovable thing, that it was possible to love me the way I was, mess and all.

This life was so close. I could taste the tang of incense as I walked past their porches and parties on my way to work. This life was so, so far from where I was. Down crowded sidewalks I walked alone again to work. Another shift, mind blurred from sleeplessness. Trying to do reading at work, trying to keep up. Unspeakable, the fear grew, twining with envy, the bitterness at the lives I imagined others had, the lives I wanted to be part of but could only watch from a distance.

What began in Iowa and followed me to college was being born again. Somewhere between the hunger, the work, the exhaustion, the anger, the desperate need for my beloved, was growing the suspicion that maybe there was no future for a person like me, a creature of trash and hand-me-downs. That there was something fundamentally wrong, unlovable, buried somewhere in me. I clung to my beloved like their love could prove me wrong. I asked for more from them, I needed more from them, needed my beloved to assure me in every moment that I was a thing worth loving. I fought when there was nothing to fight about. Through all of it, I forced my beloved to prove that they would still love me, that I was still a lovable thing, even as I texted them on nights when my beloved wanted space, even when I hid in their room to cry when they spent time with their roommates, even when I resented every moment they spent without me by their side. I asked them to prove, again and again, that no matter the force of my need, no matter how many times I made problems out of the air, that I was still a thing worth loving.

At work one Saturday at the language center when no one else was there, I started a Google Doc. I thought about that morning so long ago when I walked, shaking, toward Alex through the Portland snow, how I knew I would be safe if I could just get to his house. Sitting in an empty computer lab, I wrote a letter to him that I would never send.

THINGS I NEVER TOLD YOU
(FEB 14, 2017)

Once upon a time, I brought you coffee through the snow.

Hungover and aching, I walked in the snow to the coffee shop. I was wearing a crop top and my shoes were breaking. The coffee kept spilling when I walked towards your door. Stained and disheveled, I walked.

You opened the door, surprised, in your boxers. The television was on. You hadn't seen my text, hadn't heard me try to call.

The snow was falling on my shoulders and you let me in, sat me on your couch. The room was full and sweaty. The room was full of people who had slept there, in their pajamas and underwear.

It was cold and your house was warm.

We watched cartoons and I waited.

It was February 15th.

The night before, it had happened quick, almost without thinking. The rope, the knot.

When I was younger, I was sure that I would not live to be 25. I know, I know. This is too much for anyone. I am too much for anyone. I realize the depths of my pathetic nature, no need to remind me.

I couldn't remember the last time I had eaten a meal. My body was shaking. My fingers could hardly tie the knot.

I wanted to start over, to wash the insides of my body and my skin, to be cleansed, to be strong. I wanted to rest, finally, deeply.

Here, now, three years later, it is storming.

The other night I went to a party. I went to a party determined to get drunk, determined to get fucked up. I went to a party and wanted to let go of the anger, wanted to let the desperation rise up like bubbles, wanted to let it explode in bursts over the room.

Awake the next morning head throbbing, contacts plastered to my withering eyeballs, still wearing the clothes from the night before, still hurting, still alive in the face of it all.

This week I stayed home from school. I looked at my body, I felt my body, I thought of putting on clothing and I couldn't do it. I laid in bed in my pajamas.

I have made too many messes and none of them seem worth fixing.

Three years to the day when it snowed in Portland and I showed up at your door thrusting coffee into your hands, trembling, here I am.

I woke up in the morning, alone in my bed, jeans pressing slick into my hips, guilty, guilty, guilty.

I came to work without a bra on.

My nipples, brown and pointed, are sticking through my thin shirt.

I should be ashamed. I should be embarrassed. I am hungover or still drunk and keep reaching up to cup my breasts as if I am alone, as if my curled fingers can hide the contours of my body, trying to imagine what it would be to derive pleasure from them.

It is the middle of February and I am 25 years old, and there should be meaning in this but there is not.

The sun is coming in through the window.

Once upon a time I brought you coffee and I never told you why.

That day you made me a grilled cheese sandwich. You didn't ask how long it had been since I had eaten, and I didn't tell you.

You sat in bed with me while I ate, and you held me as I cried. Slowly, slowly, things started to feel possible again.

This time, there is no one to stumble through the snow towards.

There is just me, braless and breathing.

This time, there is no one to hold me, loose and safe.

This time, there is just me, cupping my own breasts while I sit in an empty computer lab.

This time, I still did not die.

I was dog sitting in a house across town. My beloved came to cook dinner, to spend time with me. Outside was a snowstorm, halting everything in Boston. My beloved wanted to apply for a Fulbright, wanted to live in France after graduation. I said I would help. My beloved did not say that I would join them. It was okay, I told myself. I was learning what I could ask from my beloved. I told my beloved that I was thinking of applying for a grant through the university to work at a nonprofit in another country. We would be such a power couple, I said.

Days later, when we walked back to my neighborhood through the shoveled pathways, my beloved mentioned that if I went out of town for the summer, if I were to apply for a travel grant, we would probably break up.

"It would only be a month," I said. "A month and a half, maybe."

"I just don't see this working if you're gone that long. I would want to talk to other people, pursue other people." All around us melting snow, brown and gritty.

I stayed in Cambridge that summer, didn't apply for anything. I told myself it was the right choice, it was worth it. I would have another chance to travel, I thought. I had found my love, and that was worth any sacrifice.

My beloved bought supplies from Home Depot. Their old bed was only a twin size. My beloved made a larger bed-frame, by hand, got a larger mattress, so the bed would fit us better. My beloved and I fought. My beloved and I fought often. My beloved wanted space. My beloved still asked every day if I wanted to come over. I started fights. I begged my beloved to not give up on me. Every time we fought, every time my beloved came to my house to talk, I thought it would be over. We always decided to try again. We always agreed to do something different. I got used to this feeling, the anxiety and the fear. I went to work and I came home and told myself that all this was worth it.

Somewhere on Dane Street, at a corner I would never be able to find again, my beloved yelled and I cried and I didn't know how to stop anything that was happening. I turned my head to hide from traffic. I didn't want passersby to see my face. We walked to a tiny park. My beloved sat on a swing and did not look at me. I sat among woodchips and waited for absolution. We walked to my beloved's house and we were both quiet. I apologized and promised I would change the things I didn't understand that were wrong with me.

Later, we would make dinner. Later, we would both apologize. We promised we would try new things, would find new ways to make it work. We sat in bed and my beloved touched me and I clutched at them. I don't know how many times this happened.

I wanted my beloved to take care of me. I wanted my beloved to promise they would never leave. I wanted my beloved to cocoon me in warmth until all the pieces of me were fixed. I had no idea how to do it myself. I had no idea what accountability meant. My days had turned into this. There was work, there was fear, there was my beloved.

Everything was falling apart. From the outside, everything was fine. I was making enough money to get by. With food stamps, I could even set a little bit aside every month, sometimes fifty, sometimes one hundred dollars. I was in graduate school, a good school, a school that at least partially funded my program. I smiled when I was with friends, I laughed. I had my beloved. When I was alone with myself, I closed my eyes and there was a weight in my chest that was building. I couldn't talk to anyone about what happened when I woke in the middle of the night and couldn't breathe.

Awake in the 3 a.m. darkness. Alone in bed. I made coffee. Sometimes, in the mornings, at night, when there was no sun, I closed my eyes and saw it all again. These memories, these scenes that had been tucked into the back of my mind, alive. The face so close to mine. My body was shaking. I was waiting for something to happen. My heart would not calm. There was the screaming. That house was so far away. That house was all there was.

One night, one morning, in the insomniac dark, the thought first appeared, soft and gentle. There was a way to stop this. There was a way to stop all of this. There was a way out of the house. The thought, when it came, was sweet as a lullaby. All of this, this fear, this tension, this trembling, this loneliness, this desperation, this unfixable broken creature that I was, all of this could stop. The solution, when it came, was so simple. That night, I slept past three, I slept until the sun was high in the sky.

Summer days hot and stuffy, another morning awake, another morning alone. Summer nights trying to see the moon from the space between houses. The creeping comfort in my gut taking shape, collecting images around it. The abstraction of death dressing itself, equipping itself with tools. A rope, a room, a banister. A secret comfort when my beloved yelled, when I cried, when it was another night with no one but the ghosts that would not let me sleep. The solution, really, was so simple.

I was working split shifts and two jobs. Mornings at the language center, afternoons at the library, evenings back at the language center. In the summer months when the undergraduate students were gone, everywhere was quiet, deserted, I was the only one at the language center all morning. I got there early, unlocked the rooms, turned on the lights. I sat at the desk and stared.

I was tired down to my spine. I slouched under the weight of my body, hunched in office chairs. In the mornings, my head was an empty, impenetrable mist. There is a special kind of exhaustion that encircles the bones, that penetrates the mind, when every day it is work then sleep, then work then sleep, and you become nothing but a body on the clock.

One morning, I opened a blog that I hadn't touched in months.

JUNE 21, 2017

Somedays I wake up and it's nothing, it's okay. Somedays I wake up and know that I am drowning and there is no way out. All of my shoes are broken. It is a habit of mine, wearing a pair of shoes until they fall apart, until the soles are cracked and my toes stick out. What else can I do? New things can only be bought if there is no other choice.

I walk these hallowed halls of "elite" education in broken shoes and torn clothing, my wardrobe mostly hand-me-downs and things I stole when I was brave enough to steal, when I had less than what I have now. I think I will always feel shabby.

Do you ever think about the things you could write, the art you could make, the experiences you could have, the life you could live, the moments with friends and loved ones, the books you could read, the sunsets you could see, the community you could be a part of, the rallies and protests you could go to, the other people whose struggles you could support, the unfathomable undreamed-about things you could do if not for work, if not for debt, if not for the grinding everyday neverchangingness, the truth that it is only a tiny sliver of the world who can change their position in this life?

"This is my depression," to the tune of Usher's "Confessions part 2," on repeat in my head for days.

Somedays I go home after work, walk home like I still have the energy to fight. Somedays I go home and as soon as my body rests itself supine on the mattress, I do not know how I will ever get up again.

I shared it on Facebook. Some people told me to buck up. Some posted hearts in sympathy. A woman I looked up to, a woman who had an MFA, who walked with an air of authority and knowledge, commented, said that my writing was beautiful.

It was night and we were walking. We were splurging on my beloved's favorite vegan pizza. The summer air felt like a promise. "Sara said she thought my writing was beautiful," I said. I was proud; I wanted my love to be proud of me.

"That's a pretty gendered response, isn't it?" They didn't look at me.

"What do you mean?"

"People only ever say that women's writing is beautiful. It's a really gendered compliment."

My beloved was brilliant, in the ways they kept me small.

Years later, my therapist looked at me askance when I told this story, when I tried to explain. My beloved was so smart, everything that was happening to my beloved mattered so much, it was important that I did not center myself.

That night, my beloved didn't mention anything I had written, didn't ask how I was doing, didn't ask about this thing I wrote about but could not say out loud, the words that hung between us, the way every day was a dull drip, the way I forced my smiles, how I couldn't trust what I wanted or needed, how I was losing myself. I had written about work. That was all. Working too much. There was nothing else to say about it.

We sat in a park to eat. My beloved was not speaking to me. We sat quietly and I guessed at all of the reasons for their silence. In every second, the walls were closing in.

Once, I told someone that my beloved felt like home. They shook their head. They knew something I didn't. They knew that something can be comforting when it is familiar, even if what is familiar is the thing you have been trying to escape from, even if what is familiar is a danger you lived with, the uncertainty, the fear.

When home is not safe, when home means not speaking, when home is a house of fear, when home is the place where you are feral, when home is the place you let yourself fall apart, when a love begins to feel like home, that is when you need to run.

I moved to a skinny house five minutes from my beloved, paid too much for an un-air-conditioned room that could only fit a bed. The summer heat was a hand at my throat. My room was stifling. One small window always open. One small window always open, six feet away from the window of the house next door.

Sometime that spring, that summer, I stopped being able to sleep. I woke up at three like clockwork, no matter what time I went to bed, no matter how tired I was. I lay there in the unmoving heat, in the predawn dark. Sometimes I would keep my eyes closed, hope for a few more hours of rest. Sometimes I knew it was pointless to try, would make scalding hot coffee. Sometimes I read. Sometimes, when the streets were empty, when the sky was purple, I went walking.

I walked past a hospital, brightly lit in the lavender haze of dawn. I was so tired, but no matter what time I tried to sleep, I shook awake. Full of anxiety and fear and things I couldn't quiet, no matter how much I walked.

The only time I could sleep through the night was when I was next to my beloved. My beloved hated to be at my apartment. The heat, the claustrophobic walls. My beloved slept best at their house when I wasn't there. If I stayed at their house, my beloved would ask me to leave at midnight, so at least one of us could sleep. I walked home in the darkness, past the green laundromat whose lights never turned off, and woke up three hours later.

Slow death, the gradual, daily, wearing away of a person.[6] Not quite catastrophe, something smaller, something constant. It is the slow rub of bones from too many hours standing at work. It is the mundane, the ordinary, the banalities, the things so far outside our grasp that confine, constrain us. It is another day sitting in a chair at work, your spine bent in unnatural ways, typing numbers until your mind is numb. Going home exhausted, not enough money, groceries from the dollar store, belly growling. Waking up, doing it again. The wearing away of hope when the days happen and happen and you can't see a way out of them.

"I'm sitting outside next to a river and I want to die," I said to the woman on the suicide hotline.

"Do you have anyone you can talk to about this?" the woman said.

"That's why I called you," I said. "To talk about this."

I had woken before dawn and gone walking. I sat on a hot metal bench on the banks of the Charles River and was alone with the water. I sat there until the sun came up. It was hot and I was sweating. I thought about what it might feel like to take off my shoes, leave my phone on the bench and walk into the current. There was so little, I thought, between my body and the waves. I thought about how many rocks it would take to fill my pockets, to weigh me down below the surface. I thought about Virginia Woolf. I thought about how nice it would feel, the water breaking the tension of my body.

The woman on the phone tried to end the call. I kept talking. She tried to end the call again. She said it sounded like I was okay. I began to walk home. I kept talking. There were people everywhere in Harvard Square and I didn't care about them overhearing, or what they would think if they saw my face, the snot and tears. I kept talking and crying, talked and cried until I was almost home, until I was tired enough that I knew I could sleep just a little bit more.

At home, alone, in bed, I stared at nothing. Could I tell anyone about this? Would confessing this to anyone, that I had to call a hotline, that I had begun to daydream about dying, be a narcissistic demand for attention? I already took so much from my beloved, so much time and energy, how could I tell them? What would anyone think of me if I told them that this dream of the river was beginning to be more of a comfort than anything else I could imagine? Even more comforting than the arms of my beloved, this dream of the waters rippling over my head.

I stole a copy of *The Bell Jar* from a campus bookstore. Shamefaced and dizzy footed, I could not bring myself to admit to another person the desire for this book, the hunger to see the feeling I could not name aloud mirrored back to me. It was an old, worn edition from the seventies, the spine painted a brownish gold. On the cover a black rose, casting a shadow onto the title. I'd never read it, always associated the novel and Sylvia Plath with mopey women, women who wallowed in their sadness, with young girls who clutched it to their chest as if for attention, as if to say *I am damaged and interesting*. I used to think it was shameful to let the world see you like that, until that summer, until the days when anxiety thrummed in my veins, when I shrank from people, when I could not go a full day without crying. I slipped the book from the $1 carts, slid it into my pocket when no one was looking. I walked to the plaza at the center of campus, where silver metal chairs baked in the sun. A rat darted beneath the tables.

On the first page, there I was.

"I knew something was wrong with me that summer."[7] Esther, the main character, our protagonist, our not-quite antihero, has won an internship in New York, something in fashion publishing. Moving through circles of New York women, parties, eating as much caviar as she can. She should be having the time of her life, and she knows it. But something is wrong, something within her, something that she doesn't understand, something that she doesn't know how to explain. She goes back home to Massachusetts and still something isn't right. She is in Cambridge and thinks about dying. I glanced up from the pages, at the sky edged by buildings of brick and iron.

There is a moment when Esther goes to the beach with people who are not quite her friends. She swims out into the water, far away, wants to swim out so far that her body will fail her and she won't be able to make it back. Her companions don't know anything is wrong. There is nothing to tell them. Instead, as she swims farther away, the narrator confesses to the reader.

"That morning I had tried to hang myself."[8]

The abruptness of the sentence rang through my body. The narration backtracks. Esther takes us back to the morning before she went to the beach, when she picked up a cord from her mother's bathrobe, wandered through the house trying to find a place to tie it. Eventually she gave up and went about her day as if nothing was out of the ordinary.

The campus therapist had short, silver hair, a voice that clipped. She explained to me how it worked, how I could have six sessions with her, how the campus therapists were meant to treat short-term, discrete problems. How, since it was summer and many clinicians took time off, we could meet once a month. I told her I wasn't doing okay, but I did not tell her that I had ached for the sweet waters of the Charles.

She nodded. "Let's get you started on medication," she turned to her computer.

"No, I don't—I don't want that."

She looked at me and sighed and asked why I didn't want that. Medication was so helpful for other people, she told me. She said all right, she said she was worried about me, she said we could talk more about medication in the future. She said we were out of time and she would see me again in July.

———

"Should you be reading that?" someone asked me when I showed them *The Bell Jar*, when I mentioned the narrator was a depressed girl in Cambridge who dreams of dying. My friend knew I was depressed. I never asked if she could hear something more in the way I spoke.

"It's fine." I smiled. "It's helpful," I said.

Her narrator and I were too terrifyingly alike, not in where we came from or who we were, but in how we let our desperate-mouthed sadness consume us. Reading Plath, my stomach dropped and dropped and dropped. And still I read, still I carried the book with me, sat reading it in public, gasped at every page.

———

After a fight with my beloved, the question of what would happen to us hung in the air like a pendulum above my head, waiting to sever something. My beloved was all I had. My beloved was the last thing, the last person I had to turn to.

At home, I sat on the porcelain lip of the tub in the small bathroom and stared at my thighs. There was something inside that needed to get out. There was a tension that needed to be broken. The razor was gentle on my skin, just enough to draw blood, just enough to sting. A secret with myself, these scratches. A few small marks before I went to my room. In the hot darkness the cuts bit at me, like an old, hated friend.

I walked to my beloved's door and stared at it in the darkness. I thought about knocking. I knew it would be wrong. I went home.

———

The next day when I walked to my beloved's house my thighs burned. The not-cuts rubbed against each other, singing with every step. I knocked on their door, waited for them to answer. When my beloved led me up the flights of stairs to their apartment, I collapsed onto their mattress. I cried. My beloved didn't understand why.

My beloved had nothing to tell me. My beloved had decided nothing. I didn't know if they wanted to leave, if they wanted to break up with me. I cried and my beloved held me, and as long as my beloved was there with me, what I didn't know didn't matter.

When I stopped crying, when my beloved pulled me toward them, when they slipped the skirt off my hips, when my bare legs straddled my beloved's body, when my beloved stared up at me, naked, above them, I told my beloved that I had razor burn, and they did not say anything.

———

THINGS I NEVER TOLD YOU, PART 2
JULY 25, 2017

I went walking at four in the morning and no one was there.

I told you it was razor burn, bad, and you didn't say anything. Did you know? Did it matter? You never brought it up again.

I made lists of things I wanted to do, lists of things to do before my world ended.

I have always been enchanted by apocalypse.

The willful ending of things, creation through destruction.

I'm doing okay, I tell you, when I mean to say that I am waiting for my own catastrophe to end.

You are going somewhere far away and all I can do is go the opposite direction. I claw backwards.

We stayed up late talking, something was wrong. Not communicating well, talking around each other, not meeting. Earlier that evening you had asked me to spend the night, to share the bed with you in the air-conditioned room of the house you shared with strangers. Late you turned to me after I had cried after I had opened and said you needed space, I needed to leave.

I walked home near midnight, walked home to my hot small stuffy room, walked home to the place where my housemates came home drunk loud waking me, no sleep that's a promise. No sleep no place to be. Couldn't sleep too hot couldn't sleep too many bad waking dreams.

Awake at three, just sat waiting. The hours of the clock came ticking in I sat in the darkness on the bed in the smallness and wanted to be smaller.

I heard all the words you said again and again, an invocation of my failures and I wondered what value could be attached to a body like mine. Could no longer sit with myself went walking.

I walked to your house on purpose. I knew I could be okay alone but knew I needed your voice your hands like fire. You asked me to leave and there I was back on your porch in the predawn hours staring at the locked door. Wanted to knock but too afraid to wake you up would you be mad?

Walked back the air felt purple and hot. Cried in long hours, felt the depths of patheticness.

Where does self-harm come from?

Where does value come from?

I told you it was razor burn and you believed me. The next day still crying walked back to your house you obliged, held me tight as I wept and you didn't understand why.

I am waiting for the end of my catastrophe.

Where is my moon? Where is my mythology, where is my ending?

You told me you were afraid of death and I told you half of the truth. I do not fear death, the sweet breath the finally the calm the thank god the struggle is over lie your head down to rest one long night.

In the stuffy air I am waiting.

I didn't understand what was happening to my body, why some days it was a pressure I could not get out from under. My beloved told me they were relieved when I wasn't there at parties, when I left early. They could relax when I wasn't there, they could laugh and chat and would not have to look at this girl they said they loved, who sat coiled tight, taut, about to break. I wanted to disappear until I was nothing. How pathetic, how tainted I must be if even my beloved did not want to be near me.

I bought my beloved groceries with food stamps, grinned as I paid. When we spent time together, I waited, reading, while my beloved practiced instruments. When we cooked, I washed the dishes. When my beloved cleaned their house, I swept the floors, I asked to help. I wanted to pay them back for what they did for me, wanted to smile at them and make their life easier, since I took so much, as if I could earn the things I asked for.

In *The Bell Jar*, Esther knows what will happen to her if anyone finds out that she tried to kill herself. She knows the kind of place she would be sent to, the things people would do to her, what the cost would do to her family. She doesn't tell family, friends, anyone, the thoughts, the thorned feelings that barb her daily, knowing what will happen if she tells. "When the money was used up, I would be moved to a state hospital, with hundreds of people like me, in a big cage in the basement. The more hopeless you were, the further away they hid you."[9]

I read this in the hot summer and my bones called out in answer. What would they do to me if anyone knew, really knew, the weight that lived in my chest? What would my beloved do, what would they think, if they knew that alone at home in the smothering mornings, I dreamed of all the ways I could die? What would anyone think if I told them that at night I closed my eyes and planned different ways to do it, a rope, a knot, the note to my roommates so they would call the police before they opened the door, so they wouldn't need to see what happened to my body? Would it be manipulative to say this out loud? Who would want to be with a person who wanted so badly to die? Who could love a person like me?

I had seen friends carted away from their homes by police who thought they were a threat to themselves, had seen others tucked too tightly into hospital beds, medicine crammed down their throats to make them into a normal person. Where would they move me? What would happen to me, if anyone knew? Who would pay for it?

If I were to say out loud that every day I longed for the absolution of death, I would put myself in danger. Not just the danger of abandonment, the danger of judgment, but the risk of locked doors, hospital beds, and forced medications. So many bills I couldn't pay back, so many classes missed, things I couldn't catch up on, missed shifts, lost paychecks, lost friends.

I caught truths in my throat, coated them in lies. I was all right, I said if anyone asked. I was anxious, tired. To say the truth out loud, to name the thoughts that thrummed in me like a second pulse, an ever-present ghost, would be to admit that I was broken, to shine a light on the foulest parts of myself, to risk a stranger's rough hands on my story.

———

Through *The Bell Jar* it hangs there as fact, immovable, irrevocable. Straightforward like weather, Esther's desire to die. Calm, she plans. On a day when her mother is out, she swallows the pills she has been saving, goes to the crawl space in the basement. She lies in a cranny and waits. There is a moment when, in the bottomless darkness, she calls out to her mother. It's not clear if she is still there, in the crawl space, if her mother hears her, if this is how her mother finds her or if she has already been found, or if she is crying out for her mother as she wakes up in the hospital. Did she regret it in that moment and was she asking for her mother to save her? Was she already tucked into a hospital bed, her stomach pumped, calling past the doctors? The narrative doesn't tell us. But there she is, waking up in a hospital bed.

There is a moment when she asks the nurse attending to her for a mirror, to see herself, to see what she has become. The nurse hesitates. The narration trembles.

"You couldn't tell whether the person in the picture was a man or a woman, because their hair was shaved off and sprouted in bristly chicken-feather tufts all over their head. One side of the person's face was purple."[10]

In the mirror, in the way she is seen, she is a stranger to herself, made into a thing, an object to be corrected. Nameless, without selfhood, this person in need of fixing. This person who is supposed to be her but is not her, who is at the mercy of doctors in crisp coats and nurses in scrubs who surely know what's best for her. Esther is taken for electroshock therapy, where they stick things to her head, where a nurse tells her that everyone is nervous their first time. Even if she said no, even if she told them to stop, they would know better than to listen to her. This girl who doesn't know what is good for her. This is what is done to people like her.

The cogs are in motion. Esther is rendered as an object, a girl whose mind, whose self must be corrected.

I walked through town and campus urgent, lurching, desperate. I cried in public bathrooms. I cried as I walked between classes. I cried when I walked from the campus therapy center through Harvard Square. I thought that I was the worst of white womanhood. I hated the noises I made, hated the spectacle, but still nothing could stop it. Hysterical, I opened my mouth in public places and let ugly noises come out. Some people looked at me as they passed, the spit between my open lips. The tears on my face. I cried alone in public, where I could burden everyone and no one. Where strangers could see in passing, but no one could stop, no one would have to confront the worthlessness, the paltriness, of this limp sorrow.

When I walked next to my beloved through Cambridge, when we made dinner together, I was ashamed of my stories.

I wanted to scrub the dirt out of my insides. I wanted to be the kind of girl my beloved wanted, the kind of girl who played instruments and could challenge them intellectually in all the right ways, could cook things the right way the first time and would never have to explain why I didn't know how to cook at all, the kind of girl who could have a story that began where ours intersected. If I could be the girl my beloved wanted, the kind of girl who was never too loud, never cried too much, if I could learn to be the kind of girl who knew restraint, then I might be worth something. I thought that maybe I could make myself into a person worth loving.

A wealthy author takes Esther under her wing. A patron, a benevolent benefactor. She makes sure Esther is transferred to a good hospital, pays for her treatment. Esther has a room to herself, a door that closes. A female doctor, who oversees the rest of her electroshock therapy, who makes sure it's done right, that it's useful. A doctor who understands the fear Esther feels, who starts her on birth control.

The Bell Jar ends as Esther walks to meet her doctor, just as she is about to learn if she can leave the hospital, if she can reenter the world outside. Esther stands in a room with her doctor, her mother there too, promising that this is a bad dream they are all about to wake up from.

And then what?

The novel traces the spiral, the medical treatments and institutionalization designed to fix her and left me staring over the edge of a cliff.

My beloved and I had planned a trip to see our families over the summer. We drove from my beloved's house in Ohio through and across the aching Midwest summer to my mother's duplex. I thought that finally my story would make sense, that I could point and say *look* and would not have to try to fit things inside words. I was trilling at the thought that soon I could point out the roof I had mentioned the night that we first kissed when my beloved asked me to tell them something surprising, and I told them I had once jumped from the second story of a building. I was so excited to show my beloved where I came from, to drive through the broken alley to see the apartment my brother, sister, and mother had lived in, that I did not consider that my beloved could go and keep their eyes closed.

We made the eleven-hour drive to Iowa in a single day. On the road, I asked if there was anything special my mother should get us to eat and my beloved said no. Was this where I made the first mistake? When I should have said no, listen, when I say she will not have food in the house, I mean she will not have food in the house. Instead, I nodded, smiled.

After hours of corn and nothing and corn and not stopping, my beloved was hungry. It was dark and late. We hadn't stopped for more than a few minutes all day. "What could we have for dinner?" my beloved asked. I listed the restaurants near my mother's house that might still be open. "Can we just make pasta and vegetables?" I didn't answer. "What?" my beloved said. "She won't have that?"

"No," I said. My mother's pantry was full of stale boxes from the dollar store, canned pineapples, and off-brand chips. "The grocery store is right across the street. We can stop in when we get in town."

"I've been driving all day and we didn't stop for lunch or dinner. Can she go to the store so we don't have to when we get there?"

"It will only take a few minutes for us to go there."

"Can you please just ask?"

It was close to eleven, five hours until my mother had to be at work. I knew what she would say. As I typed the message, I told myself that things were okay. This was okay, this was one request.

"She said she can pick up some groceries."

Later, my mother would joke with me that it was the first time she had gotten fresh vegetables in longer than she could remember. Later, my sister told me that when she heard this, how our mother had gotten up close to midnight, dressed to drive to Hy-Vee to buy pasta and broccoli and onions, this was the first time she knew she hated my beloved.

At the duplex at the end of the cul-de-sac, the driveway to my mother's was so steep that a person could not park on the incline. In my mother's kitchen, where I had once roasted potatoes and mushrooms to surprise her when she finished her shift, where Alex once sat, eating leftover sushi I had taken home from work, I sliced onions as my beloved boiled water. There was so much I wanted to say. My beloved was tired. It was not the time for stories. It was okay. There would be time, there would be time.

We ate pasta at the table covered with dishes and knickknacks. I showed my beloved the living room with the loveseat, the television whose antennas were never quite right. I repositioned the rabbit ears, but the local news still blurred.

My mother had insisted we switch rooms. She had already gone back to sleep in the drooping twin-sized bed, saying we could sleep in hers. Those nights in Iowa, we were chaste, barely touched. I could stretch the ethernet cord just enough, could position it on a chair in the doorway, so that we could watch television in bed.

When my mother didn't have work, we walked with her around the contours of Gray's Lake. She carried a disposable camera, took a photo of us by the water, beneath a towering oak, in the bright beautiful middle of summer, me on my toes, leaning up to kiss their cheek, their hands in their pockets, their shoulders hunched, eyes closed, smiling, embarrassed.

My mother went home, and we walked through the sculpture garden, lay in the grass under a colorless sky. Next to the public library where, as a teen, I had driven myself alone for the first time, where, as high schoolers, we escaped into the streets of a city we thought we dreamed up.

"I feel really worn out," my beloved said.

"I'm sorry," I said. "We can go home if you want, we can connect your computer to the ethernet and watch something, take a nap."

"Can we?"

At my mother's house, we reclused like hermit crabs. Like children, wrapped in blankets, watching baseball, in and out of sleep. Everything was fine, I told myself. Everything was fine.

After two days my beloved asked if it was all right if we left early, went back to Ohio. We had a long drive looming ahead of us. We could drive through my hometown, my beloved said, if I really wanted, but it was so out of the way. It would add at least an hour of driving, and didn't I want to make it to South Bend in time to have dinner with Robin, my friend from college?

"Of course," I said. Of course.

My beloved didn't like when I talked about college, so when we sat in Robin's living room admiring their plants and artwork, I didn't bring up shared memories or friends, said instead that they were both musicians and writers. Robin talked about instruments and art school, and I thought about how I had to quit band as a child because there was no longer money to rent the instrument. My beloved had already heard this story and there was nothing else to say about it.

When we left Robin's apartment, when we started to drive again into the nothing Indiana night, I cried as quietly as I could. In the passenger seat, I pushed my arm against the door, tried to press my body into the seat cushion. In the closed space of the car, surrounded by the Midwestern night, I could not hide from my beloved.

"You're crying," my beloved said. "Why are you crying?"

I wanted to tell my beloved that I would not see my mother or sister again until December. I wanted to describe the house we were leaving, wanted to tell them every detail of the place we left behind; I didn't know if they had seen a thing. I wanted to tell them about the cul-de-sac that my mother lived on, wanted to describe the way the house looked, how steep the driveway, wanted to describe the bunny ears on top of my mother's television, how that was the only way to get a clear picture, and even then most of the time they didn't work. I wanted to describe the yellow ethernet cord, how I sat on the floor in the hallway with my computer attached to it when I applied for graduate school. I wanted to describe the sagging bed my mother had slept in, the one that used to be mine, to show my beloved the car I had bought for my mother, the old Saturn whose headliner hung over our heads.

It was too late to go back, too late to change this course we had agreed on together. I shook my head, silent. I cried, and my beloved told me again that I was crying. My beloved drove without stopping until we arrived back at their parents' house, to the spare room in the basement, as if we had never left.

That summer, I worked with three other women to create a low-income student advocate group, got it registered as an official university organization. We planned, we dreamed. What could we do to make this place better for poor students? To soothe that dissonance, the discord of being poor at Harvard, to make visible the things swept under the lustrous rugs, the moments we swallowed ourselves and our stories.

We hosted a panel during the new student orientation in the fall. We made flyers, listed resources. The cheapest grocery stores, how to apply for food stamps, jobs on campus that let you do schoolwork on the clock. The hidden and not-so-hidden costs of being there, the ways the university assumed a certain financial wellspring. How, even the summer language program, which was offered to students to pass the language exams, required a $500 registration fee. How they didn't tell students that up front, how they boasted about this wonderful program and let students find for themselves the ways it was inaccessible.

I wanted to make sure that no one else felt hungry, that no one else felt alone the way I had.

During the panel, I sat at the front of the room in Andover Hall, the walls deep mahogany, windows stretching to the ceiling with thick drapes. The room was crowded, packed. There were so many of us, there to tell our stories, there to know that we were not the only ones who needed help affording this place.

I didn't know where my beloved was. In the back of the room, as if not to take up necessary space, was my beloved's roommate. He hardly said anything to me that day, sitting near the wall. Not there for himself, but there to see, to witness. I felt his eyes on me like a hand on my shoulder. He sat in the back of the room and my thoughts spiraled, circled in whirlpools: *He was here, where were you?*

When I sat in front of a crowd of new students, the room full and bustling, everyone there for a panel that I had organized, to be in community and solidarity, all I could feel was the weight of absence. Where was my beloved?

There was a day in August when I opened Facebook like I did every other day. There, at the top of my feed, an event: Memorial for Alanna. I didn't understand. I went to her Facebook page. I went to her partner's. I didn't understand. Alanna, one of my first friends in college, gone, just like that. An aneurysm, sudden, overnight. The memorial would be held in a forest outside San Francisco. I stared at plane tickets. I stared at prices. Impossible, it was impossible.

The night before Alanna's memorial, three college friends called. They were buying me a plane ticket, they said. She would have wanted you there, they said. "We're already sending you money," they said.

I flew across the sky to leave a piece of myself in a jar in a forest in California, to break myself across the dirt floor, pine needles in my clothing. Alanna Lynn, taken from this life in the middle of the night. This beacon of safety who had sat with me through panic attacks, who smiled me into being, whose hair got frizz-happy in the Portland rain, who walked with a comforter wrapped around her shoulders one cold day ("I'm from California!"), who was never and never and never ashamed of her emotions, who felt all the way, was part of the air. This girl I met through a Facebook group when I was still in high school, in a house that was not safe, in a town that was not safe, she reached across the air and let me know there was a place where I would be welcomed with open arms, there was a place where she was waiting for me.

We sat in a circle in the forest and named her. Alanna, Alanna, Alanna. We took turns, telling the stories of who she was to us. When it was my turn to speak, I made an animal noise and knew this, this was the inside of me crawling out. "Can we come back to me?" I croaked like a frog, as if begging nature to absorb me into itself. Let the redwoods catch my cracking voice, let the dirt take me, this body cannot hold the loss of her. In the crack of me was the knowing, the simple fact, repeating: It should have been me.

I returned to Cambridge breaking. I had remembered, for a moment, what it was to be home among people, and had come back to this place of slick saltwater buildings, of students' empty posturing, of people who kept their distance. It was beautiful outside and everything in me was dying.

I went to a corner store and bought cigarettes, the same brand my best friend in college had smoked. I sat on a sidewalk, low to the ground. Hidden and not. One street from campus, pretending I was somewhere far away.

My beloved was nowhere. Where were they that day? They were angry with me. I needed them, and they needed space, and they were angry every time I texted, so I sat alone on a sidewalk, feet sticking into the street. I was wearing a black tank top and long blue skirt, and this seemed important.

A few cars came close to my toes. I screamed my grief into the autumn sky. A cigarette dangling from one hand, eyes closed, tears pouring, unconcerned with who might see. Feral. I was ugly. Stained with tears, face red and crumpled. It was unfair of me to dream of dying when Alanna was gone. It was unfair of me to be here when she was gone. I wanted the heavy tangled mess of my heart to stop beating.

I screamed into the Cambridge air. The houses were close to the streets, and I didn't care if families could hear me, if passing students could hear me. I wanted the world to bear witness to the loud, lonely agony, the grief I could not contain. The grief for Alanna, the grief for all the things that would not end.

Across the street, a girl slowed down. Hesitant, she walked toward me. She sat, her knees pulled up to her chin. "You don't have to talk," she said. "But I can see that you're hurting. Can I sit with you a minute?"

I stared at the brilliant blue of my skirt and wished she was my beloved. I would have given anything for my beloved to see me then, to hear this uncontainable scream, this ugly noise. I wanted so badly for my beloved to understand.

We sat, and she listened as I cracked out an explanation. She stayed with me, told me of a friend she had lost. She began to cry. Together we made a sanctuary of that sidewalk, in that moment safe, our feet inches from passing cars, our grief unbound. This stranger who could look at me and see the ways I was collapsing, who let me see her in return.

And still in the back of my mind, two threads repeating.

Where are you, where are you, where are you?

It should have been me.

THINGS I NEVER TOLD YOU, PART 2 [EDITED]
SEPTEMBER 21, 2017

Once before I tried it, went to sleep with the noose still around my neck.

~~*You yelled at me.*~~

~~*I told you that I didn't feel loved, didn't feel special and you yelled at me. Can i tell you? I'm really not doing good. Everyone is suicidal what makes me special? Nothing, nothing, nothing.*~~

I told the woman in June that I did not want medicine. I was afraid.

It was late afternoon on a September day, warm and heady. I watched the light slant through the windows of the old house of the comparative literature department. The professor was talking, and it was there like it had never left, this thing thrashing inside me like it was a living creature. It was there with a cold certainty: Something bad was going to happen if class were to end, if I were to walk home and be in that house alone. I choked back tears and drew in the margins until class was over. I left quickly, walking down the cobblestone streets, passersby becoming long shards of static. At the fifth floor of the health center, at the intake desk for campus therapists, I began to sob.

"Can you help?" my voice sounded like a stranger, cracked and shaking. "I really need to talk to somebody." This was not the way I normally cried in public. This was something unstoppable. The nurses looked at me with wide eyes, pushed a box of tissues toward me.

"Mental health urgent care is on the fourth floor," one of them said. "One floor down, check in like you would for a walk-in medical appointment." I nodded. Took tissues. Blurred through the elevator.

On the fourth floor, sitting next to students there for checkups, for viruses and sprains, I didn't try to hide my face. In the middle of them, I was a puddle of mucus and tears. This thing wanted to get out, and I couldn't hold it in. They took me to a small room to wait for the psychiatrist on call.

A nurse with a thick Boston accent waited in the room with me. "What's got you so upset?" she said.

"My friend died," I choked. I stared at the linoleum floor.

"You have to pick yourself up!" she said. "I've had friends die too, you can't feel sorry for yourself forever." I didn't speak again until she left.

"What's wrong?" another nurse came in. I stared at the linoleum.

"I'm not doing okay," I said.

"Have you thought about hurting yourself?"

"Yes," I said.

"Have you thought about suicide?"

"Yes," I said.

"Do you have a plan?"

"Yes," I said.

"What is it?"

"Pills," I said.

They took me to a small office, where a man sat, leaning forward in his chair, as if he wanted to come as close as he could without standing.

"I'm not doing okay," I said. "Help," I said. "I want to die," I said. The man looked at me with sad eyes, with folded hands.

"Do you have a plan? Have you thought about how?" he asked.

"Yes."

"How?"

"A rope," I said. "In my room," I said.

"Let's get you some medicine," he said.

"Yes," I said. "Yes."

That night my beloved met me at my house, walked with me to the Mexican restaurant down the street, bought me dinner and I apologized for texting, for calling, for needing so much, for needing all of this.

"It's okay," they said.

"They're starting me on medicine," I said. "I'm trying, I'm really trying to get better."

The professor of my translation class had invited me to his house for tea to discuss my final project. On his back porch, surrounded by autumn air and orange leaves, he handed me a small cup of tea. He pointed to the apartment complex next door. "Nabokov used to live there," he said.

We brainstormed things I could write about. The possibilities of a paper on grammatical gender in Russian. The semiotics of Azerbaijani carpets made during Soviet rule that combined traditional Persian style with images of oil rigs and men with large red flags. We discussed doing something simple, straightforward, translating a story, accompanied by an essay defending the translation.

The world was so large. There were so many other things that mattered, and there I was with my puny sadness. I kept looking over at the brick building where Nabokov used to live, the window that used to be his. I wanted so badly to be a person who deserved to be there, a person with insights and valuable ideas, a person who could do something big and worthwhile, a person who belonged in a place like this. I was failing.

The doctors had told me I would be okay on the medicine. I thought it would be worth it, to fix whatever was wrong with me, whatever made me uncontrollable. They told me it had a black box warning. They said that sometimes, for people my age, the medicine makes things worse before it gets better. The psychiatrist tried to explain it, saying that parts of my brain were numb, asleep because of the depression, and this medicine would wake them up. At first, this would make me more aware of the pain, feel it more acutely, but I had to hold on until the medicine began to soothe.

"All right," I said. "Okay."

They read me the warning and I imagined myself sitting on stage of a black box theater, staring out at an empty room. Hamlet, all alone on stage, his soliloquy heard by no one.

"Antidepressants increased the risk compared to placebo of suicidal thinking and behavior (suicidality) in children, adolescents, and young adults in short-term studies of major depressive disorder (MDD) and other psychiatric disorders. Anyone considering the use of this or any other antidepressant in a child, adolescent, or young adult must balance this risk with the clinical need."[11]

I listened as they told me. I was already suicidal, what more could happen?

They sent me home with bags of pills, didn't ask if I had a regular therapist, and I didn't think it was important. The medicine was proof that I was trying, that I knew I had a problem, that I was taking responsibility.

"Patients of all ages who are started on antidepressant therapy should be monitored appropriately and observed closely for clinical worsening, suicidality, or unusual changes in behavior. Families and caregivers should be advised of the need for close observation and communication with the prescriber."[12]

It was a bright morning in October, one week of taking pills alongside coffee.

Something was wrong. I was wrong.

In the morning I thought: *I can't do this.* I thought: *I have to do this.* I had promised that I would restock the supplies for the improvised food pantry that the low-income student group started.

The walk to campus, my body heavy. I sat in front of the food locker, the makeshift temporary fix we'd initiated until we could get the food pantry set up. Shoved jars of peanut butter, boxes of Easy Mac, bags of rice inside. Sat and waited. There was a weight in my chest and it was breathing. There was nowhere to go and no one to call. My beloved had made it clear that they needed space, that if I were to reach out it would be a violation of their boundaries.

I don't remember walking home but there I was. My housemates were at work. I couldn't breathe. Everything was heavy, nowhere was safe. There was a fire that had to burn something.

Thousands of miles and three time zones away, the only other person I thought I could call was asleep. I stared at the time on my phone. *Please wake up soon. Please call me back.*

It started with fingernails, digging into my skin. Then nail clippers, the sharp edge leaving pale lines on my arm. I hated myself for that, how pathetic, those tiny scratches, so I got a knife from the kitchen. Lay a towel down beneath me. My throat caught between a scream and a sob. I didn't cut myself, not really. I held the knife and pressed, moved it back and forth. I sawed and cried and waited. Eleven in

Cambridge meant eight in Seattle. *Please wake up. Please pick up.*

I timed it. I called. He answered. "Alex," I said. "Alex, please help me."

His voice on the other end of the phone like a net to fall into, a blanket, wrapped tight. His voice in the sunlight, collapsing the miles and months that separated us. He was kind, he was patient in ways I didn't deserve. He stayed on the phone with me longer than I could count. He was late to work. He told me it was okay, and I believed him. I cried until there was nothing left in my body, until I was a dried-out husk. After he hung up, I closed my eyes and slept for the first time in weeks.

That night my beloved came to see me. I had acted out of turn. I had reached out. It happened like it always happened. I needed help when they wanted space. They were quiet as they walked up the stairs to my room. The shorts I wore couldn't hide the place where the blade left gashes on my skin. Two twin cuts, one on my left arm, one on my leg. The same angle. In my room, my beloved sat on the floor, away from me. I sat cross-legged on the bed. My face tearstained, body exhausted. My beloved was wearing a pale blue shirt that matched the soft twilight of the world around us.

My beloved was quiet and did not say a word about the cuts on my body. I had done something dirty that should not be spoken of. This was the proof that I was broken, proof of the ways I was untouchable. Manipulative. This thing that I did not have words for was too much for anyone to go near.

The light in my room was fading. My beloved looked so sad there on the floor, watching me with their back to the wall, that I didn't notice that they never asked if I was all right, never asked what had happened, never asked if I was inside a black box, looking out.

We never mentioned that day again.

THINGS I NEVER TOLD YOU, PART 2 [EDIT]
OCTOBER 11, 2017

~~You yelled at me.~~

~~I told you that I didn't feel loved, didn't feel special and you yelled at me. Can i tell you? I'm really not doing good. Everyone is suicidal what makes me special? Nothing, nothing, nothing.~~

in the stuffy air I am waiting

I don't know what I expected of my beloved. I needed my beloved to help me; there was no way my beloved could have given me the help I needed. I needed my beloved to give me what no human being could. I needed my beloved to convince me that I was a thing that deserved to keep breathing. I needed my beloved to convince me of something that I would never believe.

I was crying, again. In my beloved's bed in their cold attic room, they were standing, looking down at me, and I was crying, like always. I was a storm with no beginning or end.

"I need help," I said. "I need a therapist. It's so hard even finding someone. I need help finding someone who will take Medicaid."

My beloved smiled like something too good to be true. "That's all?" I watched as they typed something on their computer. Their mother had helped them find a therapist, was paying for it herself. My beloved understood the system, my beloved had an inside perspective. I wondered if my beloved was typing a message to their therapist, asking for recommendations. "There," they said. There was a vibration. I looked at my phone. An email. I read it with a bottomless stomach. The message was a few sentences, a template, an email I could send to therapists to see if they took MassHealth.

I didn't tell my beloved how many hours I had spent researching, didn't tell them that I had been sending the same message to people for weeks, that they all replied the same way. *We don't take MassHealth anymore; it must be listed wrong on the website. You can pay out of pocket though. Does that work?* I didn't tell them how many people I had called, how long the waitlists were for sliding scale. I didn't tell them that I was only allowed six sessions with a campus therapist, and I was running out of time. My beloved had done me this kindness, I couldn't ask for more.

"Thank you," I said, and smiled.

In graduate school, working three and then four jobs at a time, the ends were not meeting, and my arms were getting too tired to keep pulling them together.

I smiled to my coworkers at the library and hardly said a word. I got a cart of books, pushed it through the stacks. Rode the elevator down into the basement, one of the floors where the hallways didn't connect, where, to get to the other side, you had to ride the elevator up two floors, walk to the other end of the building and ride a different elevator down.

The Widener Library is not quite a labyrinth, but almost. It was rare, there in the basement, that I would run into another person. Headphones in, I listened to my playlist. My motions were automatic, easy. Some days, there alone in the basement, I sang along loudly, fully. Some days, I listened to a podcast and giggled to myself. Some days, days when it was never-ending, I cried in the stacks, and was sure to be quiet. A few sniffles, nothing more. Though my face collapsed, red and crumpled, though the tears came in torrents that threatened the old spines of books, I swallowed the sounds. No one would think these tiny trembling breaths were anything out of the ordinary. Just another student, stressed about their work, letting off steam. It was so nice, lucky, to have a job where I could cry, where no one would notice.

In January, I had a conversation with my beloved. Things weren't working, again, still. My beloved wasn't sure if we had a future. The nature of our relationship had to change. I nodded. I don't know how we had lasted that long.

We still walked the cobblestone streets from campus to my beloved's house. We made dinner, sat in bed and watched *Seinfeld*. I wore my beloved's pajamas, curled next to them in bed. My beloved said they loved me.

I brought my beloved a book of music, a calendar of Klimt paintings for Valentine's Day. "I'm so glad we didn't break up." I held out the presents.

"Wait," they said from bed, where we had been lying together just minutes before, "I thought we had already broken up."

I stood staring, mouth open. I didn't know if I should laugh or cry. My beloved had broken up with me without my understanding more than a month ago. I stood barefoot, wearing my beloved's gray sweatpants, my beloved's favorite large maroon shirt, offering them these tokens of affection. It was Valentine's Day and the house was freezing.

I walked home alone in the snow. I don't remember whose clothing I was wearing. I walked home through the snow and there was no one waiting.

Before things ended with my beloved, I had been friends with their housemate, Lily. We walked through Cambridge, sat in her living room, crafting. We were on the same antidepressant. We talked about brain zaps, side effects. We talked about what it meant to build community, to be in community with each other. Here, I thought, a friend who understood me.

After my beloved broke up with me and I could no longer go to that yellow house in the rich part of Cambridge, where the houses were all three floors and squat, tall and thick, I still texted Lily. Invited her over, imagined making dinner together, sitting in my room as night fell around us. Girl talk, I thought to myself. How nice to have a friend like that.

She didn't answer my messages. When she called me, days later, her voice was distant. "I can't take care of you," she said. "I can't be a support to you." I was a child being scolded for asking for something inappropriate. That was all, she said. I never heard from her again.

I understood, then. A friendship with me meant supporting me, unreciprocated. A friendship with me took too much from a person. There was something, I was sure, something so pathetic, so needy, so broken about me that made friendship impossible. Something that made even people like that, people who spoke so carefully about oppression, about justice, about building a new world, about the importance of gentleness and communication, something that made even those people know that I was not a thing to go near. I knew without doubt: people would keep leaving if they knew what I really was, if they heard the edge of it in my voice.

To tell another person of the thoughts that crowded my mind, the vines that wrapped through my days, the longing, fierce and hard, for an ending, was to burden them with something unwanted, too much for another person to hold. To share, to be open, was to demand support, was asking for emotional labor. To say these words out loud to another person, that at night when I couldn't sleep I comforted myself with dreams of ropes, water, pills, that every day I coached myself through panic with the gentle reminder that there was a way out, that I so desperately needed help, to say these things out loud was emotionally manipulative, asking for something that no one should be asked to give. This was not a thing that should be seen. This was not a thing that should be spoken.

In the morning, I looked at myself in the mirror and knew something was wrong, something in the marrow of my bones, something in the tempo of my heartbeat. Something deep down at the core of me was wrong, and to confess this to another person, to share this fact of myself, was a burden that no one deserved. There would be no absolution for a problem only I could fix.

At night, I closed my eyes and imagined how to do it in a responsible way, so no innocent person would find me. I could leave a note on the door, I thought. The note would instruct my roommates to call the police, would tell them not to open the door to my room. I thought about our second-floor porch, about ropes and knots, about how I could time it, dial 911 when everything was tied and ready, when I was perched on the banister, ready to fall into the night, so the police would come right away, so not a single neighbor or passing car would see. I thought about the river, about leaving my phone in my bed, walking across town to the shore, taking my shoes off and swimming away.

It took so much every day to get out of bed, to get dressed, to walk to campus, to go to work and class and work and keep my head up when all I wanted was to stay in bed and cry. It took so much, and for what? All this effort, and I remained untouchable.

———

February turned to March, and I didn't understand anything. I sat in class across the room from my beloved and felt my body on fire, felt their eyes on me. My beloved walked home with me, my beloved sat with me in the living room before my housemates got home, my beloved told me they missed me, missed being close to me. My beloved looked at me with eyes like clouds heavy with rain and asked if they could put their arm around me, if they could press their body to mine. I said no and stared at them across the room.

———

I was in a class on depictions of the sacred. We were reading Denis Johnson's *Jesus' Son*, the book that "Emergency" is from, the same story I had played to myself my first day on campus, the story that reminded me that it mattered where I came from, where I was, a collection of stories about Fuckhead as he does drugs and fucks up all over the state of Iowa.

I came to class giddy, so excited to talk about this thing I loved, how Johnson made the world, all of it, beautiful, worth something, worth telling stories about. This book is a homecoming. Gradually, the conversation in class became an insistence of things I hadn't imagined. Bad, some people said. Someone didn't understand why we read this. Someone called the characters monstrous.

In her book *The Recovering*, Leslie Jamison writes of Johnson's work, "His stories insisted that everything around us mattered."[13]

Nabokov says we should never identify with a character; it shrouds our "objective" understanding of the text. It is not Fuckhead with whom I identify, not the other men in the story, or the women who withstand the things the men do. It is the urgency, the sense of existing in the middle of a somewhere that is nowhere, of actions disconnected from consequences, of the jagged logic of need, the grasping for meaning on the character's own terms that pervades the work.

What can I tell you about *Jesus' Son* except I am there, in the background, a child in the corner, watching, silent and present every moment.

"I would hope I could love a person like that if I met them," a woman training to be a minister said about the characters.

I sat silent in a class at a graduate school where I was reminded daily that I could not afford to be there. At my back were all the ghosts, the ones who didn't make it and the ones who did. The ghosts lined up in the back of the classroom, unseen, waiting for me to speak. Someone was standing by the door with a baseball bat.

There were people in my town who came to school drunk, water bottles full of vodka because they knew it didn't matter. Nothing they did there, really, mattered. Surrounded by adults and police and enemies, they knew how hard it was to get out, to really get out.

"I would hope I could love a person like that."

My brother and sister are not home and do not tell me where they are. Sometimes I think it is because they do not like me. I am young and awkward, and still watch cartoons. Sometimes I think it is because they do not trust me to handle the things they put in their bodies and the people they call friends.

There is a boy I used to think was a friend. We sat in his basement smoking weed one night. "Why are you even applying for college?" He was laughing. He smiled. "No one from our town goes anywhere. Applying is a waste of time."

"What?" I said.

"You're wasting your time applying to college. You're setting yourself up for disappointment." His smile was lopsided. "I'm trying to help you." I knew that he meant it.

There were people from our town who left, who went to the University of Chicago and other distant places. But those people were not like us. Those were not the people whose houses cracked with tension, who spent long hours at Jimmy John's and Dairy Queen, who knew without needing to be told about the impossibilities of escaping the house one is born into, who breathed in drugs and poverty and desperation. In this town where the police knew my name, where they made jokes about how old I would be when I would be arrested, a girl like me was not getting out. We all found things to do to survive. Not all of us survived. Some of us drank, some of us took weapons to our own bodies.

On that day in graduate school, someone said that Fuckhead was a monster.

The professor stood in front of the class and explained the redemption arc of the stories, the way it ends, with Fuckhead in rehab, not just repenting, but helping others.

This is how the world saw us. This is how the world sees us. Monstrous. In need of redemption. Our stories and selves not worth love, not worth care, our stories and selves too messy, too raw and ugly, to take at face value, to take on our own terms. Nothing sacred in the stories themselves. The only sacred thing is when Fuckhead tries to fix the person that he is. The ghosts lined the back of the room, and in the middle of them, the phantoms of my siblings as they were in those years, and the specter of who I was. The knowledge that I was one of those characters. Inevitable, my monstrosity.

I did not speak that day in class, and left early, haunted by the condescension, the truth that these people I sat next to would hate me if they knew where I came from, who I was. What kind of monster was I? How could a thing like me ever be worth loving, ever be worth knowing in my own vocabulary?

I walked home the way I always walked. I walked home sobbing.

The next week in class, I was uncouth. I was the monster that I thought I was. I spoke before the professor did. I spoke without stopping, I brought it all to a halt. How dare we sit at Harvard and call these people monstrous? Who were we to make this false separation, that need and brokenness and poverty and the choices made out of desperation were somehow far, distant, other from where we were?

Later, the professor sent me an email. They were invoking monster theory, he said, not to insult, but to make sense of. I understand having a regional affiliation, he said.

Years later, I read the subgenre of critical theory that focuses on monsters. The basic idea is that monsters are embodiments, metaphors of the abstract things that we fear. Leatherface is not just an ax murderer, but a creature on the outskirts, targeting ideal, beautiful American teenagers. A thing that personifies the fear of an Other that is coming for American youth. We call things monster to make them Other. A monster is difference, embodied.

The characters of *Jesus' Son* were Other to the people in that class, the characters in the book were embodiments of things to fear. Metaphors of creatures best cast out, kept away from the rest of us.

Two months before I gave in to the things that had always been there, I sat alone in an apartment in Somerville, looking out at the Boston skyline. How could I ever tell my stories? If I stayed silent, no one would have to know what I was. It was in the telling that I would make myself monstrous, give myself away. These stories were not meant to be heard.

To see the people in *Jesus' Son* as in need of redemption is to ignore the terms of value of these characters, to impose one's own. There is a difference, I think, between giving someone redemption, and giving them the tools they need to be okay, to be accountable for the harm they've done and to be better. What does redemption accomplish, besides the washing away of a person, remaking them in a new image?

In that class, I do not remember what the professor thought was sacred, but I thought it was to be seen in all our brokenness, to be given a space between text and reader to hold our broken stories, our narratives in which there are no heroes, to be told that these stories matter, to be told that it is possible to be better than a hero, it is possible to fuck up again and again and again and still try to be better.

I thought that to offer redemption to Fuckhead, to offer redemption to these narratives, is to ignore the conditions that led to those actions. Fuckhead is not asking you for redemption. To offer an unasked-for redemption is to flatten something messy, something prickly, to take a testimony and claim it as another kind of story.

The first story in *Jesus' Son* is about a car crash. Fuckhead hitches a ride, and somehow sees this disaster coming, though, in his drugged-out state of mind we have to ask if he has already survived it, is telling the story after, as a sort of *ex eventu* prophecy. This story ends with Fuckhead in the hospital, with a line that could be directed to the readers, could be directed to the characters.

"And you, you ridiculous people, you expect me to help you."[14]

My professor in graduate school made much of this sentence. I can hear him saying it, the way he would lean forward just so, how his voice emphasized that first *you*. I wish I could remember the point he was trying to make, but all I remember is his voice.

Was he trying to say that here, here is our invitation to read these characters, the book itself, acknowledging the need for help? Was it here that he understood Fuckhead to be admitting some narrative need for redemption, salvation? Was it here that he understood Fuckhead to be speaking directly to the reader, telling us that there is no guidance in these pages?

I don't remember, but I remember how my body felt that day in class. How small, how ashamed.

Is there a canon of literature for poor people the same way we speak of a canon of feminist literature? I'm not sure, but if there is, surely *Jesus' Son* has a special place.

Jesus' Son is many things to many people. But it is also a response to the woman who hoped that she could love a person like that.

Well, Fuckhead says, I don't need your love. I've got my life, you've got yours. If you think you need to save me, that's your problem.

The last story in the cycle is "Beverly Home," a story in which our narrator has gotten a job at an old folks' home and is in recovery for his addictions. Fuckhead is still fucked up, staring into the windows of strangers in hopes that he will see them having sex. Near the end of the story is a line that looks back, a line that answers Fuckhead's first address to the reader, the ridiculous people who look to him for help.

"All these weirdos, and me getting a little bit better every day right in the midst of them. I had never known, never even imagined for a heartbeat, that there might be a place for people like us."[15]

Not redemption, not salvation, something softer, something smaller. To be in a safe place with others like you, to look at one another and not see *broken*, not see *monster*, to see each other face-to-face.

After my beloved left me, there was nothing left to lose by telling them that every day was a gray fog I could not see outside of. I couldn't lie to my beloved anymore, didn't have the courage or resolve. They were the only person I was honest with. I can't imagine how hard that must have been.

I told my beloved that I wasn't doing okay. I told my beloved when I was afraid to be home alone. I was manipulative. I was cornered. I said the things out loud that I'd never been able to say when we were dating. That I thought about dying, that I was so tired, that I wanted it all to end.

My beloved said that their therapist had instructed them to call an ambulance if I started talking like that. I begged them not to. Ambulances meant bills, meant things not covered by insurance, meant missed shifts and lost paychecks and skipped classes and missed deadlines.

"Please don't. Please, you can't," I said. "I don't know where they'll take me." It was a cold, hopeless certainty. There was nothing to be done but wait. All around something was pressing. A heartbeat pounding. There was an animal in my chest that wanted to get out.

I told my beloved that I wanted to die but couldn't explain how it thrashed against my sternum, how it beat against my lungs. Visceral, it was everything my body was. There was a call coming from somewhere far away, a siren song drifting over gray waters, a rustling promise that there was a way to calm this storm. This call, not always violent, not always howling, but there, steady, even and patient, waiting for me to heed it. It beckoned with soft hands and kind eyes, and I was a child in front of it, empty-handed and feral before its promise of rest. If I were to say this out loud as my beloved sat with me, their arm around my shoulders, they would have made the call with no hesitation. They would have held me there, insisting, until the ambulance came. Instead, I sat close-lipped, the melody humming through my gut, thinking about the only thing that could fix my brokenness, the only way out, this dream that, if I were to confess it, would mark me as that much more broken.

"People who are far along the trajectory toward suicide come to see death in a very peculiar light; they use terms like 'beautiful' and 'graceful' when describing it."[16]

Graduation loomed like a cliff I would jump off. There would be no more meetings with deans to talk about what else could be done to help low-income students. There would be no more emails to tell me which event had free food left over. There would be no more food stamps; I only qualified as a student. There would be no more free therapy through the school, no more student loan deferment. I couldn't bring myself to check if I was still eligible for MassHealth.

At night when I closed my eyes and thought of the impossibility of living, the inescapable debt I had no way of paying, the life that was waiting with open jaws, work and double shifts and aching feet, the dream of the rope was a comfort I couldn't deny. It was an answer to the question that had whispered me asleep. I thought of the house in Iowa, the house in which I had grown up, the house I could finally escape. I thought of my student loans, how impossibly small I was beneath them. I thought of a face, close to mine, red and screaming. I thought of my body, of the foul, rotten self that lived at the center.

Every morning, I woke up, drank acid-thick coffee. I looked at myself in the mirror and lied. "I can do this," I said aloud. "I can do this."

I started to have sex with strangers. I stared up at unfamiliar ceilings. I didn't think about what would happen when I got home. When I was with them, I didn't have to talk. I was only a body. It was, I thought, the only thing I was good for.

When I ran into acquaintances on campus, it was easy to smile, to laugh.

"How are you?" someone would ask.

"Really bad," I'd say. I would grin, cackle as if it was a joke that we knew the punchline to. They might furrow their brow. I would laugh harder. "It's fine," I said. "It's okay. I'm kidding."

The simple fact that the only future I could imagine was a future in which I was dead.

It beat at me in the mornings, a rhythm. *What am I going to do, what am I going to do?* This fantasy, this playacting of being a student at Harvard would end and I would go back to reality. What jobs were there if I moved back to Iowa? How could I pay the loans? Where could I live? What would I do?

After my beloved broke up with me, they still took me out to dinner, paid for me because they knew I couldn't afford to. I wanted to shrink into nothing. Pathetic, how pathetic. This creature of need. Sitting across from each other, I heard all the things they used to say.

"Thank you," I said.

"It's really okay," my beloved told me. *You are a black hole.*

"I really appreciate it."

"You deserve to be able to go out to eat." *You take and take and take.*

"How's everything with your new housemate?"

"It's okay. Getting better. Thanks for asking." *You always make things about yourself.*

"I'm glad."

"Take care tonight, yeah?" *What is wrong with you?*

In the snapping blue gray March air, we walked in different directions, and I looked over my shoulder, as if I could guess from the hunch of my beloved's shoulders where they were going, if they were headed to meet their new girlfriend, hold her the way they used to hold me, if they were going to tell her that she had nothing to worry about, that they were just making sure I was all right, this poor, troubled ex.

One by one by one by one, the facts of myself became a weight I could not dislodge.

I was throwing a party. I needed something to look forward to. For more days than I could count, I had nothing more than one cup of coffee in the morning, one can of soup at night. My housemates were out of town. The night before my own party, I went to someone else's. I stood in the corner and tried to be a fun person to talk to. The narrative was approaching the climax, the moment from which there was no coming back. The narrative was finally going to have a resolution. The narrative had already run its course. The narrative had continued long after it should have ended.

The fight with my friend. The night air on my walk home. The cold. I pulled my sweatshirt tighter. The whistle of the train. The sliver of a crescent moon above me, leading me home.

Dear reader, you know what happens next.

PART III

Ascencion

A woman once asked me how the world looked after I lived. If the sunlight, the trees, seemed more iridescent, if they glowed with new beauty in my freshly opened eyes.

There is the temptation, the urge, to make meaning of this thing, to make the living in and of itself redemptive, triumphant. Surely, since I didn't try again, things must be better now. It's easier, I think, to talk about wanting to die if you know the person lived through it, if they took it back later. *I was in a bad place then.* The shift into the past. *It was a problem that I had, then I got over it.*

How many times do I have to say it before you believe me? There was nothing special, nothing beautiful in the fact of living. The conditions of my life hadn't changed. It was the same with an added complication. What did this thing make me? A living suicide, a little ghost.

I had to leave Boston, had to get out of this place where I had cried on every street corner, where I went to work wondering if I would see my beloved.

Late in summer, after months of not talking, I met with my beloved, walked through the blue evening. My beloved confessed that after I left the hospital, it was hard to be around me, to talk to me. My beloved needed time to face the force of what they felt for me those days, all the love that came rushing back. The hope that my beloved still felt that we could try again. My beloved was dating someone else. My beloved wanted me to get better so we could try again. I knew I needed to leave.

I could only keep working on campus until fall classes began. The café I worked at was closing. My rent was increasing. There was no longer a reason to stay in Boston. I needed to go somewhere where no one knew what had happened, a place where I could be a stranger among strangers.

I took the commuter rail to a small town outside Salem. Bought the cheapest car I could find in the state, the cheapest car that still ran. Paid $1,500 for a twenty-year-old Honda Civic. The speakers only worked on one side. The back doors would only open from the outside. The bottom was covered in rust. Everything I owned could fit in the trunk. It was perfect.

Before I left the apartment in Massachusetts, when my housemates weren't there, I went to the kitchen. I peeled away the Band-Aids that had stayed hidden all summer between the knife block and the wall. I held them in my hands. Precious, these tokens of how bad things had been. I heard my brother's laugh when I looked at them.

There was a small box that I had bought from Goodwill. I'd wanted to get something pretty, something ornate, but what I could afford was this, a container made of pine, without a clasp to close it.

In outpatient they had told us about emergency boxes. A box or bag where you kept things that made you feel better if you were panicking, if you were spiraling. Open the box and there are the things that would calm you: sprigs of lavender, notes from friends, a note to yourself to listen to that song that you love. A candle.

My box was full of empty orange bottles, bottles I could not stand to throw away. I have told you this already. Let me tell you again. In the box, a guitar pick made from a scrap of paper. The bracelets they gave me in the hospital with my name and intake date. I taped the Band-Aids to the underside of the box's lid and thought they looked nice there, pale brown blending into the wood. My emergency box, my emergencies.

The night before I left, my beloved came to say goodbye. My beloved had moved north of Boston. I asked if it was lonely in a town by the ocean, all alone. My beloved asked if they could hold me in the blue sheets where I had died. I was foolish. I said yes. In the morning, as I was packing my car, I mentioned to a friend that I saw my beloved, said how nervous I was about their lonely house so far away. I hoped my beloved would be okay there, so far from everyone. My friend blinked, spoke slow, as if afraid I wouldn't hear. They told me that my beloved lived with a woman, the woman they began to date after me, the woman they went to see the nights after they visited me in the hospital.

I drove away. I called my beloved. I yelled. I cried on the highways. I spread my heartbreak over every inch of pavement in the city. On the phone, my beloved confessed that they wished it was me, living with them, going to sleep together at night.

I kept driving. I kept driving.

I drove until I was delirious. The road stretched past forests, hugging the coast of Lake Erie. I lost track of the hours spent singing along to my favorite songs, listening to podcasts. I took naps in rest stops. I slept in cheap hotel rooms where the air was full of cigarette smoke.

From Boston through Iowa, past Oklahoma City, I drove to Austin, a place I knew nothing about beyond the fact that there was a room in a house waiting for me, a room where I would live, where I would hide, where I would be safe from the saltwater phantoms of the East Coast. After stretches of long, unchanging Kansas fields, the rolling Oklahoma prairie, the twisting highways outside of Dallas, I drove to this new place with drooping eyes and a twitch in my leg. I turned down a small street covered in bright green trees and wide lawns. The leaves rustled in a soft wind. I parked, stood, looked at the house, down the street. The sun on my skin, on the trees, in the air.

My beloved had written me a goodbye letter. In the letter, a quote, lines from Dante's *Divine Comedy*.

It seems to me, if my understanding is right, your rising up should be no greater surprise than seeing a mountain stream flow down to the base. What should cause wonder would be if you, freed of all that holds you down, refused to rise—as if, on earth, no sound rose up from fires.[1]

This passage was not meant for me. Dante wrote that those who killed themselves would be frozen forever, ripped apart daily by harpies. Trapped not in body but in bark, unmovable roots, ungrowing branches. Our stories only heard when he snaps off a branch, when he makes us bleed. There has to be a wound, a hole, for the words of dead trees to escape.

Dante did not think we could ever ascend. We were not meant for heaven, we were not meant to go anywhere. Even when the rapture came, we would stay rooted. We had already been judged.

But maybe if we, we unliving stumps, we half-dead monsters, if we reject the narratives made for us, if we refuse Dante's story of us, if we can unfreeze our rotting limbs, if we can keep speaking, if we can make our own stories that grow in new ways, no matter how long it takes, no matter how much it hurts, then maybe, if we are free from the things that hold us down, maybe it's true that there is nothing to stop us from rising.

What are you, after you live? What keeps you going, what stops you from trying again?

The question comes to me at night, in the mornings. It comes like a friend, soft and gentle. Why not try again?

I have used up all my pills. I am afraid of getting more. I don't have the guts for knives. I no longer have MassHealth, I no longer have any insurance at all. I can't afford to be locked up again, the bills they would send me. If I were to try again, I would have to do it right this time. I can't afford to fail.

The things I hold onto are small, fragile. A student tells me they missed me while I was away. A girl tells me I helped her writing. In the morning, sometimes, the sky is pink. Sometimes, after work, I can sit outside, let the sweet Texas air lick my bare skin. Some days, it feels like an accident that I lived. Some days, it feels like a cosmic mistake with no one to blame but myself.

In Austin, the trees on my block swayed in the wind. The sky was purple at twilight. The city was full of cars. The grackles swarmed in parking lots.

I was there and the sky was lilac purple, and both of these things were illogical. I thought about calling my sister, telling the story again like it was the first time. I thought of Iman from the group in Boston who still called, still texted to check in. I thought about the other women in Boston who I would never see again. Diane, who wanted nothing to do with me, who would let no reminders of the hospital leak into the rest of her life.

I walked in the violet dusted twilight and felt things I had no names for. I looked at the world with the squinting wonder of a vampire seeing the sun for the first time, waiting for the light to hurt.

My room was in the attic of the house. The room was small, carpeted, and could not fit much more than a bed. There was a porch, a second-floor balcony, that could only be accessed from a door in my room. I wanted to sit in that attic and never leave. I wanted to lay in bed, look out the window, wait there until I remembered what it felt like to be a whole person.

I didn't know how to be around people. I had two housemates, women my age. When I heard their footsteps, I pulled my blankets to my chin. Only used the kitchen when they weren't home. I cooked, skittered to my room to eat. I left dishes in the sink, desperate to be out of sight if they came home, to spend as little time in the open as possible. Sometimes they came home before I could get back downstairs to wash my dishes, had to wait until late, until they went to bed. I sat in my bed and could hear their voices, drifting up the stairs. Tried to study how they spoke to each other. *What's up, how are you, how was your day.* The way they joked, casual, at ease, like the world was their home.

I went to a poetry reading. I introduced myself to the readers, went with them to the after-party. Under a canopy of string lights, sipping beer from mason jars, I tested sentences, practiced phrases. They asked why I moved to Austin; I answered in vague toned lies. *I had a bad time in Boston, someone I knew had a room here.* A bad time, glossed and skipped over, no need to dwell. It was cheaper here, I told them, though everyone complained about the rent, though I could still barely afford the room where I lived. I wanted to start a new chapter, I said, and smiled.

This story hid on the underside of every word. I wanted to tell everyone everything, wanted every acquaintance to know where I had been, the rooms and doors and patients and doctors, but this was not a thing to share with strangers. This was not a thing to be spoken, this thing beyond words.

It was easier to be the antisocial housemate, the girl who didn't give away a detail of her story, than to try to speak and fail. The cost of failure, the cost of saying this thing but not saying it right, not saying it good enough, the cost of speaking this thing and not being heard, unimaginable.

I wanted to hide until it all faded into nothing, until it wouldn't be a story at all. I didn't want to watch how someone's face might change, how their eyes might squint, if they would lean back, just a little, the distance they could make between us simply by bending their spine away from me, if the story started to come out.

In the novel *Frankenstein*, the creature tracks Frankenstein, the man who created him out of other bodies, stitched together, the man who cursed him with life. When the creature finds him, the creature insists on telling the story of his birth, his life to his creator. The creature was alone from the first moment he opened his eyes. As soon as humans saw him, they ran, they attacked. The creature spent months hiding next to a family's house, listening to the noises they made, learning how to speak through their example. The creature did their chores while they slept, gave up food so they could have more to eat, loved them and hoped that when they met him, they would love him back. A day came when the creature gathered his courage. He was going to talk to them. If only they could hear his story, surely these people that he loved would see past his monstrosity.

They appeared on the threshold. They screamed. Someone ran away. Someone ran toward him with weapons. The moment they saw him for who he was, they knew him as monster, a thing with no story, no past worth knowing, a thing that needed to be killed.

The creature tells this story to his creator and asks Frankenstein to make him a companion, someone like him, another creature that he would love, who would love him, so he would not have to wander the world alone. Though the creature is eloquent, though his story is heartbreaking, though he is sympathetic, though his tale is replete with allusions to Milton, with parallels to God's creation of Adam, this does not outweigh the monstrosity of what he is. Frankenstein first agrees to make the creature his Eve, then looks upon his work and knows it is nothing but horror. He destroys the half-made body of Eve, saying there can be no other being like his grotesque creature walking the earth. The creature, an Adam with no Eve, abandoned and hated by his God.

I walked through Austin choking on my own spit. There was so much to lose in the telling. There was the fear that even if I told my story so beautifully, even I filled it with poems, literary allusions, the best words I could find, when a person found out what I had done, they might still see me as a thing that needed to be locked away, a thing to be judged and defined by my most feral moments, frantic in hospitals, weeping in public.

Frankenstein's creature knows that he will never find a home in the world. Nothing he can do or say will be enough for humans to look past their perceptions of who he is. He knows that he needs another monster, just like him, someone who understands, someone who will see him as kin. Someone who will see him as he really is.

I was a monster looking for monsters, my wild, unruly creatures. My fellow outcasts, my living ghosts, my beloved apostates.

What did it feel like, the coming back? It felt like rooting in the leaves for months, mouth to the ground, eyes in the dirt, searching for anything at all that could guide me forward.

Surely, I thought, somewhere, there must be clinical standards, guidelines for practitioners and therapists. Methods for treating a person who survived a suicide attempt, what is supposed to happen next. I went looking for research. If I couldn't afford a therapist, maybe I could at least follow some of the guidelines myself. There were articles about how to prevent suicide among people who have lost someone else to suicide. There were articles about how schools should respond if a student kills themselves. There was an article suggesting that a person's primary care physician may be the person responsible for continuity of care.[2] The medical guidelines propose that office visits and brief phone calls can be used to check in on a patient. The article does not state what to do if a person does not have a primary care physician.

———

When Christ came back from the dead, he walked through the world healed. Wounds visible, closed, scarred over. A hole in his side, no longer bleeding. Pierced hands and feet that did not weep pus. Thomas ran his hands along the scars and knew where Christ had been. What he had done was indented into his skin.

When you greet your friends, when you meet new people, they will not know what your scars mean. They might not see them at all.

You stand in front of strangers and almost-friends, clumsy tongued and strange. What does a person talk about, when below every moment is a whistling hum—*Can you believe I'm still alive and here with you?* Your body will not help you, will not make it visible, will not make it known. No one will look at your skin and ask where you have been. No one will touch your hand, rub their thumb into your palm, run their fingers along your chest, look up at you with full eyes and understand where you have gone. You will not know how to find the right words or the right people to tell them to. I don't know how long you will be searching.

———

I found myself defined in terms not my own. A confined person. A suicide[3] contagion.[4] There is research that if one person kills themselves, it can inspire others to do the same. This research suggests that the contagion, the suicidal person, the one who tries and does in fact die, can spread this disease. There are articles about how to prevent the contagion from spreading and contaminating the rest of the population.

This is, of course, a metaphor. This is a metaphor that has been used before. This is a metaphor that justifies confinement, that places suicide in medical terms, an illness that lives in my body. If a person is contagious, what is there to do but quarantine them so no one else will fall ill? My body, my cells, carriers for this disease that could infect someone else if they get too close. Suicidality, a sickness that needs to be cured.

Dr. Simone Fullagar, professor of sociology, writes that the problem with this language, with framing suicide only in terms of health and illness, is not just that it obscures cultural and societal contexts. "The emphasis," Fullagar writes, "on diagnosis and treatment of suicidal ideation, depression, and self-harm as mental health problems may actually participate in the process of subjectification whereby a subject 'sees' their own self as pathological and hence shameful."[5] Sick, something wrong deep down in my body, something infectious that needs to be kept away from healthy people. The way the shame compounds. It is not just that I need help, but the person who needs this kind of help learns to see themselves as the carrier of a deadly disease, a disease that others must be protected from.

This is not to deny the proven fact that after one person takes their life, others may do the same. This is to say that the words, the metaphors, that we use matter. It is one thing to say that a person is contagious, pathological, ill, diseased, that there is something wrong with them, something wrong inside of them, that they need to be fixed, that they are sick and need to be healed, and something else entirely to say that a person is just so tired. How different to say that a person needs help that they haven't been able to find.

How different it is to say I have a disease in my brain, an illness, than to say the world has had its way with me and I can see no other path.

The day I got offered a job in Austin, I went to find a cat. There in the shelter was a small, black kitten. I knew from the moment I saw her that she was mine. Behemoth, named after the demon cat in *The Master and Margarita*. I made a promise that day that no matter what, she would have a good life with me. I would afford cat food, litter, toys. I would find a way to make a life worth living, however small, beneath the weight of things.

The first night I brought her home, she knew. Ignored my housemates, came to sit purring on my shoulder, perched, her face against my neck. She followed me up to my room though she had the whole house to explore. This thing, so small, so simple, this little ball of black fur, this little demon, who came to sleep on top of me every night.

She curled next to my ear. She draped herself over my neck when she slept. In the mornings, when I drank bitter coffee and tried to make the time before work stretch, tried to make ten minutes into an hour, she sat purring on my chest.

I got a job at a bookstore, another at a bar. The bookstore paid $11 an hour before taxes and only scheduled thirty-five hours, but, after a three-month probation period, they offered health care, insurance, and this was a thing I could not pass up. The shifts at the bar would cover the edges, stretch the money to cover the bills.

On weekend nights I drove south from one job to another. I clocked out at the bookstore, took clothes to the bathroom to change out of the uniform and into my best dresses. Waved to coworkers on the way out.

The roads between the bookstore and the bar were long, winding, intersecting highways.

There was a moment where the highway lifted, the exit ramp rose like a roller coaster, curved to the side and the car moved upward, pointed toward the clouds. As the purple-gray twilight spread across Austin, I drove into the sky. I was tired. I was hungry. But the sky was aching open around me and this, I thought, was enough for now.

I had half an hour, forty-five minutes if I was lucky, between shifts. I parked in an empty lot. Some days I closed my eyes, tried to sleep. Some days I balanced my laptop on the steering wheel and tried to write, tried to make something that might matter.

At the bar I smiled at strangers who spent more in a night than I made in a week. Kept my head down, scrubbed the dishes clean. Home past midnight, fell into bed, Behemoth next to me. Got up early, drove to the bookstore. I was not better, not really, but time was passing and the fear was distracted.

My car was breaking. At the inspection to get Texas plates, the mechanic told me the muffler was hanging on by a thread, the metal rusted through to almost nothing. It must've been the salt they use in Massachusetts in the snow, he told me. He told me how much it would cost to fix. I blinked at him, drove away, and spent months holding my breath, waiting for the pieces to fall.

On nights, in early mornings, when I had the energy, I tried to write, I applied to more jobs, got more rejections, more silence. I tried not to think about my car, tried not to think about what would happen if the loans came due and I could no longer keep up. I worked weekends, I worked split shifts. In between work and exhaustion were the ghosts.

The fact of it, the still living, snuck up on me. Out of nowhere, the friendships I had ruined in Cambridge like specters waiting in the shadows. The way my beloved would frown at me, would spit when they asked what was wrong with me. I needed to know that it was okay that I was still alive but there was no one to ask. I sat in my attic and listened to my housemates talk and laugh, put on one of their old cassettes. I sat alone and said words that felt like lies.

It's okay that you lived. It's okay that you lived.

The thing they don't tell you about coming back from the dead is that nothing gets easier. The first months in that new place were the old cycle of work, tired feet, brain sleep deprived and worn. Every month I came up short. I spent my days off in bed, desperate for another hour of sleep, feet throbbing from too many hours spent in shoes that had been worn too much, the soles thin, supporting nothing.

Working full-time, after rent, after utilities, after car insurance, after student loans, I had $43 every month for food, and gas, and anything else. I am good at getting by with little, but even I am not that good. I came home from work panicked. I came home from work lost. I opened Word documents and tried to make sentences, tried to trick myself into believing that it was worth it, this work, this writing. No matter how much I worked, the savings I had squirreled away at Harvard were disappearing in front of my eyes.

I thought of my beloved, in that town by the sea, in the house shared with a new love. I thought how shameful, how paltry my life was. I had moved so far away and had not gone anywhere.

I am supposed to hide my poverty. I am supposed to claim it as mine and mine alone, my fault, my guilt. For not working harder, for not working better. I am supposed to pull myself up by my bootstraps, even if the soles of my shoes are cracked open. I am supposed to be an inspiration: I overcame, so you too can overcome.

But I didn't. I lived on accident and kept living like a weed.

The American Foundation for Suicide Prevention writes that "many people who survive a suicide attempt begin to see [their] challenges in a new light, and realize there are people available to support them."[6] They list steps for recovery. Take care of your health, eat right, get enough sleep. Find a mental health professional. Understand your health insurance. Find a support group.

I went to work and came home, aching and hungry for food I couldn't afford. I made rice and beans and told myself it was enough. I texted my sister for advice and she began to repeat herself. I called my mother and comforted her; she worried about me. Nothing could be done. There was no money to lend, to give, nothing to do but wake up again, go again to work. At night, I kept looking, kept applying for jobs I didn't believe I could get. I waited for Behemoth to climb onto my shoulder, to purr me to sleep. I told myself again it was better to be alone, to not share the ugly fact of myself with anyone.

———

In the waiting room for the low-income, sliding-scale clinic where I could get antidepressants for free, I sat and scrolled through my phone. There was no one to text, no one to complain to about how long it was taking for them to see me, no one to send a picture to of the notice on the door stating that guns were prohibited. To tell about the bullet-proof glass the receptionists sat behind, or the other people who sat in the plastic chairs, looking at their knees. All of us desperate, all of us with eyes like wounds. Adrift, ashamed, I wanted to be nothing but a body in a void, a body with no history, but there I was, there we were.

———

The thing about eating rice and beans, microwave nachos, frozen pizza, peanut butter sandwiches, is that there will be days when no matter how much you eat, at the bottom of your gut there will be an aching. An emptiness, a hollow. I am not being metaphorical. Your insides will hurt. You will need something like protein, real protein. Carbs, bread, meat. A bright green vegetable. Things that you might not be able to get. There are some things, shortcuts, that can help: Taco Bell, In-N-Out. But access to these luxuries will be a bargain. You will need to evaluate the cost, what you are trading so that night you can go to bed and not even remember that you have a stomach because it is quiet. You might be trading a lunch, a dinner, a bag of coffee. You might need to add extra hours to your work schedule to make up for this comfort.

After days and weeks and months of calculating and constant bargaining, there is an exhaustion that settles in the feet, the stomach, the mind. I don't know how much a person needs to live. I don't know who gets to decide. I know that after days and days of not enough, a person can start to believe enough will never come.

———

My cat ate better than I did, but then again, cat food is cheaper.

———

Slow death, according to Lauren Berlant, is the physical wearing away of a population.[7] It is the *ongoingness, getting by, and living on* in the daily conditions that begin to break a person.[8] It is a million tiny cuts. What Berlant describes as slow death is something endemic, something in the air we breathe. Slow death is years of working overtime and still coming up short, it is years of hunger, years of malnu trition, year after year after year of not getting the things you need to survive.

Jasbir Puar asks us to consider "what kinds of slow deaths have been ongoing that a suicide might represent an escape from."[9]

———

We are supposed to practice self-care. We are supposed to self-soothe in moments of despair. I have not yet learned how to self-soothe an empty stomach without food.

In a dim outpatient room in Boston, a woman once said that some days, you either spend eight dollars on a salad or go another day growling.

Some days, after the dull roar in your stomach gets to be too much, you splurge. Maybe Chinese food, maybe Thai. You know that it is unjustifiable. That night, when you take it home, you feel the warmth of the bag, sit in front of the television, curl your legs up beneath you, smell the spices, the meat, the vegetables. On that night all of the things you sacrifice for that one moment, that one meal, don't matter.

Dr. Thomas Joiner writes that one of the causes of suicidal ideation is a "thwarted sense of belonging." Dr. Kim Samuel writes that poverty is relational, that is, it constricts our lives and the relationships we are able to form.[10] Dr. China Mills writes that the connection between poverty and mental health problems is "one of the most well established in all of psychiatric epidemiology."[11] These academics trace the ways that poverty can make a person feel ashamed of the clothes they wear, the house they live in, can drive a person to self-isolate if they don't want someone else to see that they can't measure up to the standards of who they are supposed to be. They show how, if a person is working constantly, there is no time to find a community to belong to.

It is, on its face, so simple. If I cannot participate in social life, if I have no money to go to the movies, to dinner, to coffee, if I am working overtime, if I spend my days off sleeping, then there is no time, no opportunity to meet people, to sit next to someone and listen to their stories, to have the small moments together that transform a person from an acquaintance into a friend. Poverty can birth isolation. Poverty can rob us of the time, the chances to build relationships. When poverty can make it impossible to feel connected to others, when poverty can make the daily work of living feel like a doomed Sisyphean task, it is no wonder, these academics write, that it can push a person toward suicide.

I don't know why this is accepted as fact by some groups of academics and entirely new to the rest of us. I had never considered it until I died, until I came back, until I saw my own death as a result, in part, of years of deprivation, years of hunger and work, years of bitterness and fear and work.

I am not sure how many days a person can live on scraps before they become anemic, before they have to go to a doctor they can't afford because they are faint, because they ache all the time. I am not sure how many days, how many weeks, a person can go without seeing a doctor before what began as an ache in a muscle turns into a tear, turns into something more sinister. I am not sure how many days a person can keep driving with the check-engine signal bright and glaring before things start to fall apart, before they must go to a mechanic who tells them numbers they don't have.

It would've been better, the doctor, the mechanic says, if you had addressed this sooner. It would've been better, the doctor says, if you had taken better care of yourself, eaten better, exercised. Things wear away, and nothing can be done to address them until the moment of catastrophe.

If we take seriously the notion that "relational deprivation is intrinsic to poverty,"[12] if we take seriously the ways that isolation, lack of belonging and connection can fuel the suicidal urge, if we consider how "stigma [of poverty] can lead to people devaluing themselves because other people assume they live a life not worth living,"[13] if we take seriously the ways that poverty can, day by day by day, crush a person, a community, then if we are serious about suicide prevention, if we are serious about suicide recovery, we need to do something about the slow deaths from a poverty that grinds away hope, grinds away a person's body, grinds away a person's idea that they might have a future at all.

Dr. Ian Marsh writes that "each age and place creates its own suicide."[14] He argues that there is no such thing as an "essential" philosophical truth of what suicide is, or what it means. Suicide in contemporary America means something different than suicide in ancient Greece, something different than suicide in feudal Japan, something different than suicide in colonial America. How could we possibly conflate an enslaved person jumping from a ship where they have been chained and imprisoned and a person jumping from the Golden Gate Bridge? There is so much that we erase, so much that we ignore, if we look at these instances and see the same thing.

Mark E. Button uses the phrase "suicidal regimes" to describe the public policies that create vulnerability to suicide. Policies that make it harder for a person to qualify for food stamps, that reduce the monthly allotment for food stamps, that make it harder to qualify for disability, that make it harder to access low-income health care, low-income mental health care.[15] He argues that suicide prevention needs to address the risk factors that foster this vulnerability. China Mills describes these policies as "hostile conditions . . . that invite suicidality."[16] Mills writes that even though these policies are not written to incite suicide, the world they design is one in which it is harder to get help. Unable to access the things they might need to survive, the tools they might need to build a life, a person can internalize the rhetoric that they are a burden to the state, a burden to others. These academics show us, again and again, that if we want to do something about suicide, we need to look at the world we have built and ask what needs to change to make it livable.

They took me to a hospital, checked my blood pressure every morning. No one explained to me why they checked my blood pressure every morning. I was not on new medicine, I was not doing anything at all. In the mornings they called for vitals and I stood in line. My problem, the despair that had only one resolution, was measured in my pulse. The entirety of a life explained in numbers and diagnoses. The problem was me, the problem was my body. Something wrong in my body. But if the problem is only housed in the body instead of the world that wears away at us, we will never be able to change the things that tried to kill us.

How can a body be separate from the world we live in? If the responsibility for "better" is always on the singular, the granular, then the responsibility is entirely on the person who should overcome their own self, their own circumstances, adapt to the jobs that fire them if they take a sick day, the banks that charge extra fees when their account is empty. The responsibility is on the person who spends hours on the phone with insurance companies, the person who works overtime and still goes to bed hungry, the person who can't get hired because of their race, their gender, the person who makes less than two dollars an hour because it is legal for companies to pay disabled employees far less than minimum wage, the person who sends email after email, who calls again and again and still can't find a therapist they can afford, a therapist who does not have a monthslong waiting list, the person who works two jobs and goes home to an empty house, with no one to call, no one to spend time with in free moments.

Sara Ahmed asks, "What if the world 'houses' some bodies more than others?"[17]

If we can't address these factors that make life, for some, unlivable, then the story will play out, again and again, in different notes, in different pitches, following the same melody, the same winding path toward a death that might begin to seem, to the desperate person, inevitable.

When Emily Malone walked out of the hospital after trying to kill herself, her debt was five figures.[18] When we leave the hospitals, we are charged for the days we spend there, for the medicines they give us, even if we are desperate to leave. I do not know how any of us are expected to get better if the places we are taken against our will can charge us thousands of dollars that we might not be able to pay back. We walk out of the hospital with a weight on our backs. What could we possibly mean by suicide prevention, suicide recovery, if that recovery puts a person further into debt and makes their life after that much harder?

They take us, they lock us up and tell us this will help us. When we leave the hospital, they send us a bill for our confinement. This, they tell us, is healing.

In *It's a Wonderful Life*, the event that pushes George Bailey to consider suicide is a bill that he cannot pay. He needs money and doesn't know how to get it. He has a life insurance policy, decides that at least if he were dead, his family would get the money they need. This is what takes him to a bridge, staring at the waters. This is what brings down the angel to save him, to show him the world in which he had never been born. When George Bailey comes back from the nightmare world, he runs through the snow, back to his crumbling house, where his wife and children wait for him.

"It's a miracle," his wife Mary says. She pulls him into the living room, pushes papers from a table. One by one, his friends and neighbors cram into his house. One by one, they put dollars, change, pennies and bills, on the table in front of George. Mary had told them that George was in trouble, that George needed money, and together they came.

But what of those of us who, one by one by one, pushed away the people in our lives? Those of us who were terrible friends, terrible partners? Those of us whose constant despair drove us to being, truthfully, not very good people? Those of us who still desperately need the same miracle that George receives? Those of us who no longer have anyone to run through the snow toward, no one coming with baskets of money to ensure that we have what we need to live?

What is recovery, what is healing to a monster?

In the novel *Frankenstein*, the creature, abandoned, forlorn, hated by all, becomes the fiend they call him. He enacts revenge, kills people that Dr. Frankenstein loves. The creature's life, from the moment of birth, is one of misery, isolation. In the last pages of the book, the creature says there is only one thing left to do. He will travel alone into the Arctic, where he will burn himself alive.

"Soon," he says, "these burning miseries shall be extinct. I shall ascend my funeral pile triumphantly. My spirit will sleep in peace."[19]

The world is no home for this creature that has been monsterized, this life that was hated from his first breath. His own death the only way for him to find rest. When he ascends his funeral pile, he will have finally found a way out of the world that hates him, a way out of the body that can only be understood as a monster, a way out of the world that has showed him again and again that for him, nothing will ever get better.

———

The thing they don't tell you about coming back from the dead is the way words fall short. The way language is a locked casket.

Shortly after I lived, Anthony Bourdain didn't. In early June, he was found dead, apparently by suicide. I sat silent behind my computer screen as friends and acquaintances made posts in mourning, my social media feed dotted with people writing about suicide, sharing lists of warning signs, what to do about them. I was a stranger in my body as I watched people who knew me, who had watched as I became nervous, overcome with anxiety, share their own thoughts about the importance of being open, of destigmatizing suicide. In an open letter about Bourdain's death, Rose McGowan wrote that it was a horrible choice, but it was his choice to make. We can read this in two ways. He was in a horrible position, facing the horrible choice, whether to die or keep living. Or we can read it as: It was horrible for him to choose this path, but he did.

September is suicide prevention and awareness month. I watch the friends who told me there was no time to talk about what had happened to me repost articles, infographics, about suicide, and I become an alien to myself.

I was right there. I am right here. What would any of them think of me? Did they notice, during those long months when my world turned gray? September passes, and I say nothing.

The stigma comes in waves, the shame moves like tides. The online performances continue. What is required of me? I imagine making a Twitter thread, an Instagram post, disclosing in these internet spaces the secrets of my still-being. The way the serotonin would flood my brain with each like, each comment. How strange, how sordid, to know that I could share these facts of myself on internet forums with people who would not have a conversation with me about it when I was standing in front of them. The posts fill up my newsfeed, and I am nowhere in them.

"Vampires, burial, death: inter the corpse where the road forks, so that when it springs from the grave, it will not know which path the follow. Drive a stake through its heart: it will be stuck to the ground at the fork, it will haunt that place that leads to many other places, that point of indecision. Behead the corpse, so that, acephalic, it will not know itself as subject, only as pure body."[20]

It was not lost on me that vampires were buried the same way as the bodies of suicides. The head removed, buried at a crossroads so if the spirit returns, it can never find the way home.

Most things that come back from the dead are creatures that are not blessed, not holy like the Christian god, not heroes like Superman. Instead, ghosts, zombies, vampires. Creatures that terrorize the living.

A thing not dead, but not the same as alive, not quite. Something closer to undead. Differently alive, alive with a twist. A monstrous kind of living, a living that goes on past when it is supposed to end, past when the story should have ended. In my body, all the things I was afraid of. Monstrous genes, something gruesome, horrible, hidden between my intestines.

The thing they don't tell you about coming back from the dead is that even if they let you keep your head, you won't know where to go next.

In her memoir *The Recovering*, Leslie Jamison tells the story of her alcoholism and her gradual recovery. Her book interrogates the place of recovery narratives and insists that the power and purpose of recovery narratives is not in their uniqueness, but in their sameness. What is important, she writes, is not the literary merit of these stories, not the singular uniqueness of the narrative or the spectacular telling. What is important is sitting in a room with others who have felt the same things, who have made the same mistakes, who have told themselves the same lies, knowing that someone new might enter the room and tell the same stories again. Her book is a symphony of stories of people's struggles, as she connects the dots to show the reader the lifesaving importance of finding sameness in our stories. Though she doesn't name it this way, this is the opposite of the dream of the American individual, the singular, bounded subject with stable and secure perimeters. Her story is porous. It is hers and never only hers. There is never a moment when she shows us where her story ends and another's begins. What Jamison gives us, instead, is a harmony of overlapping voices, making clear that none of us are as isolated as we think.

In the months after I lived, I held her book to my chest. I wished I could claim a space in the narrative in a way that felt childish, disingenuous, deceptive. I was not an alcoholic. Who was I to search for myself in the pages? When I read her book, its multiple narratives, the overlapping voices of people telling their own stories, their own personal, intertwined recoveries, I gasped with hunger. Where were the stories of we who lived? Where was our chorus, our harmony? We who had tried, who had meant it, who did not regret it, who dreamed of death like an old friend? I grasped at straws. *Was my story like yours?* I asked Jamison's silent pages. *Can it be?*

In one of the closing bits on *Seinfeld*, when Jerry is alone onstage performing his comedy routine, he looks down at the audience, away from the camera. He makes an imploring gesture with his hand. "The thing I don't understand about the suicide person," he says, "is the people that try and commit suicide, for some reason they don't die, and then that's it."

For months after I lived, if I heard the word *hospital*, if I heard the word *suicide*, I folded inward. If I was not with the people who had been with me there, my jaw clenched. Did anyone know? Could I tell them?

"They stop trying. Why? Why don't they just keep trying? What has changed? Is their life any better now?"

I walked through the world haunted by unsayable things, things too dark, too ugly to share.

"No," Seinfeld declares. "In fact, it's worse, because now they've found out here's one more thing you stink at. That's why these people don't succeed at life to begin with."

My body was a lie waiting to be found out.

"Because they give up too easy."

On my days off work I lay in bed, staring at the ceiling. My feet ached. My head throbbed. How much longer could I go without health insurance? How much longer before my savings ran dry?

"I say, pills don't work, try a rope."

I sat on my back porch in the Austin sun, the mosquitoes dancing in the air. I lit a cigarette, just for the smell of it, the secondhand smoke the strongest sense memory of Alex, of all those college friends I had lost.

"Car won't start in the garage? Get a tune-up." The audience laughs. "You know what I mean? There's nothing more rewarding than reaching a goal you've set for yourself."

I imagine someone in the audience looking down into their drink. Forcing a smile as their date chuckles, as the sound of laughter surrounds them. How their throat might tighten. On their walk home through a blue New York night, they scuff their shoes on the sidewalk, quieter than normal.

"What's wrong?" their date asks, holding their hand.

"Nothing," they say, turning their lips up in what is supposed to be a smile. "I'm just tired."

Unimaginable, that someone there, in the audience, could have survived a thing like that. A thing like that, big, and sad, and distant.

That night as they go to sleep, they might turn their back to their date, hold their arms around their own body, close their eyes and let it all wash over them, quiet and alone.

I looked and kept looking. Months passed and still all I wanted was a person, a story that would mirror my own, all I wanted was a hand to hold, anything to make sense of the life that kept going all around me.

Martin McDonagh's play *The Pillowman* is set in a dystopian police state where the writer Katurian is being tortured and interrogated. There have been a series of murders that parallel his fiction. His police inquisitors make him recount the stories he's written, so Katurian tells them the story of the Pillowman.

The Pillowman is a creature made entirely of pillows. The Pillowman appears to people when they are on the verge of suicide. He takes their hand, takes them back through time to when they were children, before they suffered, before they understood pain. Gently, he tells the little children what will happen to them, the misery they will suffer as they grow. He teaches them ways to kill themselves that will look like accidents, so their parents will never know what really happened, so that they can take their lives in their own little hands, so that they can die when they are happy children, before the onslaught of their lives makes life unlivable. He is there with them, a guide, a kind friend, ushering them through their last moments. He is there to keep them company, to let them know that they are not alone.

The Pillowman hates his job, hates his life. Hates the misery he sees, the children in pain. Big, fat tears constantly roll from his soft eyes. One day, he does what appears to be inevitable. He goes backward through time and visits himself as a child. His child-self listens to what he has to say, smiles, understands, wants to be helpful, wants to make the pain go away. His child-self douses his small pillow body in gasoline, lights a fire.

As the Pillowman dies, he experiences something he didn't expect. The screams, the cries, of all the people who, because he died as a child, he was not there to help. People who, when they had died as children, had his gentle presence there to soothe them, to ease their passing. People who now had to die alone, after miserable, wretched lives.

The tragedy of the Pillowman is not his job, or his grim, hated task of ushering children toward suicide. The tragedy is that he knows what futures unfurl in front of these children, the lives of despair and pain and abuse, and can do nothing to stop it, can do nothing to change it. What can one person, one man made of pillows, do against all of the things that make life unlivable?

Where George Bailey could change the conditions of a person's life by building them a house, by giving them a roof over their head, a loan that they could afford, the Pillowman can only visit a person when it is too late. The Pillowman can be the comfort they need in their last moments, but he can't change what leads them to that moment, can't stop a parent from screaming, can't stop the abuse, the poverty, the grinding things that wear a person down until all they have is the promise of death. The haunting tragedy of the Pillowman is that in a world that will not get better, the best and only comfort is a way out.

Someone hung a net beneath the Golden Gate Bridge to catch those of us who decided to die by throwing ourselves into the air, into the water.

There are studies that suggest that if something can halt a person's hand at the moment they try to die, if something can interrupt the action, there is a good chance they will not try again. There is research that argues that a suicide attempt happens on impulse; if the moment of crisis can be survived, things might get better from there. This net is meant to do just that, to catch people on their way down. To hold them until someone can get them up. To interrupt the moment of crisis, to give them a place to land after the impulse has faded. This net is a gesture of care from a stranger to a stranger. Whoever hung this net, this net which took years and hundreds of millions of dollars to construct, cares whether you live or die. There is a stranger you will never meet who put years of their life into making sure you survive your fall. There is a stranger who wants so badly for you to live. It is a beautiful gesture, this cradle hanging in the air over the sea.

I wish I didn't have to tell you what comes next.

The net is not a net, not really. The net is made of stainless-steel mesh. It is designed so that the waves, the salt water, the fog of San Francisco, the force of bodies hurled against it, will not move it at all. The net does not stretch. The net is not elastic. The manager of the Golden Gate Bridge says that to fall into this net feels like jumping into a cheese grater. The manager of the Golden Gate Bridge says, "We want folks to know that if you come here, it will hurt if you jump."[21]

The net hangs there as threat. The net hangs there as punishment.

They have decided that the way they can hurt us is better than the way we have decided to hurt ourselves. We who have wanted more than anything to escape from this world, we are promised punishment in new ways. We who need to be disciplined for reaching toward the only end to suffering that we could find. I stare at pictures of the net suspended below the red bridge. This thing is supposed to save us. This thing is designed to hurt us.

Some people who jumped into this steel barrier kept going. They would have been injured after falling into hard, cold iron. Likely badly injured.[22] The net hangs in a V-shape. They would have had to climb up to the edges. Crawl through, across the metal wires toward the water. Their fingers across a cheese grater. They would have had to fight the whole way against this thing keeping them trapped where they didn't want to be.

I am sorry to be the one to have to tell you that this steel mesh, these interlocking wires, begins to resemble nothing so much as a cage.

For the people who land in this net, who fall into the maw of a cheese grater, nothing in the world has changed. Even the promise of punishment, pain, is nothing new. Someone built a net to stop our fall, to hurt us on the way down. Nothing has changed to stop us from jumping at all.

Someone will read this book and say they are learning about depression, PTSD, suicide. Someone will build a barrier so I can't jump off a bridge. Someone will limit the number of antidepressants I can have at a time. Someone will make it hard for me to buy a gun.

But what will they do to alleviate the poverty that takes the food from our mouths and the hope from our futures?

Someone will take away the means that people use to end their lives, but who will do anything to make sure we have the resources to make a life worth living?

"You always have a room here," my mother told me over the phone. I saw it in my mind, the room in the back of the house that never got direct sunlight, the bed that caved in the center, the neighbors screaming. My mother and I passing each other as we went to and from work.

The attic I lived in was bright, surrounded by trees. There was so much life just beyond my reach. I dug in my heels. I would keep trying, I would look for a cheaper apartment. Things were bad, but there was a place in Iowa to fall back on, a safety net were I to fail. A house, however small, a room, however dim, a bed, however crumpled. I was, in so many ways, lucky.

Day faded into night as I stood behind a cash register, autumn shifting all around me. I went to work and I went home. I spent my days off sleeping. I didn't make any friends outside work. The bills swallowed my paychecks whole.

Why not try again?

The logic is no logic. My logic has no backing, my logic hasn't grown a spine. I don't know, I can't tell you.

Over time, it became easy enough to restock. Monthly, I went to the low-cost community mental health center for antidepressants. At the center, I sat in a room with a nurse who navigated to a Zoom call with a doctor. I would never meet this man in person. I would describe my symptoms. He would ask me a question or two about my life. When I said I couldn't sleep, the nurses handed me bottles of pills.

I would only need to wait a few months, let the pills gather like an army in wait. The method was not the problem.

What is keeping you here?

There is no answer. There is something in the no answer. There is something in the silence. Something unwordable, unspeakable and too simple all at once: I don't feel like it anymore. I might, sometime, but I don't now.

The first autumn after I lived, nothing added up. It was hard and there was no stopping it.

I texted my sister, *What do I do?*

"Rice and beans," she said again. "I'll get you more recipes."

It was the week of Thanksgiving. It was the first time I went to the food bank down the road from my house, run by a church. I came prepared with the pay stubs and documentation to prove where I lived, to prove how much or how little I was earning. I had done the research, knew what I needed, knew where to go and what to bring. They gave me a poker chip with a number written on it in thick black Sharpie, asked me to wait until my turn was called. I was ashamed in more ways than I could count.

I imagined people from graduate school seeing me there, wondering how I had failed so miserably, going from Harvard to food banks. I imagined the other people in the room looking at me askance: Was I really poor enough to be there? Was I taking food from someone who needed it more?

Without food stamps or exceptions for students, I was back where I came from.

When it was my turn to go through the line, my shame was silenced in the face of generosity. Cans of beans, cans of vegetables, bags of rice, an entire pumpkin pie for the holiday, a frozen Amy's meal, two different types of cheese, brie and Gruyère, corn-bread mix, potatoes, eggs. A volunteer had to help me carry the bags to my car, too heavy to handle alone.

At home, I was alone with the bounty. My housemates had already left for the holiday, and my cat came to inspect the bags, sniffing at the boxes. I was putting away the food, spinning and smiling in a kitchen suddenly full, when I noticed the expiration date on the cheese. "Oh no," I said out loud to no one. "Oh no."

I checked each package. Everything, the eggs, the bread, the frozen food, the pie, all of it expired. Some of it weeks ago.

"Oh no."

The midday sunlight streamed in through the kitchen window, where I sat at the table with expired things.

The first year after I lived, I had one day off work for Thanksgiving. Not enough time to go anywhere, not enough money to travel to see family. The almost-friends I had made through my job were all going to be with their relatives.

The first year after I lived, I spent Thanksgiving alone, watching movies and eating expired food. Behemoth curled up on my stomach. The pie tasted fine and it did not make me sick, and this, I thought, was enough. I stayed off social media and tried to pretend that Cambridge did not exist. That it was not a day most people were in rooms with others. The year before I had cooked a feast of vegan dishes for two, delighting my beloved. How did anyone expect this story to go? How did I? How was I supposed to spend this day, after living, after leaving? The house was chilled, and I was there, breathing.

In Hanya Yanagihara's *A Little Life*, the central character kills himself. Jude, abused as a child, abused as an adult, carries these traumas inside of him, harms himself physically, tries to kill himself once earlier in the novel before succeeding near the end.

For me, the hardest parts to read were not the brutal scenes of Jude's childhood. Not the unadorned, unsentimental moments when Jude is cutting himself. Not the passages of Jude's first or second suicide attempt. The most painful parts of *A Little Life*, the parts that made me cry bitter tears, were the months after Jude's first attempt, when his friends show up in a way that I could only interpret as magical realism.

After Jude tries to kill himself, they keep him in the hospital for an untold number of days. No one mentions insurance, no one mentions how much it will cost. His bosses are understanding. His job is not in jeopardy. His friends and adopted family take weeks away from work to sit near him, to make sure someone is always there with him, to watch, to simply be there. His best friends move in with him, sleeping on his couch so that he never has to sleep alone. In the hospital, he is kept to his bed and only ever speaks to one doctor, a kind, trustworthy man. For months and months after the attempt, his friends are exceedingly gentle and vigilant with him, aware of what is at stake. They know that just because he did not succeed, just because they let him out of the hospital, does not mean that he is not still at risk. They count the months and do not leave his side. They never once mention to him the cost it takes to provide this support. Neither the time they have spent with him, nor the money they have lost by taking so much time off work. They swallow their own feelings and collectively agree that Jude's life is more important than telling him how emotionally exhausted they are.

Has anyone had this experience after almost dying? The aggressively patient care, friends spending more than a year watching with vigilance?

Jude's friends never mention this time period again, how much they did to make sure he was safe. His closest friend never mentions that he gave up a job to stay with Jude and make sure he was okay. Jude's adoptive parents never mention the stress, or what it took to fly to him and be there when he was in the hospital. There is no resentment; the care he was given was given freely. I read these pages and curled in bed like a withering leaf.

In the hospital, they had taken a pair of scissors to the stuffed animal I'd had since I was two, severed the red ribbon that had been tied there for twenty-five years. I had promised that when I got out I would replace it.

Months passed and I stared at Wilbur's bare neck. He had been undone. Unadorned.

Months passed and I tried to find some value to myself that was not attached to degrees, to money, to tangible, measurable accomplishments. I lived among strangers, spent my days and nights working alongside people who hadn't known me before I died, who had no idea it had happened at all.

When I got home at night, I looked at this childhood remnant, this thing that was proof of where I had been. Though I still could not speak this story, though I still had no one to speak it to, this childish little thing became a reminder of where I had been. Months passed, and I knew I would never buy a new ribbon.

The god gave strict orders not to let anyone know what happened to Jairus's daughter, but still news of this spread all throughout the region. This little girl became a story, a parable, a myth. A myth that wasn't even about her, not really. I wanted to find other myths, other legends, other people who were denied a name, who were denied the endings of their stories, who kept living anyway.

After I did not die, I would have done anything to hear how this story ended. To know what I was supposed to feel like in the mornings, in the afternoons when the shadows got long. To look at my body and know if it felt different, or the same, as someone else's who died and came back. To know how long it would take for the rhythm of my breath to return to normal. How long it would take before I could be in a room with others and feel like I belonged there among the living.

The consequence of this silence is that I cannot find my fellow monsters. My fellow survivors who lived and kept living, even when they did not know how. Isolated, we remain individual cases of failure. Our stories unconnected, the similarities unnoticed.

The god holds a finger to his lips and tells the crowd not to speak of what they have seen.

I stand in rooms silent, strange, not knowing when to speak.

The little girl, raised from the dead, a film over her mouth for all time.

At first, in Austin, I called therapists and was told again and again prices I could not afford. I called low-income clinics and was put on six-month waitlists. I found a clinician through the sliding-scale clinic who cost $30 a session, who nodded as I spoke and told me it all sounded hard. I left his office with nothing but the reminder that this was hard and a bill for $30. For a while, I gave up searching. I had tried so long, so hard, and had found no one. The effort no longer seemed worth it. I decided to look for something else.

There was a church in north Austin that smelled like leftovers, lasagna and yeast. Every other Wednesday I drove north, body buzzing for lack of sleep. Posted throughout the church were makeshift signs, arrows drawn in thick blue marker on blank paper, taped to the walls, to lead us in the right direction. I sat in a straight-backed chair, in a circle with others. Waited as people trickled in the room, checked the room number to make sure they were in the right place. They tried to start on time, even as people stepped, tender and nervous, into the room.

"Welcome to NAMI," they would say, and begin to read the rules.

The National Alliance on Mental Illness—NAMI—offered these groups, led by volunteers. Blessedly free, open to anyone living with mental illness. A place where you could share as much or as little as you wanted, but either way, you knew you were not the only one like you. There were rules to follow. Keep it in the present, don't interrupt. Stick to the timers to be sure that everyone had a chance to talk.

At the beginning of each meeting, they asked everyone to introduce themselves, to share the relevant facts. I sat a little straighter, held the air in my lungs.

"My name is Madeline, and I'm a suicide attempt survivor." My eyes welled with tears. The story, the ugly parts, were coming out. I waited. No one scooted their chair away, metal legs scratching the carpet. No one blinked an eye. The conversation moved on, just like that.

There was relief in the anticlimax. Sitting in a room with others who maybe had done the same thing, who maybe knew someone who had done the same, who struggled with diagnoses and family not understanding and not being able to afford other therapy.

There was a teen sitting next to a sixty-year-old. There was a boy in college sitting next to a divorced woman. Our problems so different, our problems so similar. Uncontrollable anger, anxiety that wouldn't let us leave the house, symptoms of PTSD that we didn't know how to change. Not knowing how to communicate these things to loved ones. Not knowing how to make friends. Fighting with administrators to get disability benefits. Feeling like it was the same problem over and over.

The thing about those groups is that no one is a trained therapist. We couldn't find solutions for each other, not really. What we could do, all we could offer, was to sit in a room together, to listen to the things we couldn't say out loud to anyone else.

Sometimes during introductions, I said I had depression. Sometimes I said it was anxiety. Sometimes, when I said I was a suicide attempt survivor, there was a shift in the room, a glance. I watched how other girls looked at me. It might have been in my head, but I watched how those nights when I introduced myself with self-killing in my voice, more people were likely to mention it too, that they had tried. They would speak it, looking toward me, nodding, like I had broken a seal.

Most weeks, someone would ask if anyone had advice for finding affordable therapy. Sliding-scale, free clinics. We listed all the places we knew, all the resources we had tried to access, all the waiting lists we were on. For many of us, we were all each other had. The wait times stretched on, for months that multiplied.

The free clinic I went to for meds didn't offer therapy. I sat in a room and Skyped with a psychiatrist who gave me pills for anxiety and pills for sleep. The nurse stayed in the room, at a computer that faced away from me. At home, I looked up the sleeping pills she had prescribed. They were strong antipsychotics that cause drowsiness as a side effect. I let the full bottles begin to collect in my closet.

After I lived, no longer on MassHealth, no longer a student, no longer qualifying for food stamps or free programs, the monthslong waiting lists for sliding-scale therapy floated around me, like smoke.

Every other Wednesday we left the church, alone or in pairs. Some of us stood smoking outside, some of us waited to catch bits of conversation. *Who was that psychiatrist you mentioned? Good luck with things. I hope to see you next time. I hope you're here in two weeks.* Nothing had changed, no solutions were offered, but there was a room where we could be honest, a room where we were not alone.

Over time, over years, I learn that when I share this fact, that I tried and did not die, it can be an offering. If I can speak these words out loud, maybe others can as well. Strangers turn to me and tell me they haven't tried but they have thought about it. They tell me in a voice that begs to be heard. They have come close. I don't mention what the edge tastes like. They already know. We are all so hungry to be able to say this out loud. *I wanted so badly to die.* To find an ear that is waiting to listen, to find hands soft and strong and gentle enough to hold the stories.

Those years of lack, those years upon years of work and want, of desperate searching for something like love, those years shaped me into a person I never wanted to be. Those years shaped me into a person that I could not find my way out of alone. It's true that suicide can be a response to the conditions of your life, but sometimes the person you are is a symptom of the conditions of your life.

No one else took the lids from the pill bottles, no one else threw my head back and swallowed. No one else kept me committed to a love that pressed me into shapes I couldn't fit. No one else forced me to look at peers, possible friends, and let the anger, the resentment creep through my body. These are things that only I can change. I can learn how to be a friend who listens, a friend who can see outside myself, a friend who is not bitter about the things other people have, a friend who does not alienate others with resentment, a friend who does not assume the worst of others, a friend who does not sit in judgment of other people's lives. These are things I can learn to see in myself, things I can learn to change, things that will connect me to others. This is part of what I mean when I write about recovery: taking responsibility for the person I became, the person that I am, finding the things I need to change to become the person I want to be, a creature of blood and bone and hope.

In therapy we learn that recovery is not a straight line. There is one day that we will succeed, break old patterns. There will be other days when we fail. There might be many days when we fail and few days when we succeed. We have to believe that it is worth it to keep trying, that someday the successes will outweigh the failures. Faith, I think, is a kind of necessary stupidity.

How is a person supposed to feel, how is a person supposed to live, when they sincerely meant to die, and didn't, and woke up to a world that has not changed?

An existential, institutional crisis. Recovery is not just changing the self. Recovery is changing the things that pushed us toward the edge. It is interrupting the processes of slow death, addressing the policies that created hostile conditions.

Recovery is the ability to buy food. The ability to live a day without fear of police, of ICE. Knowing your family is safe. Knowing you are safe. Knowing without doubt that there is a future for you.

Recovery is a night I walk down the street alone, feel the honey soft Austin winter and smile. It is a woman not needing to wonder if her hospital bills will doom her. It is running across the West Texas plains, wind and sun in my hair. It is a child able to get puberty blockers, protected and safe. It is a family no longer afraid of deportations. It is a night spent alone, reading, allowed this luxury of a night off work because the bills are quiet and the money is enough. It is learning to trust, learning to look down at your body, running your own hands over your skin and knowing that you belong, here among the living. Recovery is the ability to speak of the poverty that crushes us without the judgment that poverty is our own fault.

No longer an individual, ashamed and alone and hiding and blaming only ourselves. All of us together, our stories interlaced, our lives wound tight.

There are days when I look down and realize that I am wearing the same outfit as the night I tried to die. The same pair of black jeans, a hand-me-down from my sister, the same maroon shirt I bought for $3 at a discount store. The same socks, navy blue with pink flowers on them. In those moments I become a stranger. Something is off, barely. The conversation does not pause. My feet catch, just a little. I listen. I do not smile more than normal. I am no longer normal. There is something pulling me, gently, away from the world. I have written so many words and have still never found a way to describe this.

When Christ died and came back, he was brought to God through the ascension. Luke is the only gospel that tells the story, in vague, uncertain terms. Christ was there and then he wasn't. It is in the book of Acts—written years later by Paul, a person who never met Christ except in a vision—that the story is told in more detail. In Paul's telling, this god stands in full view of his disciples. A cloud covers him, and the god is lifted from earth into the sky. In one story, Christ is on earth for forty days before he ascends. In the other gospels, the narrative ends immediately after he is brought back from the dead, with no indication of what happens next, where he goes.

When Christ died and came back, he told everyone. He visited his disciples, showed them the places in his body that bore the wounds from his death. This god knew that everyone needed this story. It wasn't pride, I don't think, that inspired the god to this telling. It was the Truth with a capital T. It was life, it was the Word of God. Everyone should hear this good news, that this blessed being knew how to die and come back the right way, who would bring everyone who deserved it back from the dead the right way.

Those of us who are rooted to the ground of Dante's hell need to find a way on our own.

In January, after so many job applications that I had stopped counting, I was offered a new job. I would make $14 an hour. I would have better health insurance. I would have a set schedule. I would work at a Title 1 high school. Because I was working at a Title 1 school, I qualified for a pause on one of my student loans. I could get part of it canceled at the end of the school year.

Things started to get easier. Fourteen dollars an hour, forty hours a week, four weeks a month. After taxes, before rent, $1,824 a month. A few hundred more each week if I kept working Saturdays at the wine bar. If I kept working at the wine bar, I could splurge sometimes, go to the fancy grocery store in town and buy pastries made that morning. I could set money aside. I could not believe how lucky I was.

I came home from work. I took a nap and when I woke up the evening was there, free, stretching long in front of me. There were hours, hours when I wasn't desperate for sleep. Six months after I moved to Austin, I bought tacos for the first time. I went to Torchy's and got the queso that everyone told me about. It was too expensive, it would never live up to the queso I had been imagining for months, but I could sit at the table alone and afford it.

I spent hours searching on CARFAX. I drove forty miles to San Marcos, traded my rotting Honda for a Kia Spectra. It was used, it was old, but there was no piece of it that was hanging by a thread. They gave me $500 for my Honda filled with rust, and I thought I was cheating them. I worried they would call me, tell me they had looked under the hood, under the car, that they wanted the money back.

When I drove home, I felt a fear beginning to leave my body, a weight lifting.

My own story, one of many, is the story of a poverty so common, so normal, a despair so pedestrian, it is nothing special, really. What I needed was so simple. Affordable therapy. The ability to take time off, to be with friends, to sit on a friend's porch in the evening and listen to the way they laugh. To live without the fear of debt taking every cent, of working overtime and it still not being enough. To live without shame. To live with the chance of becoming a person worthy of friendship.

If we think of suicide prevention, suicide recovery, as more than just medical recovery, we might see it as more than the therapist, the friends, that hold you accountable for your own life and the person you are. More than the antidepressants and medicines that can calm your mind. If we are serious about suicide prevention, we have to let the idea expand to hold all of these things inside of it. To hold these overlapping, intertwined things, to know it is all these at once: a medical response that does not assume a person is a contagion, a sickness; a world that does not create a vulnerability to despair; a way to claim the self, the people we are, and a way to claim the things we can do to change ourselves.

I would have never been able to imagine a future without therapy, but I would have never been able to imagine a future without finding a job that gave me even the smallest bit of breathing room. Therapy will never be enough to help a person who goes to bed hungry.

That spring in Austin, when the snap of Texas winter melted into endless skies, I made a choice. My student loans are so large, I thought, I will never live long enough to pay them off, but I can make a life beneath them.

I made a promise to myself that I would get therapy no matter what, no matter if it meant missing loan payments, if it meant forbearance, the interest rising. I filled out the forms to pause payments, spent hours on hold with servicers, just for them to tell me I needed to complete a different form. The correct form was not on their website, and I would call back, spend my days listening to the hold music.

I searched the database of therapists on *Psychology Today*, I googled, I called, I emailed. Some therapists didn't take my insurance; some weren't taking new patients. One night as I was leaving work, I got a call, sat outside in the clear spring air and listened as a woman from the LGBTQ+ counseling center with a sliding scale explained the waitlist, how many months it would be before I could have an intake appointment. It was the same as it had been in Boston, but this time there wasn't a student mental health center to fall back on.

Finally, someone responded. He was taking new patients and he took my insurance. He could see me next week.

I don't remember the first time we met, what he wore, or what he said to me. But he didn't blink, didn't look at me differently when I told him that I had tried to die, that I came here because I didn't know where else to go. We didn't have to count sessions, weren't working against a ticking clock of what a company decided I could have.

Once a week I sat in front of him and said all the things I couldn't say to anyone else. Honest, the facade unzipped and rolled back. One day in early spring he squinted at me at the end of our session. "You need group," he said. "It meets right after this. You're coming today."

"What?"

"Hour and a half, Tuesday evenings. You're coming."

"How much does it cost?"

"We'll talk about that later. Get your stuff," he said, standing up and motioning to me. He led me to a room where women were already waiting, women who smiled when he walked in, who smiled at me in greeting. "This is Madeline; she's starting group tonight."

The numbers kept climbing, the things I owed. There was a loan I had to take out through the government, with an interest rate of 6.9 percent. Not eligible for loan forgiveness, not eligible for income-based repayment plans. The numbers jumped. I was supposed to pay at least $200 per month, and this only went to the interest. I was supposed to pay every month, and the amount I owed kept rising.

Some nights before group I made coffee and thought of the other rooms, across the country, where I had sat sipping thin coffee, listening to other women. The women I had met in outpatient in Boston in my mind like ghosts. In Austin, I walked down the hall where the women would be waiting. Some smiled, some didn't. The chairs were uncomfortable; the room was dim.

It was different from outpatient group sessions in Boston. Here, there was no snapping, no strict rules. The same women came every week. But here, still, I told them things I couldn't speak aloud outside that room and they listened. Not friends, but not *not* friends, these women who I came to know, who came to know me. In that basement suite in south Austin, with the sky so open it would crack you in two to see it, it seemed like it was always raining.

The numbers kept climbing and I started to remember how to laugh at them.

There was so much they could do to me. They could garnish my wages. They could take my tax refunds, take my car. They could sue me. There was so much they could do to me, and so little.

Sometimes, when I began to panic in the face of this mountain of debt, I remembered, and I laughed at the secret joke I had with myself: they would not have gotten a penny if I was dead. They had come so close to getting nothing at all. They would always be there, demanding more, but I could build something good beneath them.

These numbers that grew, that ballooned, that threatened, started to feel less important, started to feel more like an absurdity. There was something mad in this laughter, but it was better than despair.

A miracle is a way of making a new world. Turning water into wine, stretching a few pieces of bread to feed a crowd. A miracle is nothing more than changing materials, changing conditions.

There was a place in Austin, where, for a little while, I could ignore my loans and sit in a room full of women and look them in the eyes. Women who I didn't feel ashamed to sit next to. Without the urgency of locked doors or insurance companies deciding how long I could stay, this, brave and vulnerable and delicate, more miraculous than calming a storm, this, learning to live within it.

There was a room where, for a few fragile months, I sat with others and thought that maybe I was not so ugly, that maybe all of this was not untellable. That maybe, to say this out loud was not a curse, not a stain, not a disease that would spread to every listener. I heard their stories, and they heard mine. I began to understand that none of this was untouchable.

Before Christ died and came back, he told everyone that it would happen. He already knew how the story would end. He wandered through towns warning people, prophesizing. He told his disciples exactly what would happen. He would be betrayed, he would be killed, he would come back. This god, omnipotent, had known how this story would end from the first moment he created the earth. It was not a promise. It was a fact that had already been decided.

There was no promise that you would die and come back. There was no prophecy, no story that anyone knew the ending to. When you come back, when you wake up to the same world that you longed for a way out of, when you wake up in the same body you longed for a way out of, there is no promise that you will ever ascend to anything better. There is no promise that you will be transformed in the living, that you will be better or worse. When you die and come back, there will be no promise of anything. Later, if you find your own definition of better, if you find your own voice, if you find your own feet, some people who know your story will applaud your progress. But this thing, this survival, this living, is not progress.

There is a violence, a disservice, in squeezing my story into an arc of overcoming my past, my diagnosis. There is a chaos in the living that will not be tamed.

The months after I lived, I didn't know if I was better, if I would ever get better. I didn't know what better meant, if better was a way of adapting myself to a world that was biting at my throat, licking at my blood. I am afraid that someone will read this and think of a person they knew, a person they lost, a person in their life who still struggles daily to keep waking up. *Madeline got better, she overcame her past. Why can't they?*

It is easy to look back and make a clean narrative. A better job led to better therapy and these things combined to make living a bit more possible, but there was no guarantee that I would get any of that. There was no guarantee that I would keep going. It took years for me to believe that it was okay that I am still here. There were nights, so many nights, years, after I did not die, when I got home and cried to no one. When I didn't understand why I was still alive, when I thought it would have been so much better if I had died that night, and there was no one to call to ask for comfort or help. If I am better, whatever that might mean, I am better because things aligned that allowed me to find the way forward, because I kept applying to jobs even after I had no hope. There was no promise that this would happen. There was no promise that I would get a better job or find a therapist. There was no promise that I would find a *good* therapist. There was no promise that finding these things would stop me from trying again. Progress is a lie we like to tell ourselves after the hard part has ended, as if we were destined to make it all along.

I had gotten so used to the work schedule, going from one job to the other on Saturdays, going to sleep early on Fridays, spending my days off asleep, curled alone, that when I blinked and saw a Friday, a Saturday, open, free, I was confused. What did a person do on the weekends? The days were bright and shining and I raised my head to meet them.

It is so simple, the things it took for my life to start getting better. I was still in debt, I still drove an old used car, I still lived in an attic, still deferred my loans, but I could go to the doctor without panicking. I could go out, I could meet people, I could go on dates. I could afford new clothes to feel good on dates. Every once in a while, I could buy a pizza. I could take a weekend off from the wine bar, drive out to Marfa with someone I was dating, just because.

When I find myself in the arms of someone new, it is there and it is not. It settles in my stomach, unsharable. I do not want to keep secrets, do not want to keep myself hidden, but this fact is not a thing to say too soon. I lay naked, exposed, and hidden. I look into a man's deep brown eyes and wonder. Do I put my lips to his ear, murmur it softly in hushed confession? Do I stare into his eyes, unwavering? Do I bury my face into the crook of his neck, fall into his unknowing warmth, sputter this story loud and harsh with his skin against my mouth?

When I'm alone, I google. How to tell a new friend that you are a suicide survivor. How to tell someone that you tried to kill yourself. The results are the same as always, pages of advice for what to do if you are the friend, if you are the listener and someone tells you they tried to die, how to respond with kindness, understanding.

I want to tell all of it, to let it all come pouring out, but this, this is not appropriate. I look into kind eyes, put my hand on his cheek, and bite my lip. How do you tell a new love, a new friend? You don't, I learn.

I speak in circles. "I'm happy to be here with you," I tell him, when what I mean is that it is a wild and unholdable thing, that I am alive and breathing, that my body is here with him. "I feel lucky to spend time with you," I say, when I mean to tell him that I am supposed to be dead. I wrap my legs around him and pull him close. I smile and tell myself that this is not a lie.

I am, in so many ways, lucky. Uninsured, I went years without a doctor, a dentist, and it was okay. The scrap of rusted metal beneath my car held on far longer than it should have. I knew where to go, where to look, kept trying until I found a therapist who made sure I could afford what I needed. I applied for more jobs even when I was hopeless, even when, exhausted, I had already given up. Eventually, I got a better job, I started to find a fragile footing.

Even now, as I write this, I do not know how I'll pay my student loans. It comes in waves, the fear. A cycle. See the numbers as they grow, begin to choke, think of all the nights working late, the sore feet, and then remember like steel. I have lived before, and I will live now.

What can I offer you besides what I suspect you already know: that it should not take so much for anyone to stay alive.

Christ rose from the dead and God made the world a promise. Christ would come back, again, a second time. When he came back it would be the end of everything. The conclusion, all stories over and done. He would decide who was good, who was bad, would separate the lambs from the goats. Would weigh every action, every creature and living thing that ever drew breath in its lungs, would decide who deserved eternal paradise, who eternal punishment. Definitive, perfect, his judgment as he decides who deserves life and who the fires of hell.

I asked my therapist to tell me if it was okay that I'm here and he shook his head. "I can't answer that for you," he told me. I drove home, cried the whole way. There was no god to turn to, no one with unclouded judgment to tell me if I belonged to life or death, nothing to raise my eyes to in heaven. I stared up as I drove. Above me the sky was thick with clouds and no answers.

What is a person supposed to do on the anniversary of the day they were supposed to die? To mark the moment that snapped the present and past into pieces, that disrupted the timeline, that cleaved the self into splinters, the anniversary of the moment that should have been it? Is it morbid to celebrate? Is it indulgent to claim the day as my own? To let the day pass like any other felt a betrayal; and there, the needling fear, what would happen if night came and I was alone?

I texted, I called, I asked, and one person came.

Michael, one of my closest friends from college, who had lived with Alex, flew from Chicago to be with me, so that time would pass over us in the same room, so I would not be alone. I told him in the vaguest ways possible why I needed someone there with me, *something happened, and I almost died but I didn't*, and he came.

One year to the day I was supposed to die alone in a cold apartment in Somerville, we drove through the Texas hill country. We climbed a rock as big as the world, stepped up its towering red slopes. Stood on top and let the wind wash our faces. Everywhere around below was green. We drank sparkling water and stared into vernal pools, looking into tiny ponds, those divots in the rocks where rainwater had gathered, where plants and creatures had forced life out of dead stone. Patches of vegetation growing on bare rock. Tiny creatures, fairy shrimp, floating amid the algae.

Michael stood next to me, there on top of the earth, and all the times that we hadn't spoken since we had last seen each other didn't matter. Years ago, Michael had driven me through Portland on the back of his motorcycle, a sunset on one side and a rainbow on the other, back before my world turned gray. We had watched each other grow, had gone our separate ways after college, and there he was, a reminder that I wasn't as alone as I'd thought. We stood on top of the world together in the sun, and there we were.

In an episode of *Law & Order: SVU*, the assistant district attorney is woken in the middle of the night by a phone call. They have been pursuing a case where a teenage boy is the key witness, testifying against his abuser. She rushes to a hospital, where she is told the witness, the teenager, has asphyxiated.

"How?" she asks.

"Aspirin and his antidepressants," Stabler answers.

The doctors appear and explain the situation. Brain damage, they say. Hypoxia, cardiac arrest, they say. Some brain activity, they say.

I sat next to a new friend, something inside my belly nesting. A surrealness that sidestepped language. On the screen the characters guess if the witness will wake up. I waited for the other shoe to drop. It was a lightness and a fire all at once. I felt hot. I couldn't look at the person I was sitting next to. On the screen, in the hospital bed, the boy is ashen. His eyes closed, a tube down his throat. Monitors beeping. Unconscious, maybe forever. Vegetative state, maybe forever.

This was how my story was supposed to end. In silence, all these words unwritten, unsaid. Sitting next to this new friend, my skin pricking with the knowledge that I was not supposed to be here.

How many of us are there, sitting silent next to new friends, feeling something we do not have words for, this thing moving through our bellies, through our bones? How much I would have given to be in a room with you, to share this story and listen as you shared yours.

I thought about pointing to the screen. Saying aloud, "That was supposed to be me." It is a vibration in my gut, a chiming, the possibility of this moment, this thing that almost but did not happen, this thing that I do not know how to explain. I stay silent.

Survival, unwieldy and impossible, settling untranslatable in our mouths.

It is a joke, sometimes. It is a punch line. "I swear to God, working a double makes me want to kill myself." An undead thing learns to laugh along with the rest. Over time, after days and years, an undead thing will not blink at the words. An undead creature must choose carefully when to reveal its nature, when is the right moment to make someone uncomfortable, to make someone catch their breath.

I nod, I smile. "I understand," I say.

I met Daniel on Tinder. He was English, an astronomer, in Austin for research. The house where he lived became a refuge. He cooked for me, made chicken wrapped in prosciutto, homemade sag paneer, breakfast tacos every morning. Gin and tonics at night, in cool, glazed cups.

On a Saturday when we were sitting on his couch, unsure what to do with the time that we had left before he had to go back to England, he asked me why I went to NAMI meetings. "What happened to you?" he said. His roof was slanted, sharp. I stared up at the windows cut into the angle, the way the sunlight couldn't reach into the room.

"I tried to kill myself about a year ago," I said. His intake of breath. His hands, squeezing me close.

"Oh," he said. He held me tighter.

He let me tell all the parts I could, let me stop at the parts I still couldn't say out loud. He didn't bring it up again, didn't pry, didn't look at me any differently. I hadn't known this was possible, outside of therapy, outside of group, to speak this sentence and not be a freak, not be an alien, not other.

His time in the states was running out. Before he left, we took a weekend, drove to West Texas. He wanted to see Marfa. I wanted to be out in the hot, dry desert air. We drove through the flowing hills to the observatory. The golden sun drenching our faces, Carly Rae Jepsen on the stereo, both of us giddy as children. We lay in the grass and he named me all the stars, the sky so full I thought I would fall into it.

On the way back to Austin, the world turned dark and heavy with storm. The hills rose and fell around us, receding into a day that looked like night. Lightning snapped so close we could smell it, sharp and musty. Thunder shaking my little car. *All Hail West Texas* thrumming from the speakers. Big, fat raindrops on the windshield. The flashes of lightning unceasing, increasing frequency, clouds lit up again and again.

I didn't know where we were, somewhere between sky and earth, the world large and open, the roads beckoning, calling, to keep going, keep going. There is something good, they promised, something wonderful waiting for you. In the middle of all of it, the two of us, alive and laughing.

The thing they don't tell you about coming back from the dead is that some days, the fact of it can make your heart skip. The intoxication. A rush in the blood, pulse beating in celebration, the old, hated refrain turned secret hymn: *I am, I am, I am.*

A day can pass like any other. And then, there will come a jolt. In the morning, the sunlight pale through the window. The coffee in the mug. The bite of a headache. Out of nowhere, the shock. I shouldn't be here, but I am, and what a wild and untamable fact.

Someone told me that I was living proof that it gets better, that people shouldn't despair. My stomach dropped, heavy and iron. The terms on which I told my own story diminished, swapped, replaced with their own.

What proof was I? Of bulletproof glass at free therapy clinics, of expired food from church pantries, of nights at work feeling life slip through my fingers, hours traded in for paychecks that were not enough to survive on, proof that beans and rice can be enough to live on, for a little while. I could not survive without help, without people bending the rules. My therapist at Harvard not cutting me off when he was supposed to. My therapist in Austin letting me pay on a sliding scale, working with me though I could barely afford it, though I could only afford it with student loans paused.

If I am living proof of anything, I am proof of this, that no one can survive on their own.

My therapist smiled at me, told me to go write a book about resilience. I didn't know how to tell him, didn't know how to hold these two things at once. That I have done something impossible, that I have lived and made a new life out of scraps and am proud of what it took, and that it should not be this hard for anyone to keep living. That I have lived this long from sheer stubbornness, and that I understand if others decide that they need to leave, that there is no shame in finding an exit. That it is our fault, all of ours, for not making a world they could stay in.

A crisis, of institutions, of systems, of selves, to shake all of us.

There is an episode of the podcast *The Mental Illness Happy Hour* where the host interviews Kelechi Ubozoh, a woman who has survived multiple suicide attempts. I listened to the episode with my heart racing. *Here I am*, I thought. *Here I am.*

At one point, when discussing her second suicide attempt, her miraculous survival, her decision to live, she remarks almost as an aside, "Life doesn't get better; you get better."[23]

It is both hopeful and true. It will not be easy, but yes, you can get better. You will get stronger, you will learn new ways to keep living, to make it through each day. A day will come when you will wake up and feel the sun on your face. It might always be there, in the back of your mind, but you can find a way forward. A morning might come when you breathe deeply and feel inside yourself something bright, something you hadn't known before.

It is both cynical and true. Life doesn't get better. But why *doesn't* life get better? We watch the rates of suicide climbing, and still we compartmentalize, still we say these people are sick, these people are individuals struggling with their own issues. What will it take to shake ourselves awake, to look around and understand that the hostile conditions that we have made are not permanent, are not unbreakable?

In September, I watch my social media feeds become dotted with articles about suicide, suicide prevention. It is easier, I think, to pretend that these individuals are just that: single, isolated individuals floating through space. It requires something more from all of us when we come to understand that access to affordable health care, physical and mental, is suicide prevention. That stopping evictions is suicide prevention. That access to food is suicide prevention. That supporting and protecting transgender people is suicide prevention. That confronting and rooting out anti-Black racism is suicide prevention. That ending deportations is suicide prevention.

That these systems in which we live, in which we are made Other, in which we are made monstrous, in which we are abject, in which the poor are kept poor, these systems can be undone, and this, this is suicide prevention.

We promise each other that *the world is better with you in it*, but too often forget that it is our job to make the world better so that you want to stay in it, to make a world worthy of your staying.

Some people, my therapist tells me, most people even, won't understand why you celebrate the anniversary of the day you didn't die. Most people, he says, will think of it instead as the day that you wanted to die. They won't feel able to tell you that, though, so they will keep their mouths closed and wonder why you revel in the morbidity.

I marvel at the failures of our language, of my language, of our imagination. How strange it would be to mark the anniversary of every day that I wanted to die. All of the moments, those years, when I could dream only of tearing a hole out of this world and running through it.

Here, the simple misunderstanding that the impulse toward suicide is brief and hard, immediate. It is a misunderstanding to think that the day, April 20, is the only moment when I held my life in my own two hands and wanted to crush it. A misunderstanding that I would like to clarify again and again and again. The day, the moment, was the accumulation of countless tiny moments, little screams, the momentum building from the first day my father pushed me to the ground, the first day that I, as a child, knew without hyperbole that I lived a life without anything like real love. Looking at the numbers of my student loans, even as I worked, even as I could barely survive, as I slumped under their weight. The first time I felt an anger that I couldn't control, that pushed others away, that confirmed my belief in what became a self-fulfilling prophecy: that I was a person not worth the trouble it took to be close to.

People will think you morbid, my therapist tells me.

Would it be different, I say, if I was in a room of people who had survived like I did?

Of course, he says. Of course.

Reader, I am trying to build you that room.

I tell a literary agent that I am writing a book about surviving suicide. They tell me that it will be hard to publish a book like this, about such a dark topic.

Where are my survivors? How will we find each other, how will we learn to speak our own stories if they are too messy, too raw, too frightening to say? If they are too dark, too morbid for anyone to hear?

The god came to a house where they said a girl had died. People in front of the house, people around her body. Mouths open. Wailing. Tongues, spit, voices of grief. "Be quiet," the god hushed them.

In one version of the story, the god tells everyone to go away. In one version of the story, the god tells them not to cry. In one version of the story, the god, annoyed, asks why the people are making such a commotion. "The child is not dead," the god says, "but sleeping." As if to tell them that their cries, their noises will wake the child. In every version of the story, the people laugh at him.

The problem, I begin to understand, is that the god is lying. The girl is dead, even as the god insists that she isn't. It is in the god's insistent negation of the girl's death that her corpse begins to breathe again. It is a performative utterance; it is illogical. The girl was dead, but the god insists that she is just sleeping, and so she has never been dead. The god wakes her from a state that she was never in. Death becomes something played with, flipped on its head, the lines between life and death porous. The people's cries turned to laughter turned to astonishment.

When the little girl opens her eyes, surrounded by noises, they have already taken her story away from her. First the people saw it as tragedy, then as miracle.

The girl gets up and walks, and there is no time for her to claim the narrative as hers. The girl gets up and walks in scripts that she did not write. The girl gets up surrounded by others that insist, again and again, that they know the meaning of her death, her life. No one asks what she felt when her breath stopped coming. No one asks if she wanted to come back.

Someone looked me in the eyes and told me that the suicidal person owes something to their possible future self.

I don't know who told them that. I don't know who told them that time works that way, that there is always a future. I don't know what I owe to something that does not exist, that might never exist. I know, I think, what I owed to my past self, the self who couldn't sleep, the self who barely ate, the self who ached, ravenous, in every moment for something like love, something like safety, a safety that I had never been able to find. If you have never felt safety, how do you know that this exists? How can you owe something to a person you might never meet?

———

Some people call it weak, giving up. The actions taken to end a life. I promise, I have never been more determined, more hopeful, more resolute, than when I grabbed fistfuls of pills and swallowed.

———

What about the people left behind? someone asks me. After a person kills themselves? Another way of asking this: Were you thinking about me when you tried to kill yourself? Another way of saying this: How selfish, to take your own life. To not think of the damage, the pain you will cause the people left behind. This question has been asked before. I don't know who this question helps. I would like to ask something different.

Dear reader, there are moments, days and years, when a person goes home and there is no one. There is no one to call, there is no one to text, no one to share the ferocity of this despair with. I do not mean that a person doesn't feel like they can share this. I mean that there is a person who has no family, who has no friends, who does not have a single person to call in their moments of crisis.

I don't know who it helps to make a suicidal person responsible for an imaginary person they might have never met. When we are asked to think of those we might leave behind, we are meant to be reminded of friends, families who will mourn. We are not meant to think of the people who have alienated everyone in their life, who know that if an acquaintance hears of their death they will not be surprised, who know that the world sees them as disposable, a contagion.

The story of Jairus's daughter is told in different books. Every story ends without her saying a word. Every story is a little different. In every version of the story, when the god says that the girl is sleeping, the people laugh. Ridicule. She is gone. She is beyond anyone's help.

He takes her hand. He tells her to get up. She walks.

"Get her something to eat," the god says.

Here is a girl, dead to everyone. Here is a girl that everyone has given up on. A girl beyond all help. And here is a god, offering her his hand.

The god takes her hand in his own, eases her return back to the living.

This god who could walk on water, this god who could feed five thousand people with five loaves of bread, this god who chased money lenders from the temple, this righteous god doesn't listen to the laughter of the people all around, the people who say it's too late.

Even when no one else will help, when the idea of this girl ever healing is laughable, when the people around her have no hope that she will ever get better, this god sees something they can't. This god sees life where everyone else sees death.

Maybe this is the real miracle of the story. Not that Christ brings her back, but that he looks at her on the ground and knows that she can get up, even as everyone around her believes she is too far gone.

When Christ died and came back, he led his people into a great big field. The Gospel of Luke doesn't tell us what the sky was like, if it was calm or full of clouds. Christ blessed the people around him, and just like that, went away to heaven. Luke doesn't say how he got there, or where, exactly, he went. One moment he was there, the next there was only open space.

After you die and come back, after you die and keep living, you stand alone beneath a sky that will not tell you anything. You shouldn't be here, but you are. There might not be anyone to lift you up. There will be no god blessing your return. There will be no crowd staring at you, watching, waiting for you to ascend. The sky will crack open above you, rain will begin to fall on your face. Somewhere in your body, all the stories, all the moments and memories that you can't fit into narrative. Sometimes, this will be all you have. Sometimes, this will be enough.

There is a man in the Christian gospels who tears at his chains. He rends his clothing, wanders the tombs outside the town. In his body, a swarm of demons. The story does not tell us how many. The townspeople are disturbed by him, his shouts that carried in the air. When Christ comes, he puts the howling spirits into the bodies of pigs that run screaming to drown in the water. They don't consider that maybe the demons had something important to say.

Christ is led to Jairus's home immediately after he drives the pigs into the water. From this god is born life, from this god is born death. The many-voiced beings that rush into the waves, the little girl who gets up without a word. One of these is supposed to be holy. One of these is not. I can't separate one from the other. My story is in the mouths of the drowning pigs, my story is the man beating his own chest, cast out and hated because of the things inside of him. My story is in the first steps of the unnamed girl. The screams that no one wanted to hear, the exile, the banishment, and the silence that comes after.

There is so much that can be lost in the telling. There is so much at stake in speaking this story. The way a person might inch away, the way a person might nod, unsurprised. The way a friend may not react at all. Once, I shared this with a friend, that I had tried and didn't die. She did not look up. "Okay," she said. She went back to cleaning her apartment. In my chest rose the pain, the embarrassment of sharing my ugliest self with a person who didn't want it. A person who, maybe, just didn't care. Sometimes, you will not know how a person will react. Sometimes, a person will break your heart. Maybe, more often than not, a person will break your heart. But sometimes, a person will listen. Sometimes, a person will still love you for the monster you are. Sometimes, a person will need your story.

In the months, in the years after I did not die, I was desperate for all the stories I needed to hear. All of the stories silenced by shame, silenced by fear. You who thought your story was too much for anyone, who worried about who you might alienate if you spoke this thing out loud. To you who are reading this, who did not die, I needed you. I needed more than anything to hear your stories. I needed to know where you went the first day after you did not die. I needed to know the first thing you ate, if it was hospital food, if you could eat at all. I needed to know who the first person was who held your hand as you told them your story. I needed to know when you began to feel normal. I needed to know if you never felt normal again. I needed so badly to know how your story kept going, long after it should have ended.

The first thing I ate when I woke up in the emergency room was a cookie, brought by friends, that I could barely taste. The first thing I ate when I left the locked ward was a bowl of Cream of Wheat, tan, sprinkled with cinnamon, so sweet I thought I might cry. I drank coffee at three in the afternoon that day just because I could. The things that made me think that, maybe, it was worth it to stay alive were a hospitalization program in Brookline paid for by the state, and a job at a café, where every day I carried home slices of leftover pies, boxes of pecan, chocolate bourbon pecan, mixed berry, Dutch apple. There was no one to hold my hand, not even in therapy, until I met Daniel, more than a year after I left the hospital. I can't tell you when I began to feel normal.

What I can tell you of my own recovery is this: It was nothing spectacular. It was nothing beyond waking up in the morning and trying to do things that I thought were wastes of time: applying for better jobs, writing essays, waking up at all. It was a job that paid $14 an hour and a therapist that worked with me on a sliding scale. It was being able to understand, finally, what brought me to the loving desire for death, and what I could change about myself, about the world, to make a life that I didn't want to end.

It was being able to say this out loud, without shame, that I am a suicide attempt survivor.

The thing they don't tell you about coming back from the dead is that it happens slowly. You open your eyes, stand next to your bed, your crumpled sheets. Look down at where you were lying just a moment ago. Minutes with hands like strangers stretch into hours, that become days, that spread into weeks, and still, there you are, breathing. Your body in the sunlight, your own skin beneath your fingers. How much time, how long, before you know that you are alive, that you are back?

There is no tomb, no rock rolled away, no one there to bring oils for your body. There is no crowd, no witness, no prophecies for you to make. There is no holiday to mark your resurrection, nothing special about that day. Maybe someone will come to sit with you, maybe no one will. But you are there, and you are breathing. Nothing more, nothing less. And this, maybe, is the only proof you will grow to need.

The thing they don't tell you about coming back from the dead is that only you can decide when you have come all the way back, when you have arrived. Maybe, truthfully, there is no end point. Maybe you will spend your life arriving, again and again. Maybe you will never be sure if you got there.

You can still walk through the world with your head up. Just as no one else can see that you were supposed to die, that you, undead, defy your own narrative, no one else can tell you that you are supposed to be alive. You might have friends that love you in long, tired evenings, over dinner and wine. You might sit alone every night with no one to call. Your family might hold you close, might make your favorite food for your birthday. Maybe a lover who knows, who kisses you a little harder on the anniversary of the day you should have died. Maybe you will have no one, maybe you will come back and lose yourself in the silence that can feel unbreakable, impenetrable.

No god can whisper in your ear, speak down from the heavens and convince you. No lover's hands will be enough to prove to yourself that you should still exist. There will be no climactic moment, no crowds gathering to celebrate your resurrection. And still, you wake up, again. Your sheets will be the same ones you tried to die on until you buy new ones, without ceremony, without meaning beyond this: You wanted new sheets. You get up, look in the mirror. Remind yourself that Superman probably felt like a freak. That he was alien and strange. With the tips of your fingers against your cheek, inhale. The narrative is yours to claim. You know, somewhere deep in your body, that it can be okay to stand up and walk, even if you're not sure where you're going.

On the fifth anniversary of the day I did not die, I didn't tell anyone. Not ashamed, not confused, but sure. This day is mine, and I don't need to publicly claim it to know that every speck of sun in the sky, every breath of cloud, is for me.

There might come a year when you look at the calendar and know that today there is nothing special that you need to do. The knowing is enough. You might not ask for the day off work, might not take yourself to the Italian restaurant in town that you have only ever heard of, never stepped inside, unable to justify the price. When you are at work, it will start to rain. Just for a moment, a precious minute, you step outside. The drops on your skin. The chill in the air.

Things you know you weren't supposed to be alive to feel. You weren't supposed to make it this far, but here you are.

You will stand beneath a sky that is silent except for the rolling thunder, raindrops beading on your bare skin.

Sometimes, silence can be an assurance. That you know without needing to say, that your living, the sensation of rain, your own cold breath, is your own private celebration.

The rain will fall in your hair. On your still-living body. You will breathe and taste the water in the air. You will go back inside, smile at colleagues and coworkers. No one will know the wonder of your being, but this doesn't matter anymore. You know. In the steady beat of rain, you know the riotous, uncontainable fact: You are. You are. You are.

Someone asked me what living felt like. The coming back.

I don't know how else to explain it except to say that I like to walk in the rain with no umbrella. I like the drops on my skin. The way my clothes get wet. The way the water hits my body, the way each drop is a reminder. *Here you are. You are here.*

Sometimes, I show up to work drenched and have to find an excuse. I lost my umbrella. The rain just started. I didn't think it would be so bad.

How can I explain how delicate, how precious, how strange, the sensation of water is on living skin?

There is no agreement on exactly what happened to Jairus's daughter in the moments before her death or how, exactly, she died. Her body, laid on the ground with tender hands. Chest motionless. Around her, the tears, the wailing. The story doesn't say how long she was there, unmoving, before she came back. It could have been hours. It could have been seconds. The story doesn't say if she was sick, if this was something her family had worried about for days or weeks, or if it happened suddenly, without warning, all at once.

When Christ brings her back from the dead, for a moment, maybe, she hears the crying turn to stillness. Eyes still closed, she could have heard the shortest gasp.

There is no time for her to relearn what it is to be alive when everything around her says she should be dead. There are no marks on her body. She wakes to all of it, surrounding her. The sounds of people, surrounded by open mouths. Someone is there, standing over her, telling her to get up, to walk. Her father is weeping. She doesn't understand why her father is weeping. Someone offers her their hand. She holds on to this stranger's hand, rises to her feet. She takes a step, her muscles stiff. No one knows to ask where she has been, what she has seen.

She walks. She opens her mouth. She breathes.

A day might come when you get home from work, close the door behind you, when you look at the calendar and pause. There is something special about this day, but you can't quite remember what it is. You blink. The math might not seem to add up. Has it been that many years? Has it been that few? Time is not on your side, not that day.

You blink again. Someone is calling to you. You are late for dinner, and they have made your favorite meal, with meat so tender your own mouth melts around it. Someone is calling to you, night is falling across your shoulders in pale blue hushes, and you are wanted, you are waited for. You might sit across from a friend who is closer than your own heart, smile at each other and know without having to say. All of it, there in front of you, there behind you, in your own hands, in your own eyes, bursting and calm at once.

The god knew there was life where everyone else saw death. The god knew to hush the crowd. The god knew that once she stood up, she would have to find her own way forward, even as he helped her to her feet.

Dear reader, I can't offer you a single path. I can't tell you where you will need to go. There will be so much that stands in your way. There is no straight path to follow.

Talitha koum, the god says.

My name is Legion, for we are many. My many, my horde, my broken, crooked stumps. My beloveds who gave up on the world, we who the world gave up on. My beloved suicides, my living ghosts.

Though our stories are dark, though others may not want to hear them, though they would bury us in forlorn places so our spirits would never find each other, would never find our way home, though Dante planted us in the soil of hell and promised us we would never rise, though they lock us in hospitals, call us weak, call us failures, call us contagions, call us diseases, what I can offer you is this: there is nothing that can keep a good ghost down.

They used to bury us under crossroads so we could never find the way home. So our spirits could never curse anyone with our presence, so our bodies couldn't contaminate the sacred space of cemeteries, our bodies that no longer deserved to rest there. They buried us alone, isolated from each other.

When you come back from the dead, you might find yourself there. Cast out from life as it is supposed to be lived, in the middle of a road whose end you can't see. You might never find your way back to the home you used to have, the body you used to have. You might stand paralyzed and alone in the center of that crossroads. Surrounded by fog and mist and no clear way forward. There will be no sign to mark your way. But if you close your eyes, maybe, you will hear me calling to you. I can't tell you which way to go, but I can tell you that you are not alone.

I can't tell you what it is supposed to feel like the first days after you open your eyes. I have lived and kept living and have never found out. I have scoured libraries and medical databases and never found an answer. I don't think my story will be an answer to yours. I can't offer you an answer to any of the questions that thrummed in my blood those first days after I lived.

All I can offer you is this, the story of my death, the story of my coming back. All I can offer you is this, that you know, when you open your eyes, that you are not the first person to wake to this thing outside language. That someone else has stumbled through those first bright days. That someone else fumbled through each moment, not sure where any of it was going. That someone else had no words to say and no one to say them to. That someone else didn't have anyone to share this fact with, outside of therapy, outside of locked doors. That someone else stood among people and felt alien, separate and outside the world. That someone else looked up at the sky and waited for an answer that never came.

All I can offer you is this book, these words, so that you know, always and always and always, that you are not alone. Not doomed, not cursed, not untouchable, not untellable, my hands waiting for your story, my story in yours.

AFTERWORD/ TO THE READER

To you who have survived, you who have lived and not known where to go from there, you who have imagined it but never tried, who may think of it like a recurring dream from childhood that never leaves, who did not get a church service honoring your life, or a party with your coworkers or even a hug from a friend when you came back, or a wave of posts on social media, or someone looking down on you, there to bring you comfort like George Bailey's angel:

I may never meet you, I may never see your face, but I would like to throw you a party. I would like to buy you champagne, good champagne, to pop the cork and watch your eyes sparkle because you know the bubbles are for you and you alone, for the mere fact of your being. I would like to fill a room with all of your friends, or strangers if you'd prefer, and put on your favorite songs, take your hand in mine, dance with you and watch you sing with your fullest voice. I would like to hold you up, put you on a stage if you feel like it, let you tell your story, all of it, all of the parts you thought you could never say out loud, and let you know that your story is not too ugly to be heard. I would like to buy you flowers on the first anniversary of the day you did not die (years after too, if you'd like), would like to know if you prefer roses and lilies or snapdragons and baby's breath. I would like to stand you next to a Christmas tree, run through town and get dollars from every person, collect them in a basket for you, to do whatever you'd like with the money. On the first day that you come home from the hospital, I would like to make your favorite dinner, watch the movie that always brings you comfort, and sit with you until your breath starts to feel normal again. I would like to walk with you down the street, so when you run into people you know, people who might never guess the places you have been, you will know that you are seen. I would like to come with you when you go back to work, so you know that someone there understands where you have gone and how miraculous your return. I would like you to know that though we may never meet, you are not alone. If it helps, I can be your ghost, invisible and imagined and with you.

If you are reading this, if you have closed your eyes and hoped they would not open again, and woken up anyway and kept living, holding on to some ragged scrap of hope, I would like to tell you that I am proud of you. And I am so, so glad you are still here.

ACKNOWLEDGMENTS

Thank you to my editor, Maya Fernandez, for ushering this book through the stages of editing and revision, for helping to bring this to the world. Thank you to my agent, Ayla Zuraw-Friedland, for taking a risk on an artsy debut memoir about suicide. This book would not have been possible without you both. What a privilege to have an agent and editor who are not afraid of the dark. Thank you to everyone at the Frances Goldin Literary Agency and Beacon Press for your support.

I have been privileged to have the support of literary organizations. Thank you to the Aspen Institute and Aspen Summer Words, Tin House, and Writers' League of Texas. Thank you to Paul Lisicky and the editorial team at Ploughshares. Thank you to Pete Rock for all your support and mentorship. Thank you to my early readers at Alabama: Wendy Rawlings, Kellie Wells, and the cohort in my novel class who let me workshop sections of this memoir, even though you really did not sign up for it. Thank you to my workshop leaders at Aspen Summer Words and Tin House, Gregory Pardlo, Emily Rapp Black, and Cecily Wong. To Margaret Juhae Lee and all my agent siblings. To my colleagues and peers across the Liberal Arts, Humanities, and Communications division at Austin Community College.

Thank you to my Tin House cohort: Anna Cabe, Megan Doyle, Melissa Uyên-Thi Lê, Anna Hui Tran, Amy Grote, Bethany Marcel, Kevin Lê, Kristen Hamelin Tracey, and Sophia Huneycutt. I am so, so lucky to write alongside you all. I can't wait to read your books.

Thank you to Edward. I wouldn't have gotten here without your help and guidance. Thank you for kicking my ass when I need it, for making me accountable, for holding me to a high standard and helping me get there.

Thank you to all the girls in all the groups. You know who you are.

Thank you to the peers and faculty at Harvard who supported me even as I fell apart. To the women of the Low-Income Student Advocates, to the woman who cried with me on a sidewalk, to the TAs who let me submit creative pieces instead of academic essays. To Dr. Ann Braude. To Halyna Hryn and the staff at the Ukrainian Research Institute.

To all the people who helped me survive in Boston. To Rachel and Ted for the most important cup of coffee I've ever had, for still being my friends despite the mess that I was. To Greg Given. To Kate Mason. To every single one of you at Petsi Pies. Thank you for not firing me; thank you for making me feel like part of your family.

Thank you to the friends from college that supported me over the years. Thank you for teaching me what home could be. To David. To McNutt. To everyone in Team Bautista.

To Celia Bell, for reading early drafts, giving notes on final drafts, fielding anxious texts, and Wade Redfearn, for keeping me out dancing until five in the morning. To Ciaran, for being a voice of reason and support across space and time. Thank you for letting me leave slightly unhinged voice notes at any time of day. Thank you for being my friend through all of it.

Thank you to John Darnielle and the Mountain Goats. There were years when your music was the only thing keeping me alive.

Thank you to Behemoth, my perfect demon. I hope I die before you do. You can eat me if I do.

To all the loves, all the friends. Thank you, thank you, thank you, all of you. I could not survive this world without you.

NOTES

PART I: AN ARCHEOLOGY OF THAT SILENCE

1. D. T. Chung et al., "Suicide Rates After Discharge from Psychiatric Facilities: A Systematic Review and Meta-analysis," *JAMA Psychiatry* 74, no. 7 (2017): 694–702, https://doi.org/10.1001/jamapsychiatry.2017.1044; Rebecca Musgrove et al., "Suicide and Other Causes of Death Among Working-Age and Older Adults in the Year After Discharge from In-Patient Mental Healthcare in England: Matched Cohort Study," *British Journal of Psychiatry* 221, no. 2 (2022): 468–75, https://doi.org/10.1192/bjp.2021.176.
2. General Laws of Massachusetts, 123 M.G.L., Section 12, https://malegislature.gov/Laws/GeneralLaws/Parti/Titlexvii/Chapter123/Section12, https://www.mass.gov/doc/admission-and-discharge-rights/download.
3. Mental Health Legal Advisors Committee, "Your Rights Regarding Admission to and Discharge from a Hospital Under Massachusetts Mental Health Law," https://www.mass.gov/doc/admission-and-discharge-rights/download, accessed June 18, 2025.
4. Michel Foucault, *History of Madness*, ed. Jean Khalfa, trans. Jonathan Murphy and Jean Khalfa (Routledge, 2009), 95.
5. Kay R. Jamison, *Night Falls Fast: Understanding Suicide* (Vintage Books, 2000), 15.
6. Jamison, *Night Falls Fast*, 15.
7. Jamison, *Night Falls Fast*, 15.
8. Sergei Yesenin, "До свидания мой друг" ("Goodbye My Friend"), 1925; translation by the author.
9. Mark E. Button, "Suicide and Social Justice: Toward a Political Approach to Suicide," *Political Research Quarterly* 69, no. 2 (2016): 274, https://www.jstor.org/stable/44018009.

PART II: A PLACE WITH NO EXIT

1. Matthew Ratcliffe et al., "What Is a 'Sense of Foreshortened Future?' A Phenomenological Study of Trauma, Trust, and Time," *Frontiers in Psychology* 5, no. 1026 (2014): 2, https://doi.org/10.3389/fpsyg.2014.01026.
2. Vincent J. Felitti et al., "Relationship of Childhood Abuse and Household Dysfunction to Many of the Leading Causes of Death in Adults: The Adverse Childhood Experiences (ACE) Study," *American Journal of Preventive Medicine* 14, no. 4 (1998): 245–58, https://doi.org/10.1016/S0749-3797(98)00017-8.
3. Thomas Joiner, *Why People Die by Suicide* (Harvard University Press, 2005), 46–93.
4. Deborah Treisman, host, *New Yorker Fiction Podcast*, "Tobias Wolff Reads Denis Johnson," May 8, 2009, https://www.newyorker.com/podcast/fiction/tobias-wolff-reads-denis-johnson.
5. Joiner, *Why People Die by Suicide*, 122.
6. Lauren Berlant, "Slow Death (Sovereignty, Obesity, Lateral Agency)," *Critical Inquiry* 33, no. 4 (2007): 754–80, https://doi.org/10.1086/521568.
7. Sylvia Plath, *The Bell Jar* (Bantam Books, 1978), 1.
8. Plath, *The Bell Jar*, 129.
9. Plath, *The Bell Jar*, 130.
10. Plath, *The Bell Jar*, 142.
11. Allergan USA, *Lexapro (Medication Guide)*, (2016): 1–26, https://www.fda.gov/media/135185/download.
12. Allergan USA, *Lexapro (Medication Guide)*, 3.
13. Leslie Jamison, *The Recovering: Intoxication and Its Aftermath* (Little, Brown, 2018), 24.
14. Denis Johnson, *Jesus' Son: Stories* (Farrar, Straus & Giroux, 1992), 12.
15. Johnson, *Jesus' Son*, 160.
16. Joiner, *Why People Die by Suicide*, 132.

PART III: ASCENCION

1. Dante Alighieri, *The Divine Comedy: Inferno; Purgatorio; Paradiso*, trans. Allen Mandelbaum (Penguin Random House, 1995).
2. Denis J. Lynch and Catherine Goertemiller Carrigan, "Managing Suicided Attempts: Guidelines for the Primary Care Physician," *Primary Care Companion to the Journal of Clinical Psychiatry* 5, no. 4 (2003): 169–74.
3. Mary Anne Walling, "Suicide Contagion," *Current Trauma Reports* 7 (2021): 103–14, https://doi.org/10.1007/s40719-021-00219-9.

4. Madelyn S. Gould and Alison M. Lake, "The Contagion of Suicidal Behavior," in *Forum on Global Violence Prevention; Board on Global Health; Institute of Medicine; National Research Council. Contagion of Violence: Workshop Summary*, 2013.
5. Simone Fullagar, "Wasted Lives: The Social Dynamics of Shame and Youth Suicide," *Journal of Sociology* 39, no. 3 (2003): 301, https://doi.org/10.1177/00048690030035076.
6. American Foundation for Suicide Prevention, "After an Attempt," https://afsp.org/after-an-attempt/, accessed June 14, 2025.
7. Lauren Berlant, "Slow Death (Sovereignty, Obesity, Lateral Agency)," *Critical Inquiry* 33, no. 4 (2007): 754.
8. Berlant, "Slow Death," 759.
9. Jasbir Puar, *The Right to Maim: Debility, Capacity, Disability* (Duke University Press, 2017), 11.
10. Kim Samuel et al., "Social Isolation and Its Relationship to Multidimensional Poverty," *Oxford Development Studies* 46, no. 1 (2018): 83–97, https://doi.org/10.1080/13600818.2017.1311852.
11. China Mills, "The Psychiatrization of Poverty: Rethinking the Mental Health-Poverty Nexus," *Social Personality and Psychology Compass* 9, no. 5 (2015): 214.
12. Samuel et al., "Social Isolation and Its Relationship to Multidimensional Poverty," 3.
13. Samuel et al., "Social Isolation and Its Relationship to Multidimensional Poverty," 17.
14. Ian Marsh, "Suicide and Social Justice: Discourse, Politics and Experience," in *Suicide and Social Justice: New Perspectives on the Politics of Suicide and Suicide Prevention*, ed. Mark E. Button and Ian Marsh (Routledge, 2020), 28.
15. Mark E. Button, "Suicidal Regimes: Public Policy and the Formation of Vulnerability to Suicide," in Button and Marsh, *Suicide and Social Justice*.
16. China Mills, "Strengthening Borders and Toughening Up on Welfare: Deaths by Suicide in the UK's Hostile Environment," in Button and Marsh, *Suicide and Social Justice*, 71.
17. Sara Ahmed, *The Promise of Happiness* (Duke University Press, 2010), 12.
18. Emily Malone, *Cost of Living: Essays* (Henry Holt, 2022), 5.
19. Mary Shelley, *Frankenstein* (W. W. Norton, 2021), 168.
20. Jeffrey Jerome Cohen, "Monster Culture (Seven Theses)," in *Monster Theory: Reading Culture*, ed. Jeffrey Jerome Cohen (University of Minnesota Press, 1996), 4.

21. Olga R. Rodriguez, "It Took Decades, but San Francisco Finally Installs Nets to Stop Suicides off Golden Gate Bridge," Associated Press, January 3, 2004, https://apnews.com/article/golden-gate-bridge-suicide-nets-san-francisco-11020bcfa279ba68eb72f72c0c5a2eef#.
22. Rodriguez, "It Took Decades, but San Francisco Finally Installs Nets to Stop Suicides off Golden Gate Bridge."
23. Paul Gilmartin, host, *The Mental Illness Happy Hour*, episode 354, "Surviving Suicide—Kelechi Ubozoh," October 27, 2017, https://www.everand.com/podcast/505495051/354-Surviving-Suicide-Kelechi-Ubozoh.

BIBLIOGRAPHY

Ahmed, Sara. *The Promise of Happiness.* Duke University Press, 2010.

Alighieri, Dante. *The Divine Comedy: Inferno; Purgatorio; Paradiso.* Translated by Allen Mandelbaum. Penguin Random House, 1995.

American Foundation for Suicide Prevention. "After an Attempt." https://afsp.org/after-an-attempt/. Accessed June 14, 2025.

Berlant, Lauren. "Slow Death (Sovereignty, Obesity, Lateral Agency)." *Critical Inquiry* 33, no. 4 (2007): 754–80. https://doi.org/10.1086/521568.

Button, Mark E. "Suicide and Social Justice: Toward a Political Approach to Suicide." *Political Research Quarterly* 69, no. 2 (2016): 270–80. https://www.jstor.org/stable/44018009.

Button, Mark E., and Ian Marsh. *Suicide and Social Justice: New Perspectives on the Politics of Suicide Prevention.* Routledge, 2020.

Case, Anne, and Angus Deaton. *Deaths of Despair and the Future of Capitalism.* Princeton University Press, 2020.

Cohen, Jeffrey J. "Monster Culture (Seven Theses)." In *Monster Theory: Reading Culture*, edited by Jeffrey J. Cohen. University of Minnesota Press, 1996.

Felitti, Vincent, Robert Anda, Dale Nordenberg, David Williamson, Alison Spitz, Valerie Edwards, Mary Koss, and James Marks. "Relationship of Childhood Abuse and Household Dysfunction to Many of the Leading Causes of Death in Adults: The Adverse Childhood Experiences (ACE) Study." *American Journal of Preventive Medicine* 14, no. 4 (1998): 245–58. https://doi.org/10.1016/S0749-3797(98)00017-8.

Foucault, Michel. *History of Madness.* Translated by Jean Khalfa and Jonathan Murphy. Routledge, 2006.

Fullagar, Simone. "Wasted Lives: The Social Dynamics of Shame and Youth Suicide." *Journal of Sociology* 39, no. 3 (2003): 291–307. https://doi.org/10.1177/0004869003035076.

Gilmartin, Paul, host. *The Mental Illness Happy Hour*, episode 354, "Surviving Suicide—Kelechi Ubozoh," October 27, 2017. https://www.everand.com/podcast/505495051/354-Surviving-Suicide-Kelechi-Ubozoh.

Gilmore, Leigh. *Tainted Witness: Why We Doubt What Women Say About Their Lives*. Columbia University Press, 2017.

Gould, Madelyn S., and Alison M. Lake. "The Contagion of Suicidal Behavior." In *Forum on Global Violence Prevention; Board on Global Health; Institute of Medicine; National Research Council. Contagion of Violence: Workshop Summary*, 2013.

Jamison, Kay. *Night Falls Fast: Understanding Suicide*. Vintage Books, 1999.

Jamison, Leslie. *The Recovering: Intoxication and Its Aftermath*. Little, Brown, 2018.

Johnson, Denis. *Jesus' Son: Stories*. Farrar, Straus & Giroux, 1992.

Joiner, Thomas. *Why People Die by Suicide*. Harvard University Press, 2007.

Joiner, Thomas, Jessica D. Riberio, and Caroline Silva. "Nonsuicidal Self-Injury, Suicidal Behavior, and Their Co-Occurrence as Viewed Through the Lens of the Interpersonal Theory of Suicide." *Current Directions in Psychological Science* 21, no. 5 (2012): 342–47. https://doi.org/10.1177/0963721412454873.

Kaysen, Susanna. *Girl, Interrupted: A Memoir*. Vintage Books, 1994.

Kotrosits, Maia. "Queer Persistence: On Death, History, and Longing for Endings." In *Sexual Disorientations: Queer Temporalities, Affects, Theologies*, edited by Kent Britnall, Joseph A. Marchal, and Stephen D. Moore. Fordham University Press, 2018.

Leenaars, Antoon. "Suicide and Human Rights: A Suicidologist's Perspective." *Health and Human Rights* 6, no. 2 (2003): 128–48. https://doi.org/10.2307/4065433.

Lynch, Denis J., and Catherine Goertemiller Carrigan. "Managing Suicide Attempts: Guidelines for the Primary Care Physician." *Primary Care Companion to the Journal of Clinical Psychiatry* 5, no. 4 (2003): 169–74.

Malone, Emily. *Cost of Living: Essays*. Henry Holt, 2022.

Marsh, Ian. *Suicide: Foucault, History, and Truth*. Cambridge University Press, 2010.

McDonagh, Martin. *The Pillowman*. Faber and Faber, 2003.

McRuer, Robert. *Crip Theory: Cultural Signs of Queerness and Disability*. New York University Press, 2006.

McRuer, Robert. *Crip Times: Disability, Globalization, and Resistance*. New York University Press, 2018.

Mills, China. "Strengthening Borders and Toughening Up on Welfare: Deaths by Suicide in the UK's Hostile Environment." In *Suicide and Social Justice: New Perspectives on the Politics of Suicide and Suicide Prevention*, edited by Mark E. Button and Ian Marsh. Routledge, 2020.

Musgrove, Rebecca, Matthew Carr, Nav Kapur, Carolyn Chew-Graham, Faraz Mughal, Darren Ashcroft, and Roger Webb. "Suicide and Other Causes of Death Among Working-Age and Older Adults in the Year After Discharge from In-Patient Mental Healthcare in England: Matched Cohort Study." *British Journal of Psychiatry* 221, no. 2 (2022): 468–75. https://doi.org/10.1192/bjp.2021.176.

Plath, Sylvia. *The Bell Jar*. Bantam Books, 1972. Originally published in 1963 by Heinemann.

Puar, Jasbir. *The Right to Maim: Debility, Capacity, Disability*. Duke University Press, 2017.

Ratcliffe, Matthew, Mark Ruddell, and Benedict Smith. "What Is a 'Sense of Foreshortened Future?' A Phenomenological Study of Trauma, Trust, and Time." *Frontiers in Psychology* 5, no. 1026 (2014): 1–11. https://doi.org/10.3389/fpsyg.2014.01026.

Rodriguez, Olga R. "It Took Decades, but San Francisco Finally Installs Nets to Stop Suicides off Golden Gate Bridge," Associated Press, January 3, 2004. https://apnews.com/article/golden-gate-bridge-suicide-nets-san-francisco-11020bcfa279ba68eb72f72c0c5a2eef#.

Samuel, Kim, Sabina Alkire, Diego Zavaleta, China Mills, and John Hammock. "Social Isolation and Its Relationship to Multidimensional Poverty." *Oxford Developmental Studies* 46, no. 1 (2018): 83–97. https://doi.org/10.1080/13600818.2017.1311852.

Seah, Rebecca, Kirsty Dwyer, and David Berle. "Was It Me? The Role of Attributions and Shame in Posttraumatic Stress Disorder (PTSD): A Systematic Overview." *Trends in Psychology* (August 2023). https://doi.org/10.1007/s43076-023-00315-6.

Sgobin, Sara Maria Teixeira, Ana Luisa Marques Traballi, Neury Jose Botega, and Octavio Rizi Coelho. "Direct and Indirect Cost of Attempted Suicide in a General Hospital: Cost-of-Illness Study," *Sao Paulo Medical Journal* 133, no. 3 (2015): 218–26.

Shelley, Mary. *Frankenstein*. Edited by Michael Bérubé. W. W. Norton, 2021.

van der Kolk, Bessel A. *The Body Keeps the Score: Brain, Mind, and Body in the Healing of Trauma*. Penguin Books, 2015.

Walling, Mary Anne. "Suicide Contagion." *Current Trauma Reports* 7 (2021): 103–14. https://doi.org/10.1007/s40719-021-00219-9.

Weinstock, Jeffrey Andrew, ed. *The Monster Theory Reader*. University of Minnesota Press, 2020.

White, Jennifer, Ian Marsh, Michael J. Kral, and Jonathan Morris, eds. *Critical Suicidology: Transforming Research and Prevention for the 21st Century*. UBC Press, 2016.

Yanagihara, Hanya. *A Little Life*. Anchor Books, 2015.

Yesenin, Sergei. "До свидания мой друг" ("Goodbye My Friend"). 1925. Translation by the author.